VALUABLE

I am sure this will become a very val' else who has described faith and life witl I am certain that most readers will gain Personally, I have gained a lot through this book. The many good examples keep the message down-to-earth, relevant and understandable. This book will certainly help many to see the life God desires to lead his children into. I have been inspired to bring this perspective more into my preaching.

Svein Granerud – theologian, author, speaker,
Normisjon, Norway

TIMELY

I have had the pleasure of knowing Daryl Krause for many decades. I first knew him as a university student, a very talented and caring young man who was already very God-focused yet practical and down to earth. I have followed his spiritual walk closely and have been very impressed with his commitment to the cause of Jesus. *Father-Life* is very timely book for a generation struggling to know the goodness of God.

David Mok – author, life coach, founding pastor of
International City Church, Brisbane, Australia.

RELEVANT

The message of *Father-Life* is important and seems to be increasingly so for the Church in our day. The book is timely and very relevant for preparing and strengthening us in the increasingly post-Christian society of the Western world.

Tarjei Cyvin – pastor, Mission Covenant Church,
Trondheim, Norway

DEEP TRUTHS

This is not a book to read fast. There are so many deep truths coming in short succession – a bit like reading the Letter of James. I like it a lot when I feel I want to re-read what I just read.

Sofie Seglem – mission leader,
YWAM, Norway

THOUGHT-PROVOKING

This book has led me via easy to follow, thought-provoking but logical progression to a more mature relationship with my Heavenly Father. It in no way diminishes the work of Jesus Christ as Saviour or of the Holy Spirit as teacher inspirer but rather enhances each of their roles in leading me to a more abundant life in my Heavenly Father. The insights into target practice, covenants and contracts, grace, adoption and so much more left me feeling as if I've been wearing blinkers all my life and only now am I starting to understand what I should have known all along.

Heather Schmidt — retired school teacher,
Biloela, Australia

ENRICHING

As a young missionary, I had many valuable conversations with Darryl. He taught me to read the Bible in fresh ways and not just through my 'Norwegian glasses'. It is a pleasure to see that the heart of Darryl's message is now available in book form. This book can help us to break free from many of our cultural assumptions as Christians. It has enriched my own views of God's character and his purposes for his children.

Andreas Nordli — author, speaker, mission director,
YWAM, Norway

REFRESHING

The writing is refreshingly simple and uniquely straightforward, almost like an analytical Hemingway. The formatting and general organization of the book is "soft" enough to read it semi-casually in a cozy armchair, but has enough instructional framework for a self-studying scholar, a youth group, or even as a daily devotional. Almost all the ideas in *Father-Life* are drawn directly from scripture. There's a lot of perspective to be found, and I have plenty of interesting rereading of the Bible ahead of me. *Father-Life* cleared up several apparently conflicting or unclear points in the gospel for me, and I think it will prove to be a key waypoint in my journey with God.

Gene Park — university student,
Korea/Australia

COMPELLING

This is an inspiring book with fresh perspectives. Most Christians have a clear understanding of Jesus, a bit less about the person of the Holy Spirit, and the Father seems even more obscure. Darryl's work in *Father-Life* brings out new insight and compelling traits which can help believers to 'warm' up to the Father.

Alv Magnus – author, speaker, former mission director,
Norway

RELATABLE

What a lovely book! It has given me a renewed longing to know the Father better and allow his character and views to continue to form my life. Darryl invites us to journey closer to the Father and deeper into a living relationship with him. The many good and relatable examples stir hope and a longing for all the Father has for us. The clear layout with many section headings makes the material readily accessible. The summary of key points at the end of each chapter kept the message clear, and the suggestions for application and reflection are a gold mine for personal growth or as a resource for groups. I recommend *Father-Life* to all who desire a deeper life with the Father as his beloved sons and daughters.

Marianne S Braseth – preacher, speaker, mentor,
YWAM, Norway

Father-Life

FRESH PERSPECTIVES FOR FULLY LIVING AS A CHILD OF GOD

DARRYL KRAUSE

Ark House Press
arkhousepress.com

Cataloguing in Publication Data:
Title: Father-Life: Fresh Perspectives for Fully Living as a Child of God
ISBN: 978-0-6457514-8-2 (pbk)

Cover design: Esther Krause
Author photo: Bendik Krause
Illustrations: Jan Willem Middag

APPRECIATION

I am amazed and humbled by the fact that I have actually written a book. At times, I felt more like an observer as the message developed and took shape. I am convinced God has been at work in this process and has guided me through to completion.

Along the way, however, many others took part and made valuable contributions. These include those who gave repeated encouragements to write a book, and the countless friends, colleagues, family members, authors, editors, and even casual acquaintances who helped shape this work through feedback and input. I am deeply grateful for all of you. Special thanks go to Jan Willem for creating the drawings which enhance the textual illustrations.

One person stands out in the crowd, one whose participation has been essential: my magnificent wife, Magni. Thank you for backing and encouraging me in this incredible adventure.

CONTENTS

-    Author's Note   1

PART ONE - KNOWINGTHE FATHER   3

1. Awakening to Father - Life   5
2. Rediscovering the Fatherhood of God   15
3. The Father's Target   25
4. Our Own Targets   33
5. Embracing True Goodness   43
6. The Good Father   53

PART TWO - RELATING TO THE FATHER   63

7. Relationship?   65
8. Pursuing Relationship   75
9. The Hopes of the Father   85
10. Our Inheritance in the Father   93
11. Faith is Foundational   103
12. Confident Faith   113

PART THREE · ALIGNING WITH THE FATHER 123

13. Jesus the Game Changer   125
14. Our Righteous Father   135
15. Becoming theRighteousness of God   147
16. Grasping the Game Change   157

PART FOUR · THE FATHER-CENTRED LIFE 167

17. From Fences to Wells   169
18. The Father's Eyes of Grace   179
19. Grace that Flows Freely   187
20. Finding Freedom in Submission   197
21. Living Righteously by Faith   207
22. Spiritual Growth   217
23. Worshipping the Father   229

• Suggestions for Study   239
• Endnotes   243

AUTHOR'S NOTE

DEAR READER,

If you're anything like me, you want your relationship with God to be alive, growing, and flourishing. That's what this book is about, helping Christians grow.

BACKGROUND

Many of the examples I share come from my own walk with God, including over 30 years of service in Youth With A Mission. I grew up in a loving Christian family in Australia, yet that gave no assurance of a problem-free walk with God. During my studies in engineering I had several milestone encounters with God, including a revelation of the Lordship of Jesus, a personal encounter with the Holy Spirit, and a calling to cross-cultural mission. Yet I still found myself struggling with areas of tension in my relationship with God. Even being in full-time Christian ministry and training others was no guarantee of having it all together.

The things we say we believe – the sermons we hear and the books we read – don't automatically manifest themselves in godly living and fruitful relationships. How can we bridge the gap between theology and lifestyle? I think my problem-solving mindset has shaped my pursuit of God and my desire for harmony between theory and practice. As I kept digging for answers, a growing revelation of the Father's goodness led me into greater freedom, fresh life, and confidence in God.

PROCESS AND PURPOSE

Writing this book was prompted by increasing pressure from others to share what they considered unique and helpful insights. Yet the fact that my message seemed unique was also a concern. Therefore, more than ten years have gone into writing and editing this book, while I have studied the Scriptures, checked reliable references, and sought the input of a wide range of godly men and women. I don't assume to be correct in every detail and I don't expect you to agree with all my conclusions. Yet in this mix of familiar and fresh perspectives, I am sure you will find at least some 'meat' to help you grow.

MEAT TO CHEW

Are you ready to embrace fresh perspectives about God and your relationship with him? That will require re-evaluating or even discarding some current views, and it can have consequences in other areas and relationships. Growth means change, and 'meat' needs to be chewed. If you want deep growth, then don't rush your reading and allow yourself time to process. Each chapter ends with suggestions for reflection or application, but feel free to process in the way that gives you the best fruit. Engaging with your spiritual family can also be significant, so suggestions for individual and group study are included at the end of the book.

PRAYER

May you be deeply blessed through this book, and may God be glorified in your life as you continue to grow in the fullness of the Father-life that flows from him.

In his grace and love,
Darryl Krause
Kristiansand, Norway

PART ONE

KNOWING
THE FATHER

The early apostles did not simply promote a new religious system; they taught a completely new way of being human. Jesus paved the way for us as he lived in perfect harmony with the Father. His whole life in human form was 'Father-life' – it flowed entirely from the Father. This God-intended way of being human spreads life to others and glorifies the Father.

For us, living this way comes from knowing who we are – or more importantly, *whose* we are. These first chapters lay some important foundations in knowing the Father for who he is. We will reflect on the life that flows from him, common misunderstandings about his character, and the goodness of his father-heart towards us.

> *May the glorious Father give you*
> *the Spirit of wisdom and revelation,*
> *so that you may know him better.*
> Adapted from Ephesians 1:17

1

AWAKENING TO FATHER-LIFE

The time of worship had been rich and meaningful. As we now sat quietly, drinking in the goodness of God's presence, someone started to describe a scene that had come to their mind while worshipping. It was a depiction of God's father-heart for his sons and daughters.

This scene, which I will soon describe, gave me fresh insight into the type of dynamic relationship we can have with our heavenly father. It affected me then as a young adult, and for 40 years it has continued to stay with me and reveal new truths. It gives us pointers to the type of life that flows from the Father of Life, and it can teach us how to live well with others.

IN THE GARDEN TOGETHER

Picture a father working together in the garden with his young son or daughter. It is a beautiful, sunny day, and they are enjoying the moment. The father is a skilled gardener. He knows where to dig to help nourish the plants, and what to remove. While often pulling out weeds, he sometimes takes out healthy plants to make room for others to grow.

The child lacks understanding, but is full of enthusiasm and proud to be 'helping Daddy'. When the child digs in the wrong places, the father often lets it go for a while and occasionally gives some gentle directions: "That's really good. Now, how about you dig over here?" The father knows there hasn't been any major damage; he can fix things up, one way or another.

The child sees the father pulling up weeds and has a go. They often get it right, but sometimes have no idea what they are pulling up. Out of the corner of his eye, the father notices too late as his child uproots a healthy plant. He smiles to himself and thinks, "I had plenty of those anyway." Another time, he gently intervenes, "I think we'll leave that one there for now, but here are some weeds you can pull up."

A casual observer may be troubled and consider the situation chaotic. Yet the father would say everything was perfect; he would not have it any other way. He loves the way his child just wants to be with him, doing whatever he is doing. The child's shortcomings are hardly a concern as the father sees their desire for relationship. The father relishes the moment and enjoys the fulfilling intimacy of doing things together.

LOVE AND TRANSFORMATION

The Bible can be described as a love story. Yet we tend to focus on just half of the story: God's love for us. He is also working to transform us into sons and daughters who fully love him and live in tune with him. The garden illustration is about more than the beauty of the moment. It is also about growth and transformation.

When did the father first allow his child to join him in the garden? When there was a certain level of skill or ability to do everything correctly? No, there wasn't a test to pass. A simple desire for relationship and involvement is all the father looks for. The father also desires relationship and wants the child to develop and grow. How does that happen? Not by striving or checklists, but by being there and responding to the father. It is all very relational.

The skills of a good gardener are similar to the skills of a good father. They both know how to nurture, nourish, and promote growth. They can transform chaos into beauty. A skilful father promotes growth in his child and in their relationship.

The father in this scenario does not do a daily evaluation of his child's performance. That would quench their spirit and stunt growth. Yet he doesn't just let the child do whatever they want all the time. That would also weaken their relationship and inhibit his child's development.

SYSTEM OR RELATIONSHIP?

For much of my life, I failed to grasp the relational perspective. I thought of my relationship with God in terms of a system or checklist. Salvation was: confess, repent, believe and receive. Living as a good Christian followed a simple system: go to church, read your Bible, pray, etc.

I had grown up in a loving Christian family in Australia. For as long as I can remember, I believed in a God who cared, and I wanted to honour him with my life. Yet as a teenager, I responded to at least three different altar calls at various evangelistic meetings. I was not sure if I was really born again because I did not live up to all the ideals for being a good Christian. I believed in the Father's love, but he seemed to be quite demanding at times.

As I read the Bible and tried to understand what God expected of me, I was subconsciously looking for a *system* to follow. Yet I couldn't crack the code and find a system that worked. I eventually learned that relationships cannot be reduced to a system.

My spiritual journey has been a process of breaking out of the limitations of system-thinking and discovering the relational dynamics of life as God intended. I love sharing with others the things that have given me this fresh perspective and transformed my walk with God – things I wish I had known earlier. May you also experience some of that same paradigm shift as you learn to view familiar topics from a new angle.

A FATHER WHO SAVES

A key part of the transformation in my relationship with God has been a deepening understanding and love for my heavenly Father. Previously, I tended to focus on Jesus. He was centre stage – the One who saves us. The Father seemed to be in the background. I had even heard that Jesus intervened to take the brunt of the Father's wrath towards us – as though they were at odds!

The truth is, our Father is slow to anger and longs to forgive. He sent Jesus because he wants to forgive. Jesus even claimed, "it is the Father, living in me, who is doing his work" (John 14:10). It was God – Father, Son and Holy Spirit in unity – who worked our salvation. Yet crucially, it was the Father who completed the process by raising Jesus.

I had just glossed over the Father's role in our salvation, thinking the whole point was to *believe that Jesus died for my sins*. Yet Paul talks of God crediting righteousness to those "who believe in *him who raised* Jesus our Lord from the dead" (Rom 4:24). We are to believe in the Father. Surprisingly, the saving faith described here does not build on the finished work of Christ but the work of the Father after the Cross.[1]

RESURRECTION NOW

Throughout the centuries, the Eastern Orthodox Church has consistently emphasised the Resurrection. Easter Day is, by far, the most important day on their calendar. In recent decades, a growing number of evangelical scholars have realised how central the Resurrection is in New Testament teaching.[2]

By over-focusing on the Cross, I had an incomplete view of the Resurrection. I thought the Easter was all about the sacrificial death of Jesus, the most important day being Good Friday. The Resurrection merely validated the Cross and gave us the hope of future resurrection (as in 1 Corinthians 15).

On closer examination, however, I find many passages speak of the significance of the Resurrection for life *here and now*. For example, Paul wrote:

And if the Spirit of him who *raised* Jesus from the dead is *living in you*, he who raised Christ from the dead will also *give life to your mortal bodies* because of his Spirit who *lives in you*. (Rom 8:11)

This isn't just about 'eternal life' after our physical death but life to our *mortal* bodies, through his indwelling Spirit. Paul prayed that the Ephesians' eyes would be opened to know God's "incomparably great power for us who believe". This power, he explained, "is the same as the mighty strength he exerted when he raised Christ from the dead" (Eph 1:19–20).

There is a powerful resurrection-life currently available to us. It is from the Father, through *his* Son and by *his* Spirit. This is *Father-life*!

A NEW WAY OF LIVING

I had thought 'eternal life' was just something to look forward to, a new *form* of existence after our physical death. This is valid, yet only part of the story. John claims believers already have eternal life (John 3:36; 1 John 5:13). Elsewhere, he describes it as something that can reside in us (1 John 3:15).

'Eternal life' is the life that flows from the eternal One. For us, it is a dynamic *type* of life and a fresh *way* of living to enjoy here and now. It is a new way of being human. Through the Father's saving grace, this life is available to us. Paul appeals to the Colossian believers to actively engage in this new resurrection life:

Since, then, you *have been raised* with Christ, *set your hearts* on things above, where Christ is, seated at the right hand of God. *Set your minds* on things above, not on earthly things. (Col 3:1–2)

Firstly, we note that Paul is saying they are already raised and he implores them to intentionally tap into this new life. They are to intentionally set their hearts and minds on 'things above' rather than 'earthly things'.

Secondly, we need to explore what Paul is contrasting when he speaks of 'above' and 'earthly'. In the past, I read this as the typical opposites: sacred versus secular; lofty spiritual matters versus the mundane things of this world. Yet context is king! Paul goes on to describe the things of our 'earthly nature': lust, greed, anger, slander, lying, and such (Col 3:5–9). These things destroy life and relationships. In contrast, setting our hearts and minds on things 'above' is very down to earth. It means to 'clothe' ourselves with compassion, kindness, humility, gentleness, patience, forbearance, forgiveness and love (Col 3:12–14). All of these things promote and release life.

GOD IS LIFE!

These life-giving characteristics are the essence of resurrection life. God himself is the true source of these qualities, and they all carry his life. In fact, "every good and perfect gift is from above, coming down from the Father" (Jas 1:17). As we set our heart and mind on these 'things above' – clothing ourselves in compassion, forgiveness, and so on – our daily lives and relationships are infused with life from above. Heaven invades earth through us and touches those around us. We cannot live this Father-life only within a private *me-and-God* bubble. These life-qualities make us more alive and lead us into healthier relationships with both God and neighbour.

Do you want to *clothe yourself* in this way? The more we know him – Father, Son and Spirit – the more easily we can set our minds on the things he values. To know him *is* eternal life, according to Jesus (John 17:3).

There is a *type* of life which is the very essence of God. This 'eternal life' has always existed, and Jesus was the full expression of this *Father-life*. John proclaims, "That which was from the beginning ... the Word of life ... the eternal life ... was with the Father and has appeared to us" (1 John 1:1–2). He later re-emphasises this key concept: "He is the true God and eternal life" (1 John 5:20).

God himself is life. We can embrace the fullness of life he intended for us only through truly knowing Him. It is crucial, however, to know him as our Father: The Father of Life.

A PLACE FOR LIFE TO FLOURISH

To better understand the life God intends for us, let's go back to where it all started, the Garden of Eden. The book of Genesis describes how the Father of Life gradually fills the earth with a rich diversity of plants and animals and we read the repeated observation, "it was good". Yet after the initial work

> **« God intends human life to flourish within a framework.**

of creation is done, activity continues in a new direction. The Creator takes elements of his creation and fashions a garden. Originally, God *spoke* creation into being, yet now, he *planted* a garden (Gen 2:8). More creativity is released as various plants are intentionally planted and organised.

Intentionality distinguishes a garden from raw, untamed nature. Someone is involved in creating order by establishing defined areas, boundaries, pathways, and such. Yet significantly, a garden is a place of *nurture* where life flourishes within the given framework.

Similarly, God intends human life to flourish within a framework. Originally, God placed mankind into the prepared garden. Since then, he intends that we be born into a family. Ideally, parents provide a secure framework for growth and the necessary nurture to stimulate life. Even as adults, we live within the frameworks of society.

This basic model of *life flourishing within a framework* is a recurring theme, and we will explore it from various angles. It connects with the idea of shifting our focus from systems to relationships. A gardener has a system and order in the garden, but the focus is on promoting growth within that framework. God gives us some boundaries and a moral framework for life, yet he is not satisfied with simply having law and order. He desires that our relationships with him and others are alive and flourishing within that framework.

Jesus came that we may know abundant life (John 10:10). There is something spectacular about life that flourishes and abounds. Where I live, in Norway, there is a dramatic display of fresh life every spring. The gardens, fields, and forests explode with renewed growth. The dynamic seasons are quite a contrast to the perpetual green of my childhood in tropical Northern Australia. Yet also there, the rain forests are vibrant and teeming with life. How much more glorious it is when God's sons and daughters flourish in the abundance of his life.

FATHER·LIFE

I have chosen the term *Father-life* to describe the dynamic type of life which is both life itself and the One who is Life. We could just speak of 'resurrection life' or 'eternal life', but those terms evoke many popular assumptions. To me, the concept of Father-life covers:

- The type of life that flows from the Father and is the very essence of God
- The life with the Father which he desires to draw us into
- Living the kind of life the Father has in mind for us
- Taking hold of the Father's hopes and dreams for us
- Desiring to live in harmony with the Father
- Drawing on the Father as our daily source of life
- Allowing the Spirit of the Father to direct our life
- Aiming to be like the Father, as he shapes our character and values
- Aiming to be with the Father and doing what he is doing

If you desire any of these things, keep reading. The aim of this book is to increase your knowledge of the Father and your love for him.

FRESH PERSPECTIVE

A major part of embracing Father-life involves learning to break out of our natural system-thinking and gaining a more relational perspective. If there is to be growth, then something needs to change. This transition from familiar patterns to new paradigms can be demanding, but also refreshing and significant.

Perhaps you've heard of the captain of a large navy ship who, upon seeing the lights of another vessel directly ahead in the mist, sent an urgent signal ordering that vessel to divert. His whole view of the situation suddenly changed when it became clear that the lights were from a lighthouse. That moment of insight quickly resulted in a change of course.

Sometimes, all it takes is some fresh information to help us see in a new light and make better navigational choices in life. This has been my experience. The things that have helped me see my heavenly Father in a fresh way have had a profound impact on the way I live.

As we continue to focus on the Father in this book, please be aware that we are not turning our attention away from Jesus. In one sense, Jesus will always be central: "No one comes to the Father except through me" (John 14:6). Yet note that the point in that verse is that we come *to the Father*. Furthermore, one of the prophecies about Jesus calls him "Everlasting Father" (Is 9:6). Jesus and the Father are barely distinguishable from one another. Focusing on God as Father, however, helps us to recognise him as the source of life itself. We will explore that next.

—

KEY POINTS

- The Resurrection opened the way for a new *way* of living here and now.
- 'Eternal life' is both God himself and life as he intended.
- Like a good gardener, the Father desires to see human life flourish within the given frameworks for life.

REFLECTION AND RESPONSE

Take a moment to meditate on this prayer:

I keep asking that the God of our Lord Jesus Christ, *the glorious Father*, may give you the Spirit of wisdom and revelation, so *that you may know him better*. I pray that the eyes of your heart may be *enlightened* in order that you may know the hope to which he has called you, the riches of his glorious inheritance in his holy people, and *his incomparably great power* for us who believe. That *power* is the same as the mighty strength he exerted when *he raised Christ from the dead* and seated him at his right hand in the heavenly realms, far above all rule and authority, power and dominion, and every name that is invoked, not only in the present age but also in the one to come. (Eph 1:17–21)

Afterwards, pray your own response to the Father, using this passage as a basis. Ask him to release this same life-power in your life.

2

REDISCOVERING THE FATHERHOOD OF GOD

Have you ever struggled to make sense of a large jigsaw puzzle without knowing what image it would form? The challenge would be even greater if you suspected that all you had were random fragments from different sets.

This was how I felt concerning God. I struggled to relate to him as Father, particularly in relation to all the other descriptions in the Bible. My journey of rediscovering the fatherhood of God started with an encounter with a young Muslim:

STRUGGLING TO CONNECT THE PIECES

I was 30 years old and leading a small missionary team in the dusty provincial town of Erciş, in eastern Turkey. There, I met Ahmet, a Kurdish teenager keen to practise his English. Like many Muslims, he was also very open to discussing spiritual matters.

"Tell me, Ahmet," I asked, "you believe that when you die, you will stand before the Creator in judgement. Should he let you into heaven?"

"Well ..." he hesitated, "I have tried to live a good life, and he is merciful, so I think he will let me in."

"But," I questioned, "isn't God holy and just? You know you have often done things against his will. How can a holy God allow rebellion to go unpunished?"

This clearly posed a challenge for Ahmet. He pondered for a moment before concluding, "Well, since he is holy, then perhaps it would be right for him to condemn me."

I tried to explain how the death and resurrection of Jesus resolved the apparent conflict between God's holy justice and his loving mercy. I did not manage to convince Ahmet that day, yet in the following days, I gradually realised that I also had questions.

I was convinced that Jesus had fulfilled God's holy requirements and the righteousness of his judgement, while fully expressing love and mercy through his selfless sacrifice. But that seemed more like a description of the 'mechanics' of salvation. It still left me with a sense of tension between the 'God of the Old Testament' and the 'God of the New Testament'.

I struggled to see the big picture of who God is. I liked the idea of him as a caring father, but I did not always see how that related to him being my king, or a potter shaping my life as he chose. Moreover, how did all this fit with him being a shepherd, a consuming fire, or a rock?

OUR VARIOUS VIEWS OF GOD

Over time, we develop various views about God. Where do they come from? Ideally, from the Bible. Yet many other factors, such as our experience, values, and worldview, shape the way we understand the Bible.

We all have some experience or thoughts regarding earthly fathers and authority figures that inevitably distort our views of God, even if our experiences have been good. Sermons and teaching we have heard, and people who have discipled us, also tend to colour what we see. For example, if we have regularly heard that he is a God of order, we may think more in terms of systems and miss seeing the relational perspective.

Some of the strongest yet most subtle influences upon our views of God come from cultural assumptions. I had to learn how Western individualism coloured my views. I tended to look at God through a *me-and-God* lens. Western thought tends to look at things in isolation, and it emphasises differences, rather than show how things connect. We can easily assume, for example, that God's justice conflicts with his mercy. The world around us tends to think *either/or*, yet the Kingdom is usually a matter of *both/and*.

The Bible uses many different names, adjectives and images to describe God. Because of Western thinking, we need to consciously search for the connections to see the whole picture and not just isolated fragments of truth. In doing this, we need to understand the limitations of biblical imagery.

THE POWER AND PERILS OF ALLEGORY

As a Bible teacher, I am inspired by the way Jesus used parables, and I love the skilful use of allegory in the Narnia books by C. S. Lewis. Allegorical stories can give rich insight into reality. Yet, as they say, you should not force an allegory to walk on all fours.

Allegories, parables and other biblical imagery provide *some* points of connection with the reality they illustrate, but only some. We must not try to draw parallels on every point. For example, in the Narnia stories, Aslan the lion has some strong connections to Jesus. But we must not read too much into the parallels or expect Aslan and Jesus to be identical. Similarly, saying Jesus is a shepherd doesn't mean he is motivated by financial gain or providing for his family, like human shepherds.

We must apply wisdom in how we understand the various descriptions of God in the Bible. When a word is used figuratively, it no longer carries all of its literal meaning. For example, God is like a bridegroom, yet we must not read too much into the bride/bridegroom imagery. As we identify the intended meaning of biblical images, we find that they help to define each other, giving us a more complete picture.

THE WHOLE PICTURE

While biblical metaphors such as shepherd and gardener are similar to the idea of a caring father, others seem at odds with the parent-child relationship. One example is the husband/wife imagery of the Old Testament, which illustrates a formal covenant commitment. Another contrasting image is that of the lovers in the Song of Songs, which has inspired many to pursue deeper intimacy with God. Similarly, we have the image of the bride and bridegroom in the New Testament.

Are these contrasting views (husband/lover/bridegroom) in conflict with the view of God as our Father? Only if we take them out of context and read too much into their figurative meaning. When properly understood, they help define what kind of father God is:

- Our Father is very committed to the relationship, even when we are as rebellious or wayward as an unfaithful spouse.
- He longs to be with us and enjoy oneness of heart, like the desire and satisfaction between two people in love.
- He looks forward to a day of greater trust and closeness, when we are even more involved in each other's lives and passions, like how a bride and groom anticipate their marriage and purposeful life of togetherness.

The opposite is also true; knowing the character of our Father helps define what type of husband, lover, or bridegroom he is presented as being. The same principles apply to other imagery the Bible uses to describe God. We must seek to understand the intended meaning of each 'piece' and how it fits neatly with the others. In addition, our view of the Father must be in harmony with our views of the Son and the Spirit.

The Bible also has imagery for how we can view ourselves in relation to God, such as child, servant, friend, disciple, sheep, clay, and branch. Here too, we

must not take any single view out of context. For example, we are called to have faith as *little children*. Yet focusing only on the image of a helpless little child may hinder us from growing into our role as *adult heirs* of the Father. Similarly, we are both *born* as his children and *adopted*. Bringing our own cultural assumptions to such terms can create conflicting views. The deeper our understanding of what the Bible means by the various ways we can relate to God, the more we can live out *all* of them simultaneously.

WHAT IS FATHERHOOD?

The view of God as our Father is quite unique compared to other descriptions in the Bible. It occurs frequently and touches on many aspects of God's character and our relationship to him. It also goes beyond being an image or metaphor. God is not merely *like* a father, he literally *is* our Father. We have some important foundations for this in the Old Testament, where God's fatherhood is mentioned both directly[3] and indirectly.

In the Hebraic world of the Old Testament, fatherhood had the following three ideas at its core. When *any one* of these appears in relation to God, his fatherhood may be implied, even when 'Father' is not used.

1. Above all, the father is *the source or origin* of a family or clan, so it is he who provides an *inheritance*.
2. A father *protects and provides* for his children.
3. *Obedience and honour* are due to the father; otherwise, *correction or discipline* may be given.[4]

Which points have been strongest in your view of God as Father? Personally, I have tended to focus on the second point (provision and protection) and occasionally, the third (obedience/discipline). However, these points are not unique to a father as provision, protection, and discipline can come from a mother, local authorities, or governments. Yet in the Hebraic worldview, the father alone is the source of the family and thereby the one who gives an inheritance. This first point was central to their understanding of fatherhood.

Thus, the Jews consider Abraham to be their literal father. Yet in terms of being their source, God's fatherhood is just as literal. He is the one who took the initiative with Abraham long before they existed as a people. There are also many references to God giving his people an inheritance, each expressly implying that he is their Father.

I missed seeing these aspects of source and inheritance for two reasons. Firstly, my Western individualist idea of fatherhood only covered one generation, while the biblical view covers countless generations. God is both our personal Father and our collective ancestral Father.

Secondly, my view of inheritance related to death. I rarely considered my inheritance as an *heir of God* (Rom 8:17), and only thought in 'spiritual' terms, and in connection with life after death. Yet some of the biblical references to us as heirs relate to life here and now, and our role in God's plans.

THE FATHER OF US ALL

Understanding God as our source means that his fatherhood isn't limited to his people. He is the source of *all* life, so he literally is the Father of all humanity. Significantly, mankind was created "in his image" (Gen 1:27), just as Adam later had a son "in his image" (Gen 5:3). We are all descended from Adam, the "son of God" (Luke 3:38). The fact that God is our Creator means he is our Father (Deut 32:6).

I had often reflected on Psalm 139:13 – "For you created my inmost being; you knit me together in my mother's womb" – and did not hesitate to apply those words to myself. Yet it never occurred to me that, if the verse was true for me, then it was also true for everyone. The Psalms remind us that we *all* come from him and belong to him: "The LORD is good to all; he has compassion on all he has made" (145:9); "The earth is the LORD's ... and *all* who live in it" (24:1).

> **"** *Our true Father already values us, so he is looking for trust, not performance.*

While speaking in Athens, Paul presents God as the global Father: He has made and guides "all the nations". He desires relationship and is "not far from any one of us". Paul concludes by including his pagan audience in the proclamation, "We are his offspring." (Acts 17:26–28.)

OUR VALUE IN THE FATHER'S EYES

The fact that he is the source of all life – that we are all his offspring – gives everyone an inherent *value* in the Father's eyes. *This* is why God provides salvation by faith, not by works! 'Redemption' means God buys back what is already his.

We are all his 'children', regardless of how lost we are. Our 'works' have nothing to do with salvation because our performance has nothing to do with our value in the Father's eyes. Our true Father already values us, so he is looking for trust, not performance. He longs for us to trust him (have faith in him), so we can have a relationship together. The parable of the Prodigal Son illustrates this.

The foundational facts that we are his offspring and belong to him give us a framework for knowing him as Father. Everyone has this basic framework, but this alone is not relationship. The Father pursues life in the framework. He knows us, cares about us and desires to bless us, even before we are born again.

To better grasp your value in God's eyes, you must go beyond just thinking of your heavenly Father giving you his love, care and provision. Remind yourself regularly of the solid foundation you have in knowing he is the *source* of your life; you belong to him! Remember also that you have an *inheritance* in him; you have a purpose in his good plans.

Understanding our value in the Father's eyes should give us confidence in approaching him, no matter what has gone wrong. It should also transform the way we view others. When we start to see others as the Father sees them and to value them as he does, it then becomes much easier to love our neighbour. Then Father-life becomes a fountain within us.

GRACE TO GROW

Our views of God and others are inseparably connected. Some of the deepest lessons I have learnt about God came through my relationships with others. One such lesson came following my encounter with Ahmet, while I still had questions about the apparent tension between God's holiness and his love.

I was back in Greece, where our mission team had been based for a few months, yet we were soon to leave. As I walked through a forest, praying and worshipping God, I suddenly had flashbacks to various situations with the team. It was as if God was bringing to mind specific incidents when I, as team leader, had been unnecessarily hard on the others.

I was shocked. While earnestly seeking to be a godly leader, I had fallen short of my goal in numerous situations. No, I was more than shocked; I was upset with my heavenly Father and offended at his timing: "Fine, this is great, *now* you show me?" I protested. "Why couldn't you have shown me these things earlier, to help me be the godly leader I was aiming to be?"

The response from God seemed immediate. I didn't hear audible words, but the warm, gentle thoughts that came were crystal clear: "Calm down. I am your Father and I know how to help you grow. You had other things to deal with earlier. I am revealing these things to you now, so *now* is the time for you to respond. This is my grace to you. I guide you through a process; I don't ask you to deal with everything at once. Because I withheld this revelation, I extended grace to the others. I helped them to cope with your immaturity."

Wow! That suddenly put things in a new perspective. I realised immediately that my being offended at God was an expression of pride. I had 'aimed' to be a good leader, but what I had in mind was *to be able to look back and see that I had followed the system and done a good job*. I was more concerned with getting a perfect 'scorecard' and impressing my Father.

By showing me my shortcomings, God ruined my hopes of having a perfect scorecard. Yet even my prideful reaction was met with the Father's gentle correction. I even sensed God affirming my misguided efforts to be a good leader.

However, the fact that God allowed me to remain ignorant at first did not change my responsibility for my actions. I knew I had to talk to the team and ask for forgiveness. Fortunately, we were to have a team gathering just after my walk. As I asked for forgiveness, they unanimously responded that it was fine.

They explained that they understood that I had been focused on many practical things, and my behaviour had not bothered them.

SPACE TO GROW

The Father had extended His grace in the midst of my immaturity, and had given others the grace to help them live with me. Meanwhile, I had expected too much of others and was irritated at their apparent lack of maturity. How ironic!

God was clearly teaching me more about his father-heart. The Father's grace often involves 'breathing space' and room to grow. I am so glad God isn't like an inspection mechanic after a mechanical safety test: "Here is the list of all the problems with your car. Come back and show us when they're fixed." No, our Father takes into consideration our level of maturity and insight, and the condition of our heart. He desires to shape our hearts and the way we live but, as a good father, he knows the importance of having space to grow.

Let's connect this to the garden model of *life in a framework*. In Greece, I was too focused on the framework and the way things 'should' have been. I was good at 'pruning' the team but weak at promoting life and giving space for growth. I was more focused on systems than relationships. God's response, just like in the scene of the father and child gardening, was to first hold back and then later, bring gentle correction.

DESIRING CLARITY

A few weeks earlier, in Turkey, my talks with Ahmet had stirred up questions about God's character and the underlying tension I felt. His holiness appeared to demand perfection, while his love seemed to be about accepting anything. My distorted view of God's holiness is why I was so demanding of the others on the team.

God's gentle dealings with me in Greece gave a fresh understanding of the Father's grace. I started to sense that this new view of grace answered my questions about God's holiness and love – somehow. Yet tension remained. Even as I understood that God's grace was not a matter of *either/or*, I still struggled to see the *both/and* perspective. I 'knew' grace was the answer to everything, but I did not want mere theory – I wanted life!

As I prayed and asked God to help me better grasp and live the truth, fresh insight soon came in the form of a vision that left me sleepless for hours. I was overwhelmed by the refreshing sweetness of Father-life. I'll tell you about it in the next two chapters.

—

KEY POINTS

- The Bible gives us a variety of imagery to help us know God. We must understand his fatherhood in connection with the other perspectives.
- God's fatherhood extends to all humanity, giving each one of us value in his eyes.
- God gives his children breathing space and the grace we need to help us grow.

REFLECTION AND RESPONSE

Do you need help to see others as the Father sees them? Perhaps recognising the value God sees in all humans will help you to better understand how he views you. If the Father is highlighting this as an area of growth, then he will help you in that process. Pray and ask for the grace to grow.

3

THE FATHER'S TARGET

The vision came to me many years ago, yet still influences my life. It was not a vision I could see with my physical eyes; it was more like a vivid dream. It helped me to resolve the apparent tension between the Father's holiness and his love.

THE ARCHERY LESSON

I was in an open field, and an archery target was in the distance. A bow and a quiver of arrows were placed in my hands as I heard the Father's words, "I have one goal for your life: Jesus, my Son. Be just like him. Be one with him; he is one with me. You must aim at the target."

The words were warm, yet clear and firm. The words themselves were not frightening, yet the task was daunting. The target was so far away. How could I even hope to come close, let alone hit the target?

The enormity of the challenge churned through my mind, yet my anxiety dissipated as I felt a comforting arm on my shoulder. I heard the same warm voice of the Father again: "Whatever happens – whatever the result – do not lose hope.

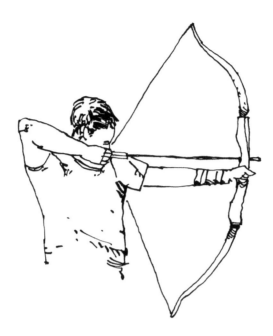

Wherever your arrows fall does not change your value in my eyes. You are my child, and I love you and accept you just as you are."

This seemed like another metaphor of the tension between God's holiness and his love. Sure, there was acceptance, but there was also the impossible target. As I considered the scene in my mind, however, new hope filled me. This was different. There was no tension here, if I focused on my aim rather than the results. I sensed the Father explaining further:

"When your aim is pure, what happens after you release the string is not the issue. Do not let an arrow that falls short of the target become a source of discouragement. Neither let an arrow that hits the target be a source of pride.

"Do not ignore the results, as being aware is important in improving your aim. Just do not let the results define you, as they don't change who you are. This is not a competition; this is life. I am your Father, and you are my son. Let your aim be to aim well. I look to *the heart* and the integrity of your aim. I see where you are really aiming."

A FRESH PERSPECTIVE

This vision gave me important insights into the heart of the Father. Who else but a father or mother is so able to meet us with both *total acceptance* and *high ideals*? Those two things are naturally in conflict when focusing on behaviour and results. When results are the focus, the ideal becomes the *standard* for acceptance.

For example, you may struggle with some area of habitual sin, such as gossiping, worrying, dishonesty, anger, or something else. If you set yourself the standard of never doing it again, you will feel condemned at the slightest failing. By focusing on the heart, we can know the Father's acceptance and humbly and confidently keep aiming for the ideal, even while failing repeatedly.

Total acceptance and high ideals can work together, like life flourishing within a framework – the garden model. We have the impossible ideal of perfect oneness with the Father and a clear framework of moral absolutes. Within that framework, however, he meets us with the life-giving acceptance and nourishment we need to grow. Our growth needs the Father's acceptance (giving room for growth) and his ideals (something to stretch towards).

The archery field example gives us an integrated understanding of the Father's character, and reminds us of his focus on the heart.

THE FATHER LOOKS TO THE HEART

The fact that God looks to the heart was not new to me. The Bible tells us, "people look at the outward appearance, but the LORD looks at the heart" (1 Sam 16:7). I had 'known' this as a theological truth, yet it had not yet transformed my view of God and my perception of how he viewed me. I still focused on performance, behaviour and appearance – external things. I had assumed that the Father focused on these things also.

It isn't that the external aspects of your life do not matter to God; they do. Yet they don't matter in the way we assume. They are simply the fruit, or the outworking, of the heart. The Father views the external workings of your life not *only* in light of his absolute, divine standards, but also in relation to the state of your heart. This is the core of the Gospel message. If the condition of our heart changes – if we have a repentant heart – then God no longer views our sin in the same way.

King David had a clear understanding of the need for heart repentance. His actions were horribly out of line when he got Bathsheba pregnant and had her husband murdered (2 Sam 11–12). Yet David knew his wrong actions came from deep within. He knew God was looking to his heart and it needed sorting out: "Create in me a pure heart, O God, and renew a steadfast spirit within me" (Ps 51:10). David also knew that his heart response was the most meaningful response he could make and that God would not look down on this: "My sacrifice, O God, is a broken spirit; a broken and contrite heart you, God, will not despise" (Ps 51:17).

God had given the people of Israel many commandments, including laws for ritual sacrifice. However, he was not interested in having a people that simply followed rituals and conformed to a pattern of behaviour. The sacrifices were a way of expressing love for God. If their hearts were not in it, then their outer obedience was meaningless, as highlighted by Isaiah:

> "The multitude of your sacrifices – what are they to me?" says the LORD. "I have more than enough of burnt offerings, of rams and the fat of fattened animals; I have no pleasure in the blood of bulls and lambs and goats. When you come to appear before me, who has asked this of you, this trampling of my courts? Stop bringing meaningless offerings!"
> (Is 1:11–13a)

God himself had given instructions for bringing sacrifices. Yet there is no point in trying to impress him by doing the 'right' thing if our heart motives and attitudes are all wrong. He may rightly ask, "Who asked you to do this?" and proclaim that our actions are meaningless.

PARENTAL GRACE

This emphasis on the heart means our heavenly Father differentiates between wilfully wrong actions and acts of ignorance or immaturity. Every good parent understands the importance of grace when dealing with their child's shortcomings. In the gardening story (Chapter 1), the father acted graciously in response to his child's lack of skill. Our heavenly Father most certainly knows how to exercise such care in bringing up his children.

As I began to understand this, I started to see that, in one sense, *the aim is the aim*. Now, I would say that *relationship is the aim*. It's as though the Father is saying, "I never thought you would always hit the target, but I want you to

> **" Sin is when we value other things more than relationship with God.**

always have a pure heart, a pure aim. Aim at me, at having a relationship with me, and at oneness with me."

Life is more than trying to *achieve* a perfect aim. We must not be so focused on how well we aim that this then becomes another area of performance or striving. Our goal is relationship, and the process of learning and growing is part of that. God doesn't leave us to sort out everything alone. Our heavenly Father is with us, helping us, encouraging us, and teaching us. He wants our relationship with him to grow deeper and our trust in him to grow stronger.

MISSING THE MARK

While the archery field analogy gave fresh insight and was appreciated by others, I was not certain if it was entirely biblical. I had heard preachers explain that the New Testament Greek word for sin – *hamartia* – meant to 'miss the mark'. If that was God's view, then it was not enough to simply aim well.

Interestingly, *hamartia* was used in archery, meaning literally to 'miss the mark' or 'fail to hit the target'. Yet in Greek thought and culture, it was also applied figuratively, to any form of human shortcoming or failure. Even singing off-key was *hamartia*. Basically, 'sin' was failure to live up to a defined system or standard.

I later discovered, however, that the typical Greek usage of *hamartia* was not what the writers of the New Testament had in mind. They built upon Old Testament concepts of guilt and evil intention, giving *hamartia* a distinctive new meaning.[5]

Biblical usage of *hamartia* focuses on the moral shortcomings of a heart aiming at anything less than the Father's highest. When we are 'off-target' in the Father's eyes, it is our aim that is off, not merely our results. Sin is when we have rejected his target, when we value other things more than relationship with him. While the world views sin simply in terms of a system, the biblical view is relational. This understanding of sin connects well with the archery field example.

THE AIM OF THE TORAH

While looking for biblical perspectives, what I found most interesting was the Hebrew word *torah*. This is usually translated as 'the Law' (referring to the Law of Moses) or just 'law'. The word *torah*, however, derives from the root verb *yarah*, which was used in archery. It meant 'to take aim, to shoot'. In this sense, the Torah is not so much a rule book to rate your performance as it is a guide from the Father, defining the target for his people.

The essence of the Torah – the bullseye of the target – was to have healthy relationships. Jesus highlighted this relational aspect when He said that the greatest commands were to love God and neighbour. The rules provided a framework for doing so, yet the point was to have relational life in the framework.

Anyone who has tried to learn archery knows that repeated practice is required to improve one's aim. This was a part of the whole deal for Israel – it was OK to keep trying and improving one's aim. As long as they kept trying and humbly realigned their heart when needed, God would not disqualify them for poor performance. We saw earlier that King David had grasped this.

God even assumed that people wouldn't always hit the target. The Torah included instructions about what to do when they had failed to aim well or had missed the mark. There were prescribed ways of dealing with sin, expressing repentance, and making restitution.

The Father's grace is also evident in his instructions for the Day of Atonement. Once a year, God wanted everyone to wipe the slate clean and start all over again. Never in the history of Israel did the Father ever redefine the target of loving him with their whole heart. His approach was always to give new chances and encourage His people to improve their aim.

Even if someone made a total mess of their life by getting into serious debt, losing their family farm, or ending up in slavery, there was still hope. Every fifty years, the Year of Jubilee was a major 'reboot' for the whole community. Never in the history of the world has there been a god so keen on giving broken relationships a fresh start, setting captives free, and restoring lost inheritances. The Torah is amazing.

THE AIM OF IT ALL

As Christians under the new covenant, our target is not the Torah, yet the goal of loving God wholeheartedly – the bullseye – remains the same. Our new target is clear: Christ in us, us in him. We aim to be one with him, as his resurrection life flows through us. It is as if the Father is saying, "I have one goal for your life: Jesus, my Son. Be just like him. Be one with him; he is one with me." We are to aim for depth of relationship, not simply a defined system.

Yes, complete oneness is impossible in terms of performance. Yes, we will never fully achieve this goal, in that sense. Yet we can keep aiming and realigning our aim every time we recognise the need to do so. We can keep taking new risks and trying again, practising and developing our aim and our understanding of what we are actually aiming at. Our heavenly Father is more than willing to help us in this process. He desires relationship with us.

In the next chapter, we will further explore insights from the archery field.

—

KEY POINTS

- The Father looks to the heart more than performance, and he desires growth.
- In looking to the heart, there is no tension between his total acceptance and his high ideals.
- Knowing the above points frees us to keep aiming at his target, regardless of our performance.

REFLECTION AND RESPONSE

Take a moment to reflect on what you have just read. Does the fact that the Father looks to the heart challenge some of your views of God? Invite the Father to give you a deeper revelation of how he views you, especially in your times of weakness or failure.

Finally, read the poem on the next page. It was written by a friend as she processed her impressions from the archery field story. You could also write a poem or a song, draw a picture, or make your own creative response to the archery field.

AIMING

Pursuing You
in a pool of tears.
While others
keep score
and pronounce judgement.

You alone know
whether I was disobedient
or just blind.

I will pursue You only
as theories,
sounding so wise,
call and tempt me.

Some demand, "Hit the bullseye!"
Others plead, "Don't even try!"

But how can You know
whether I love You?

I embrace all your precepts;
I will not forget them!
So I etch your Name
into my quiver
with my nails.

Your eye is not on my arrows,
as they sail way off course.
You follow my eye
and the integrity
of my
aim.

Synnøve Kapelrud, 2008 (translated by Darryl Krause, used with permission)

4

OUR OWN TARGETS

Have you ever experienced 'spiritual ping-pong'? For me, it was all about the apparent tension between God's holiness and love. My encounter with Ahmet (chapter 2) brought this tension to light, but it had been an underlying issue for a long time. I needed to understand how distorted views of the Father impact our aim and our relationship with him.

SPIRITUAL PING-PONG

As a young believer, I had a desire to grow and develop, though rarely saw much progress. How was spiritual growth supposed to happen, anyway? What part could I play in the process? Did I even have a part to play?

I would pray and ask God to help me grow in some area, and then I would try to be diligent and put effort into the process myself. This led to frustration and an abiding sense of condemnation about my shortcomings. All this connects with a legalistic view of the Father, where his holiness, justice and hatred of sin are dominant aspects.

After a while, however, someone would remind me of the Father's love and mercy: *"We can't change ourselves. We have to let God do the changing."* I was reminded that the Father knows our weaknesses, yet loves us regardless. This 'all love' view of God seemed to say, *"God loves you just the way you are. In fact, he loves you so much that he is going to leave you this way; growth is not important to God."* This was just as discomforting as the condemnation of the first view. I did not want to stay as I was. I had struggles and insecurity; I wanted to grow and be set free.

The problem was that both of these views of the Father seemed to be true in isolation but not when put together. So I continually bounced from one view to the other, in spiritual ping-pong. That is the problem with spiritual ping-pong; you are the ball! It is not *you* playing; rather, ping-pong is being *played on you*. That is certainly not fun.

Can you identify with this sense of tension or ping-pong? How have you dealt with it? Some people accept the apparent tensions, either consciously or subconsciously. Others have pushed aside certain 'pieces' of the puzzle that don't seem to fit. One common approach is to try to *balance* these two sides, yet that does nothing to resolve the tension or bring things together. For me, the archery field gave a completely new understanding of what was going on.

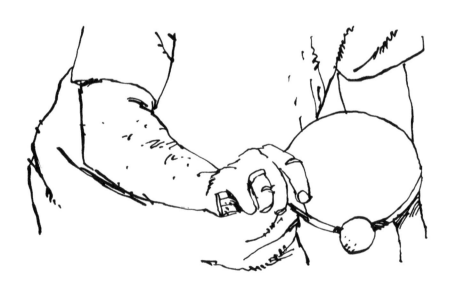

THE ARCHERY LESSON CONTINUES

The first part of the archery field vision gave me a more integrated and truthful view of God's character. The next part exposed the lies I had believed about God. What can happen when we forget that the Father looks to the heart, when we don't look to him for help, and when we take certain things out of context?

Two new scenes illustrating how I had lived came to mind. These scenes exposed the deception of the spiritual ping-pong I had experienced. While these two scenes seemed to take me in opposite directions, both led to the same surprising result.

THE LEGALIST

In the first scene, I was preoccupied with the phrase, "You must aim at the target". That resonated so strongly with me that I dwelt only on this phrase and its apparent implications. It was clear what I had to do. (Or so I thought.) I was focused on my performance and I imagined God was, too. I continued the train of thought and assumed the seemingly logical conclusion: "You must aim at the target ... *therefore you must hit the target.*"

In this scene, God seemed like a strict father. I felt I had to please him by performing well. I could also feel a pervading sense of failure and condemnation as one arrow after another went astray: "Oh no, not another arrow way off course." (*For example, as a young Christian, I would decide to read my Bible every day, but couldn't even do so for two consecutive days. I also felt like a complete failure regarding Christian 'duties' such as evangelism.*)

So far, only a few arrows had come near the target, and sudden gusts of wind had carried many in new directions. The hopelessness of the situation was almost too much to bear. Then, to top it all off, I fumbled while releasing the next arrow and it fell at my feet.

This was not working at all well; something had to change. If only the target was not so far away. While wallowing in the misery of my very literal shortcomings, I noticed a tree stump off to one side. Perhaps this was something I could hit?

I carefully placed a new arrow on the bowstring with a fresh sense of hope. I drew back and released. "Wow. That was close." Anticipation mounted as I released the next arrow. "Yes! I finally hit something." (*For example: Always being truthful was too hard; I was regularly a little deceitful, or pretending to not hear something. Yet I could manage to avoid any serious lies or major deceit.*)

This fresh sense of achievement led me to choose the tree stump as a 'better' target for my life. However, as the challenge wore off, I chose another object a little further away. Not everything worked out as I had hoped, but at least I felt some satisfaction with my achievements. Deep inside, I hoped my Father would be pleased with my performance.

Occasionally, I would catch a glimpse of the original target. "Shouldn't I really be aiming over there?" Doubts troubled me briefly, before being dispelled by the comforting words of reason, "Yes, but that was impossible. You have to be realistic; God knows your limitations." Yet I couldn't ignore the lingering sense of unrest deep in my conscience, as I pursued the satisfaction of my redefined goals. Results had become more important than relationship.

THE LIBERALIST

The second scene started quite differently. "You must aim at the target" faded from consciousness as the latter words resounded through my heart and soul: "Wherever your arrows fall does not change your value in my eyes." Oh, those words of the Father – so warm, accepting and reassuring.

Again, my reasoning and assumptions led me astray. This time, I dwelt on the total lack of pressure to perform. I extended the sentence: "Wherever your arrows fall does not change your value ... *therefore you don't even need to aim at the target.*"

I started aiming at the target but quickly discovered how impossible it was. But what did it matter? Before long, I was shooting all over the place at whatever I chose. (*For example, there were situations in my life where I would define for myself what was OK or not OK.*)

As I continued, the liberty of shooting anywhere and rarely hitting anything became meaningless. Soon, an element of the previous scene was repeating itself in mirror detail. A nearby tree stump caught my attention. After several attempts and a few close misses, I finally hit it. (*For example, I was habitually ignoring certain road rules because I didn't want to be 'legalistic'. When I sensed the Holy Spirit convicting me about my lack of respect for civil authority, I only adjusted my driving to the level of what most people were doing. That much I could do.*)

Aiming at something on the archery field was certainly more rewarding than aiming at nothing. Yet after consistently hitting my chosen target, the

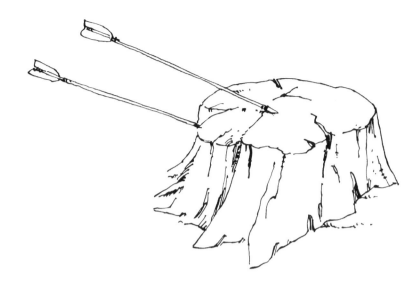

challenge would wear off and I would select another. After all, wasn't that a better target?

MY OWN TARGETS

I was lost in my world of struggles and failures on that archery field as I tried to digest these conflicting scenes. Suddenly, a voice penetrated my thoughts, like an echo from the dawn of time asking, "Where are you, Adam?" Those were not the exact words, but they could have been. In my unfolding vision of the archery field, the Father, who had seemed absent while I struggled alone, was now clearly present. A firm yet warm voice questioned, "What are you aiming at, my son?"

This simple, penetrating question was directed at both of the two scenes I had just seen myself in. I went from one scene to the other, searching for words to defend myself:

"I really did try." I protested, as the character in the first scene. "But it just wasn't working out; it was practically impossible. You must understand how hard it is. Anyway, look at the tree stump way over there. See how far away it is. Yet I can hit it, or at least come very close."

In the second scene, I was just as defensive: "Well, you said wherever my arrows fall does not change my value. You must have known I could never hit that target, or you wouldn't have said that. But look at this tree stump over here; I can hit it always, and that one over there, nearly always."

"But, my son," responded the familiar voice of the Father. The firm, warm tone was seasoned with sorrow and pain, as he summed up both of the scenes: "You have chosen your own targets."

THE PROBLEM AND THE SOLUTION

Everything was suddenly clear to me. The scenes in my mind were realistic and hit home with shocking accuracy. I used to see myself as a victim of spiritual ping-pong but now, I could see my part in creating the tension.

We tend to focus on outer things, such as performance and 'liberty'. These distract us from the importance of aiming well and focusing on the Father of life. In turning our attention away from God, we lose focus and develop distorted views of his character and what life is all about. This leads to regularly choosing our own standards, our own targets. Typically, we end up with a confusing mix of different standards for different situations. This was certainly true in my life.

The Bible has a word to describe situations where we bow and submit to something of our own making: idolatry. Instead of 'idolising' our heavenly Father, aiming to be like him and in relationship with him, we set up our own 'idols' of what to aim for. We value other things more than our relationship with him.

As I reflected on the archery field, I felt a sense of guilt and shame for my part in all of this. Yet at the same time, there was a powerful sense of hope. Here were answers; here was a way of escape. The key to avoiding 'spiritual ping-pong' and the hidden idolatry it leads to is to keep the focus on our aim and not our results.

LOOKING BEHIND OR MOVING ON?

Performance and results are, by definition, in the past. On the other hand, our aim is focused on the future – what we hope to achieve, what we would like to happen. Perhaps Paul was thinking of this important shift from results to aim when he wrote of "forgetting what is *behind* and straining toward what is *ahead*" (see Phil 3:12–14).

> **❝** *Instead of 'idolising' our heavenly Father,*
> *we set up our own 'idols'.*

It is our human emphasis on external things, such as results, that causes us to focus *behind* – at what has happened. Imagine a child sitting on the floor playing. A second child walks past and accidentally stumbles on one of the first child's feet.

"Hey! Don't kick me," the first child shouts.

"Well, you shouldn't stick your feet out," the second child retorts.

"No, you should watch where you're going!"

What is happening here? Both children are looking back at what just happened and are trying to defend their innocence. But it is an *outer* innocence of performance they have in mind, and it causes them to accuse and be suspicious of each other.

If our focus is on our aim rather than the result, then we can look ahead and our goal is *heart* innocence. Imagine if this was the aim of the second child. Perhaps they would say, "I'm sorry. I wasn't looking. I hope you are not hurt." The focus would be on life and relationship.

If we are aiming at innocence of behaviour, saying "sorry" is admitting we have failed to behave well. Typically, we think in terms of systems rather than relationships, focusing on frameworks more than what brings life. We then use standards to defend our innocence and to accuse one another – sometimes even God. I know I have brought some of these elements into my relationship with God, either acting this way myself or imagining God to be similarly focused on standards. When I focused behind, rather than ahead, I ended up justifying my actions, felt condemned and blamed my Father.

TWO FORMS OF DECEPTION

Our views of God – and of life itself – get blurred when we shift our focus away from the Father of Life. Instead of his intended framework for life, we end up with the twisted frameworks of legalism and liberalism[6].

Legalism gives us a complex framework, which puts the focus on performance and striving. It leaves us with a sense of condemnation for any failure and a feeling of pride for any achievement. Our identity is tied to our performance and life is all about *doing*.

Liberalism, on the other hand, has a simpler framework. It puts the focus on acceptance and discourages trying: "God loves me no matter what. I'm OK as I am." Life is all about *being*. The feeling of 'liberty', however, can lead to apathy or poor self-esteem.

A legalistic mindset is so focused on reaching the standard that it ends up making a standard it can reach, perhaps not all the time, but at least some of the time. While the thought that we should be aiming for a higher standard lingers, the achievement of reaching the chosen standard justifies the digression.

A liberalistic mindset argues that we don't need a standard; anything goes. Of course, we shouldn't do *this* or *that* – like rob a bank or murder. But as long as we don't do anything from our pick-and-choose list of things, then anything goes. Again, we end up making our own standard. We define a system and aim for that rather than relationship and oneness.

REBELLION OR TRUST?

Legalism and liberalism appear to be opposites, yet both lead us to setting our own standards. Ever since the Garden of Eden, humans have had an inner conviction that we alone know what is best for us. This conviction, driven by pride and rebellion, leads us away from the One whose very essence is Life. Instead of feeding from the Tree of Life, we turn to the Tree of Knowledge, thinking we can figure out for ourselves the best framework to live by.

Recognising this underlying rebellion gives a clearer understanding of sin. Sin is not so much about a failure to perform or be perfect as much as it is about the rejection of God's target for our lives – we fail to aim at relationship with him. The renowned minister and author, Oswald Chambers, says it clearly:

> Every other view of sin, other than the Bible's view, looks on sin as a disease, a weakness, a blunder, an infirmity. But the biblical revelation shows sin to be an anarchy – not merely a missing of the mark, but a refusal to aim at the mark.[7]

The alternative to rebellion is trust. Choosing to aim at the Father's target – to aim at life with him, as he intended it – is an initial expression of our trust. This trust in the Father will deepen as we continue to pursue relationship and aim well. This is especially true at times when nothing is working out as we had hoped, or it feels like we have been abandoned.

One thing that helps our trust to grow – even during hard times – is having an integrated and trustworthy view of his character. The archery field gives us a simple model of how God's love and mercy work together with his holiness and justice. It clearly illustrates how the Father meets us with *both* total acceptance *and* high ideals.

In time, the archery field also helped me to grasp more of the immeasurably rich goodness of God. He truly is a good Father, as we will see in the next two chapters.

—

KEY POINTS

- Our tendency to focus on outer things leads us to make assumptions about God.
- Legalism and liberalism are both based on distorted views and lead us to set our own standards (define our own targets).
- We can escape 'spiritual ping-pong' as we gain a holistic view of the Father and learn to fully trust him (aim at his target).

REFLECTION AND RESPONSE

What aspects of legalism or liberalism can you identify in your own life? How about 'spiritual ping-pong'? Have you chosen some of your own targets? Take a moment to reflect or discuss. (If you are not sure what I mean by *liberalism*, have a look at endnote 6.)

To be free from such things, you need a fresh revelation of the Father and his focus on the heart. However, your ability to recognise these things will be limited if you feel a sense of condemnation. The Father has high ideals for us, yet meets us with total acceptance. Receive the Father's acceptance now as you invite him to reveal more of his character and his target for your life.

Thank you, Father, that you love and value me, and that your love and acceptance are not based on performance. Help me to see where I have set my own targets, that I might realign to your high ideals. Teach me to value what you value and to aim at relationship with you.

5

EMBRACING TRUE GOODNESS

One day, someone asked Jesus, "Good teacher, what must I do to inherit eternal life?" Jesus responded with a new question and a surprising statement: "Why do you call me good? No one is good – except God alone" (Luke 18:18–19). In other words: God alone is *truly* good, and human goodness is always less than ideal. How can we understand this sort of goodness?

WHAT IS TRUE GOODNESS?

Imagine I tell you about a friend who is a 'good person'. I explain that he is really warm and loving, never gets angry, and is always ready to forgive. He is, however, not entirely dependable. He will often promise to do something then not keep his word, and he isn't entirely honest in all his business dealings. Can I really use the term 'good' to describe him? Is being warm and loving enough? Or is there a moral side to true goodness?

Let's consider another 'good person': This one is always dependable, meticulously law-abiding, and upright in all she does. Yet she is a bit hard on her children and somewhat demanding of others. She isn't the first person you would invite to a fun party. Can we honestly describe her as 'good'? Is the uprightness and dependability of moral goodness enough? Or is there a need for compassion and tenderness to be fully good?

Understanding true goodness needs a *both/and* perspective. We need to integrate *both* aspects of warmth *and* uprightness. We must see *both* the heart goodness of compassion and forgiveness, *and* the moral goodness of integrity and dependability.

Is there any person who fully meets this description? No. Human goodness, even at its best, is always distorted or lacking. It tends to emphasise either one aspect or the other. Human parents, no matter how good they are, will always be less than ideal. Truly, no one is good – except God. The Father alone is the defining reference point for true goodness.

WARM OR COLD?

To better understand true goodness, let's compare various character traits. Consider these four simple words that can describe someone's character:

- warm
- soft
- firm
- cold

It is easy to see how some of these words are opposites:

- warm vs. cold
- soft vs. firm

Yet which of these words belong together? It may seem natural to connect these pairs:

- warm and soft
- firm and cold

Thinking about goodness in these ways can affect our view of God. If we tend to view our heavenly Father as warm and soft, we may end up with a liberalistic view. If words like firm and cold dominate our view of the Father, then we easily slide into legalism. As long as we connect warm with soft and firm with cold when thinking about God's character, then we are set for a game of spiritual ping-pong. These word pairings are not helpful when it comes to understanding the Father's character.

So, how is God? God is good – in the *full* meaning of true goodness. He is both *warm* (caring, loving, merciful, mindful of our weaknesses, quick to forgive), and *firm* (solid, dependable, unwavering, truthful, holy, just).

We can connect this to the archery field by saying God is:

- **Firm** ("you must aim at the target")
- yet *not* Cold ("therefore you must hit the target")
- **Warm** ("wherever your arrows fall does not change your value")
- yet *not* Soft ("therefore you don't need to aim at the target")

Remember, there is no conflict here as long as we keep in mind that our heavenly Father focuses on the heart. The Father has high ideals for his children, yet he loves and accepts us as we are, even as he helps us to grow.

AIMING FOR BALANCE?

How can we grow to know God in this way? How can we be careful to avoid the extremes of legalism and liberalism? One way of avoiding two opposing extremes is to aim for *'balance'*. This is a very popular solution – we find it in both Eastern philosophy and Western values. The problem with this middle way of 'balance' is that it is not a well-defined target. It is only defined by what to avoid, thereby increasing the tension.

As a young Christian, I would hear advice like: "Avoid the ditches. Don't be *too* legalistic. Don't be *too* extreme in your liberty." Yet, how much legalism is *too* much? How much liberty is *too* extreme? Should we aim to be 50% legalistic and 50% liberalistic? No! These things – even in small amounts – hinder us from knowing our heavenly Father. The pursuit of balance isn't what the Bible teaches, and it is a road to nowhere. How can we find a better road?

DIVIDING WISELY

Let's go back to the four words we looked at earlier and use them in a series of simple diagrams. We'll start by placing them in a grid:

Firm	Warm
Cold	Soft

Next, we'll split the diagram. This illustrates the opposing views of God and the associated spiritual ping-pong. There is a clear tension here between the legalistic view of God as 'firm and cold' and the liberalistic view that he is 'warm and soft'.

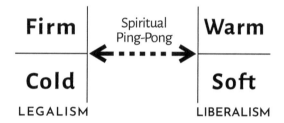

What is the source of this tension? Is there tension within God? No, the tension comes from our underlying assumptions. Because we naturally focus on outer things, we think about the level of performance God expects of us. We assume if God is *firm*, he must also be *cold* (not warm and caring). That is legalism. Similarly, in liberalism, we assume if he is *warm*, he must also be *soft* (not firm, no high ideals). The diagram below illustrates this double tension.

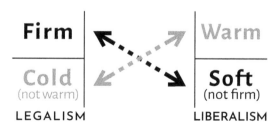

The distorted views of legalism and liberalism are a mixture of truth and lies. That is the source of the tension. Lies and deception are, by nature, at odds with the truth. Let's abandon the confusion of the spiritual ping-pong model and the pursuit of balance. We'll go back to the original grid, with added labels to identify the truth and lies about God's character:

Firm TRUTH	**Warm** TRUTH
Cold LIE	**Soft** LIE

Perhaps a better way to make sense of this would be to start by separating truth from lies. We'll sort out the 'rubbish', being careful to keep what is valuable. This is starting to look better:

Firm	**Warm**
Sorting out ↑ the rubbish ↓	TRUTH
	LIES
Cold	Soft

Dividing things this way gives a very different perspective. In rejecting lies about him, we see more clearly that God is both firm and warm. Let's illustrate the wholeness of God's character by joining 'Firm' and 'Warm' into one unit. God is truly good, and we find double security in his total acceptance and his high ideals. The road we need to be on is now clearer.

GOD IS GOOD! (**Firm & Warm**)

↑ This road is going somewhere!

LIES (Cold / Soft)

As we seek to embrace God's goodness, we begin to journey out of lies and into truth, out of darkness into light, out of confusion into revelation, and out of fragmented tension into wholeness. This road is going somewhere. We are no longer simply trying to avoid ditches and stay out of trouble. This new road leads us into closer relationship with our Father. It also leads us into wholeness as we embrace the wholeness of who he is.

KEEPING THINGS TOGETHER

The Bible is an important resource as we seek to grasp the wholeness of God's goodness. Yet we need to see the whole message of Scripture and not take things out of context. For example, the Bible tells us about God's 'warmth' and acceptance – he is a father who knows our weaknesses and remembers we are dust. Yet we can easily draw our own conclusions about what that means, thereby distorting God's word. Here are some typical thought patterns:

"God knows I am weak ... *therefore he lowers the standard to my level.*"

"The Father accepts me as I am ... *therefore I'm fine just as I am and don't need to grow.*"

"God remembers I am dust ... *therefore he doesn't expect me to be any better.*"

That is not what the Bible says. All of the Scripture passages I have found that speak of God knowing our weaknesses also speak of the high ideals he has for us. For example, in the Psalms, David reminds us that God "knows how we are formed, he remembers that we are dust" (Ps 103:14). Yet the same psalm tells of how God wants to show love and compassion to those who recognise his high ideals – those who *fear* him and *obey* him (vv. 11, 13, 17 & 18).

In the New Testament, we read that God is able "to sympathize with our weaknesses" (Heb 4:15). Does that mean our Father gives us the 'grace' to stay weak? No, the very next verse encourages us to "approach the throne of grace with confidence, so that we may ... find *grace to help us* in our time of need" (Heb 4:16). This help is offered in connection with God's high ideals. Just a couple of verses earlier, we are reminded that he is the One who "judges the thoughts and attitudes of the heart" (v. 12), and the One "to whom we must give account" (v. 13).

Similarly, James declares that the Lord "is full of compassion and mercy" (Jas 5:11). However, only a couple of verses earlier, he warns his readers (who were 'saved'

> **" *True goodness is the very essence of his being and character.*

believers) of God's impending judgement for the seemingly trivial matter of grumbling against each other (v. 9). Our Father has high ideals for his children.

We need to understand what the Bible tells us about God in context, otherwise we lose the ability to see vital connections and our view of His goodness becomes distorted.

GOD'S GLORIOUS GOODNESS

There is an interesting incident in the life of Moses that brings together these two sides of God's goodness. It starts with Moses requesting, "Now show me your glory" (Ex 33:18). Before this, Moses had already seen many physical expressions of God's glory. Now, God's response to Moses shifts the focus, as he declares, "I will cause all my *goodness* to pass in front of you ..." (v. 19)

What does goodness have to do with glory? Has God missed the point of Moses' request? Or could it be that God's goodness is the most glorious thing about him? God goes on to say that he will proclaim his *name* in Moses' presence:

> And the Lord said, "I will cause all my goodness to pass in front of you, and I will proclaim my name, the Lord, in your presence. I will have mercy on whom I will have mercy, and I will have compassion on whom I will have compassion. But," he said, "you cannot see my face, for no one may see me and live." (Ex 33:19–20)

Moses was already familiar with God's name, *Yahweh*. Yet "name" in the Bible is most often about reputation. When God proclaims his *name* in this way, he is making a statement about who he is and what he wants to be known for. What does he proclaim about himself?

Even before the passing-by part of this incident, God's explanation of what is about to happen gives us a foretaste. He makes a brief statement about the two interwoven sides of his goodness: There is the *warm*, caring aspect expressed in his mercy and compassion, and there is the *firm*, pure, other-than, holy aspect expressed in, "no one may see me and live."

God then explains how Moses is to be placed in a cleft in the rock to be shielded as he passes by. While passing by, he proclaims his *name*:

> And he passed in front of Moses, proclaiming, "The LORD, the LORD, the compassionate and gracious God, slow to anger, abounding in love and faithfulness, maintaining love to thousands, and forgiving wickedness, rebellion and sin. Yet he does not leave the guilty unpunished; he punishes the children and their children for the sin of the fathers to the third and fourth generation." (Ex. 34:6–7)

Again, we see both aspects of goodness as God proclaims his name: There is the *warm*, caring aspect expressed in compassion, love, faithfulness, slowness to anger, willingness to forgive. Yet there is also the *firm*, pure, holy aspect of not leaving the guilty unpunished.

It is the *goodness* of God – his holy, loving goodness – which sets him apart from all human forms of goodness and all false gods. True goodness is the very essence of his being and character. Yet we need revelation to see it. We are so easily blinded by our human ideas of goodness that we miss the immense glory of the rich goodness of God – a perfect integration of warmth and firmness; faithfulness and truthfulness; compassion and dependability; forgiveness and judgement; love and holiness.

HOLY WHOLENESS

The goodness of God is the purest and most whole form of goodness. Our heavenly Father is not 50% holy and 50% loving. He is 100% holy and 100% loving. That means that his love and holiness are inseparably connected.

Just look at the description of genuine love in 1 Corinthians 13 (patient, kind, not self-seeking, etc.). This is holy love – the ultimate expression of pure, whole, undiluted, uncorrupted love. Similarly, the Father's goodness is holy goodness.

When we think of God's holiness expressed in wrath and judgement, we must also recognise his love at work. It is his love for all that is truly good, his passion for all that promotes life, that is at odds with all that destroys life and undermines relationship with him. Yet he is slow to anger, giving grace to the humble. His holiness is loving holiness; his goodness is loving goodness.

Do you see the beautiful wholeness of the Father's character? He is the perfect Father; he meets us with *total acceptance* and *high ideals*. God is truly good. The more we grasp that, the more we desire to be one with him.

—

KEY POINTS

- Human ideas of goodness are distorted and limited.
- True goodness is both 'firm' and 'warm'.
- Our heavenly Father is the very definition of true goodness. We must grasp the wholeness of his character.

REFLECTION AND RESPONSE

Have you tried to have a 'balanced' view of God? In what ways can the idea of balance reinforce the apparent tension in God's character and hinder you from trusting the Father's goodness? (Pause to reflect or discuss.)

Take a moment in prayer. Invite the Father to give you a fresher, richer revelation of his goodness. Ask for a renewed understanding of both his holiness and his love. Be ready to respond to that revelation in new ways in the coming days and weeks.

6

THE GOOD FATHER

How does our heavenly Father express his goodness to us? It might be helpful to contrast how he acts towards us with what he is *not* like. Perhaps a parable can shed light on God's father-heart.

THE PARABLE OF THE DISTRAUGHT DAUGHTER

Anna was six years old when her parents were expecting their second child. Shortly before the birth, Anna was sent via airplane to stay with her grandparents for a few days.

On her flight back home, Anna's heart bubbled with anticipation at the thought of seeing her baby brother. She spontaneously shared with the lady sitting next to her about her brother and proudly showed the new dress her grandfather had given her.

"What a cute girl," the woman thought, as she offered Anna some chocolates. In all the excitement, Anna forgot her father's parting words of caution. He told her to be careful about what she ate and to avoid sweets because she sometimes suffered from travel sickness. Anna was not rebellious; she was simply caught up in excitement. She continued to talk – and to eat chocolates.

After a while, however, the plane encountered turbulence, and a growing nausea soon left Anna's new dress covered in chocolate vomit. A flight attendant made a futile attempt to clean her up, but had other duties as they prepared for landing. The mess was now smeared well into Anna's dress.

After landing, one of the ground staff kept Anna at a safe distance as he guided her through the terminal building. As soon as he realised who the father was in the crowd, he left Anna to walk the last few paces alone.

Anna was in emotional turmoil and lowered her gaze. Her joy and excitement about reconnecting with her family and seeing her baby brother were now smothered by an overwhelming sense of despair. How could she face her father? She had disobeyed his instructions; she had eaten chocolate.

Much more than the guilt of disobedience, Anna was numbed by shame. Her stained dress displayed how she felt inside. How could she meet her father like this? Anna hesitated briefly. She hardly dared to look up as she slowly dragged her feet towards her father.

WHAT HAPPENS NEXT?

How will Anna's father respond as he greets her? Will he be shocked, disappointed, indifferent or even ashamed of her? Would it help if I give you a clue and say Anna's father is a good person? How would a 'good person' respond?

Let's look at three different versions of this father, which correspond to three views of God's goodness. In each alternate ending, the father will be 'good' in some sense and will offer some form of forgiveness. First, consider this legalistic father, who represents a 'firm and cold' view of God:

FIRM AND COLD

Anna glanced up and saw her father in the crowd; she also saw the shock on his face. Her emotions were in turmoil. She ran to her father sobbing, "I'm sorry Daddy. I'm sorry. I know I shouldn't have eaten the chocolates."

Her father held her at a distance as he tried to assess the situation. "I'm sorry," she repeated, still trying to connect with her father.

"It's OK. I forgive you," he said hesitantly, as he bent down and gave her a restrained peck on the cheek, seemingly preoccupied. "I'm so surprised you would do something like this," he continued. "You've obviously eaten sweets on the flight, even though I told you not to. Well, this certainly changes our plans. I told Mummy we would go straight to the hospital, but you're not going anywhere looking like this."

"But I want to see Mummy. I want to see the baby."

"That will have to wait until tomorrow. I forgive you, but you need to understand there are consequences when you do something wrong."

Anna knew there was no use protesting. She silently followed her father to the car, weighed down by shame and worthlessness. Her father's words of forgiveness barely touched her sense of failure and her aching heart.

WARM AND SOFT

What if Anna's father illustrates a 'warm and soft' concept of God?

Anna glanced up and saw her father in the crowd. His initial look of surprise quickly turned to a smile, then a chuckle. At first, Anna was a little confused, but soon she too started to chuckle and found herself moving confidently towards her father.

"Well, this was a surprise. I didn't expect to see you looking like this. Seems like you had some fun on the flight," he said, trying to lighten the situation.

"I'm sorry Daddy," Anna started but was abruptly cut off.

"Nonsense, don't worry about it. I forgive you. It's just a dress," her father said casually, as he bent down and gave her a careful shoulder hug. "It's OK. Don't think about it," he added, as he held her briefly.

"But I wanted the baby to see me in my new dress, and now it's all ruined." Anna was obviously still distressed.

"It's OK, Anna. It's just a dress. Let's see if we can clean you up a little in the washroom." A few minutes in the washroom removed some of the worst staining, but now bits of fibre from paper towels were added to the mess.

"Come on, Anna, let's just go. Don't fret about the dress. It's no big deal. I forgive you. You know Mummy and I love you just as you are. Come on; cheer up. Let's go see your brother. It's going to be fun; he may even smile at you."

Anna knew she was forgiven, and she tried looking forward to the hospital visit. But the messy dress reflected her abiding sense of shame and failure as she silently followed her father to the car. His shallow forgiveness did not heal her deep shame.

FIRM AND WARM

Is it possible to find a third view that isn't just a mixture of the other two, nor the point of 'balance' between them? What if Anna's father was godly in the full sense of the word? What if his character was very much like God's? Let's imagine a truly good father, who is both firm and warm, who has both total acceptance and high ideals. How might he respond?

Anna glanced up and saw her father in the crowd. For a moment she thought she saw a look of surprise on his face. She glanced away and hesitated. By the time she looked up again, his face was beaming as he ran towards her. Anna ran the last few steps as her father bent down and swept her up in a big reassuring bear hug.

"But I'm all dirty, Daddy," Anna tried to protest. Her father didn't care at all. She clearly needed a change of clothes, so what did it matter if his clothes also got dirty. Besides, he was thinking more about his daughter than his clothes; she looked like she really needed him.

"I'm sorry Daddy," she sobbed. "I know I shouldn't have eaten the chocolates."

Her father's heart went out to her. He could see she had already suffered terribly. He could see she was repentant too, so he certainly wasn't about to crush her broken spirit by chastising her. He continued to hold Anna firmly while comforting and reassuring her: "It's all right, my precious girl. I forgive you; don't cry."

"But my new dress is ruined, Daddy."

"Oh, it was such a beautiful dress too," he replied with warmth and sincerity. "But don't worry; let's go home and clean ourselves up first. Then on the way to the hospital, I'll buy you another new dress."

"But it's all my fault," Anna protested.

"Yes, it wasn't a very clever thing to do. But I know you didn't mean it, and I'm going to help you fix everything up."

"I love you, Daddy," Anna exclaimed as she relaxed her head onto her father's shoulder. Her heart relaxed also, as she now knew everything was OK. She was again at peace with her father and with herself.

"I love you too, Anna," he whispered as he carried her out to the car.

GRACE RESTORES

The father offered forgiveness in all the versions of the story. Yet in the first two, Anna was left with an abiding sense of shame. It was only in the last version that the father brought deep restoration. He alone extended grace and dealt with Anna's shame.

Human forgiveness is often more technical and external, dealing with the 'legal facts' of guilt. Grace is relational and goes much deeper. True grace deals with the inner feelings of failure, worthlessness, and low self-esteem, in order to rebuild relationship and trust. Shame runs deep and needs more than mere forgiveness.

One of the most surprising things about God's character is how he engages in our lives and is committed to finding solutions. This is how firmness was expressed in the last version of the story – the father was firmly committed to pursuing the best relationship possible. And, just like that father, our heavenly Father is even willing to get himself dirty as he helps us out of the mess we've made. He desires to reconcile and restore. He restores honour, dignity, and relationships. The Father's goodness is expressed in actively helping us grow – his grace empowers.

RECOGNISING THE COUNTERFEITS

In contrast, a legalistic view of the Father can leave us feeling helpless and debilitated. We focus on limits, standards, shortcomings and the need to strive. We carry a sense of condemnation and an awareness that things are not as they *should* be. We imagine God our Father increasing our guilt and shame by saying things like:

- "You *should* do better."
- "You *shouldn't* do that."
- "That's *not OK*."
- "That's *not good enough*."
- "When will you ever learn?"
- "OK, I forgive you, but don't do it again."
- "You *should* pray more."

On the other hand, some of us with a legalistic view of God may feel like we have it all together and that the Father is pleased with us for our good performance. We may then find ourselves judging others, thinking they *should do better*, etc. It doesn't matter whether we view others or ourselves in this way, or imagine

God viewing us this way. Any emphasis on the way things 'should' be indicates legalistic thinking and a legalistic view of God.

A liberalistic view of the Father can seem different. Rather than striving, we may tend to make excuses, or minimise or ignore problems. We probably focus on '*freedom*', often with a sense of shamelessness. We imagine the Father saying things like:

- "I love you *just as you are*, so stop aiming to be better."
- "It's *OK* to just stay weak and sinful."
- "You *don't have to* be that good."
- "You *don't have to* pray if you don't want to."
  (Somewhat true but not helpful.)
- "It's important for you to be *free*."

With such a view there will typically be an emphasis on the finished work of the Cross and all that is done and finished in our lives. These things are important, but what is done and finished is only part of the story, giving a framework for an ongoing relationship.

THE FATHER ENGAGES AND EMPOWERS

The Father doesn't just want us 'saved' – he wants our transformation into oneness with him. That is one important aspect missing in both legalism and liberalism. Where is the grace to restore? Where is the help to grow? Legalism judges but offers no help. Liberalism says you're OK just as you are, you don't need to grow. But what if I want to grow? What if I want to be more like my Father?

God the Father will, at times, expose some area of weakness in our lives or show us where we fall short. Legalism has that part right, though it tends to overemphasise this aspect. Whenever the Father exposes a need for growth, he only does so as a *first step* towards offering help and restoration. He only exposes our shortcomings in the context of such help. (This is what I experienced in Greece when God highlighted an area for growth in my life. See Chapter 2.) God doesn't just leave us with the awareness of weakness and the associated sense of failure and condemnation.

Liberalism highlights how the Father accepts us in our weakness, which is true. Yet the liberalistic view of acceptance is passive. God doesn't just accept us; He encourages us to grow, helps us to repent when necessary, and actively empowers us. He gives "grace to *help* us in our time of need" (Heb 4:16). The Father of Life seeks to release his life deep within us. He aims for deep transformation at the core of our being.

DEEP TRANSFORMATION

Legalism will generally lead to shallow outer *conformity*, with little growth. We may end up 'doing the right thing' while our hearts are hard and our motives and attitudes are not right. In legalism, the 'grace' extended in forgiveness touches guilt, but not the deeper root of shame.

Liberalism, on the other hand, can lead to *non-conformity*. We may appear to conform in many situations, but only to the degree it suits us. There may be little or no desire for growth; it may even be seen as unnecessary. Any forgiveness is shallow, generally trivialising sin or shame but not dealing with them.

Yet our true Father does not focus on simple conformity or our 'freedom of choice'. In his true goodness, he aims for deep inner *transformation* of our heart – our values, our motives, our character – as we *grow* increasingly closer to him and more like him. His grace goes deep, removing shame and restoring identity. As he transforms us, we find ourselves freely choosing to conform to his image.

THE ACTIVE GRACE OF GOD

The more we grasp the fullness of the Father's goodness, the more we can comprehend and receive his grace. This is because grace is the *practical expression* of goodness; it's how true goodness acts.

I often hear grace spoken of as a synonym for forgiveness, which is partly true. Yet grace is so much more. Forgiveness can be passive (like in the first two versions of Anna's father). In the softer form, it may be expressed as: "Just forget it; don't worry about it." In such cases, ideals may be brushed aside or the standard reduced to the shortcomings of the person.

In contrast, a harder person may say: "OK, I forgive, but you don't deserve it. Now go away and don't do it again." The high standard is firmly upheld and the forgiveness is more of a legal technicality than a heart expression of compassion and warmth.

Neither of these distorted forms of forgiveness expresses grace or depth of relationship. Forgiveness addresses guilt about what has been *done*. That is a step

> **❝** *Grace is the practical expression of goodness;*
> *it's how true goodness acts.*

in the right direction, but grace takes it further. Father-grace goes to the core of our *being*, our identity, who we *are*. Life flourishes when we are set free from shame and start to discover who we are in the Father. His grace stimulates growth by coming to us with total acceptance and the high ideals that provide a framework for growth. Both parts work together; acceptance alone isn't enough.

LIVING IN GOD'S GOODNESS

We must grasp the firmness *and* the warmth of who God is. We need to live within the double security of the Father's total acceptance *and* his high ideals. That is where life flourishes. The thing that brings his acceptance and ideals together is the fact that he is more than willing to get involved and help us. This was the key with the third father (the truly good one) in Anna's story.

Gaining insight into the true goodness of the Father has helped me grow in two ways. Obviously, it has strengthened my trust in him. It has also helped me to know how he calls us to live with those around us. As I have allowed the goodness of God to shape how I interact with others, I have, in turn, gained a deeper knowledge of the Father and more confident trust in him. Loving God and neighbour are not two separate issues; they are inseparably integrated (Matt 22:36–40).

Later chapters in this book will focus on how our understanding of God's goodness can impact the way we live. For now, in the coming chapters, let's shift our focus to what it means for us to be in relationship with God.

—

KEY POINTS
- The heart of true goodness and grace goes beyond mere forgiveness; it addresses shame and seeks to restore.
- Recognising counterfeit views of the Father can help us to know the truth about how he views us.

- The Father engages in our lives to bring growth and transformation – his grace is active and empowering.

REFLECTION AND RESPONSE

Have another look at the "Recognising the Counterfeits" section of this chapter. Pay attention to some of the keywords there. Certain words – *should, shouldn't, OK, not OK, good enough, not good enough* – can alert us to distorted views of God in our thinking. Even if these words appear in our thoughts about our self or others, they are usually a reflection of our view of God. Which of these thought patterns are most relevant for you?

Invite the Father to increase your awareness of when you are thinking such thoughts, especially during the coming weeks. As awareness increases, be ready to reject the lies and embrace the true goodness of the Father.

PART TWO

RELATING TO
THE FATHER

I wish I had a dollar for each time I heard someone say, "Christianity is not a religion; it is a relationship." Unfortunately, many descriptions of our relationship with God seem static, lacking relational dynamics.

What makes a healthy relationship? What sort of relationship does God hope to have with his children? Moreover, how can the relationship grow and deepen? After exploring these questions in the coming chapters, we will turn our focus to an essential ingredient in all deep and meaningful relationships: Trust. This is also known as 'faith' and is one of the purest elements of Father-life.

> *Come near to God*
> *and he will come near to you.*
> James 4:8

7

RELATIONSHIP?

How can our relationship with the Father be deep and meaningful? What makes any relationship dynamic? Let's start at the human level and consider a marriage that seems to be lacking something important.

A HOLLOW RELATIONSHIP

Suppose you have a cousin you don't see much because he lives in a distant city. He has married since you last saw him, and five years have passed before you finally meet again. As you talk with him, your concern about his marriage grows. He says he still loves his wife, yet he hasn't seen her for a while and only visits her occasionally. By now, you need an explanation.

"Don't get anxious," he says, with a calm smile. "Our marriage is fine. This is just the way we do things. At first, we lived together all the time. Then I started reconnecting with some of my old friends. Sometimes, I didn't come home at night, or I'd be away for a whole weekend. Eventually, I ended up buying a separate house for her to live in."

Now you are even more confused: "Being separated doesn't sound like a good marriage. Are you getting divorced?"

"No, we are not formally separated. It's just a practical arrangement. You see, I would sometimes bring other women home and –"

"What! There are other women?"

"Calm down. I could see this created tension in our relationship. I really care about my wife, so I thought it best if she had her own place to live. But hey, I go there regularly to spend time with her or do some odd jobs."

"But, there are other women. Doesn't she want a divorce?"

"No, she's just terrific about it all. It doesn't matter what I do, she always forgives me and says she is committed to standing by me, no matter what. We are determined to stay married. It's really just a matter of identity and knowing your standing as a spouse. Once you get married, then you are married; you *are* a spouse."

By now, you just have to tell it like it is. "That is just nonsense. Being married is about more than the wedding and the facts of being a spouse. It's about growing closer and investing in the relationship."

"Well, if you think you must put something into it to make it work, then you haven't understood the significance of what happens when you get married. I had doubts at one stage, so I checked with the pastor. He remembered our wedding clearly, and he could assure me everything was in order. All the proper procedures

were followed, the right words said, and the papers were all signed in the right places. We were 100% married. You don't have to try to make a marriage work; you just need to rest in the assurance that you are married."

"But, where is love in all this? You have to show that you love her."

"I do love my wife, and I show my love to her in my way. I'm not going to fall into the trap of thinking I must *do* certain things to be her husband. I *am* her husband – that is my identity. If I was trying to be a 'good husband', then that wouldn't be real."

By this point, you feel like you're talking to a brick wall. He speaks about being real but has a very hollow understanding of real relationships.

THE FRAMEWORK NEEDS LIFE

This is a rather absurd illustration, but I hope you get the point. I have never heard anyone talk like this about marriage. Unfortunately, I have met many Christians who talk about their relationship with God in a similar way. The emphasis is typically on our *position* in Christ, who we have now *become*, and all that is done and *finished*. These are important foundations, yet they become distorted by the split-thinking that says life with our heavenly Father is all about *being* and not at all about *doing*.

Perhaps you have seen the film *Green Card*. An American woman agrees to marry a French man, purely as a technicality, so he can obtain residency status. They don't intend to have an actual marriage beyond the paperwork. The authorities, however, want to check that this is a genuine relationship: Are they really *relating* together as husband and wife? The question of what they *do* together is vital.

The initial act of *getting* married – or *getting* right with God – provides a framework for the relationship. Yet there needs to be life in the framework for it to be a real relationship. The life comes, and the relationship flourishes, through the things you do together. A good example of this is the father and child gardening together (Chapter 1).

CONTRACT OR COVENANT?

As mentioned in Chapter 2, the Bible regularly uses marriage as an illustration of the covenant commitment our heavenly Father wants with his children. For many years, I thought of a covenant merely as a special type of contract. Yet, compared with contracts, the biblical view of covenant gives us a *very* different approach to relationships – one that is easily misunderstood.

Contracts are generally a practical arrangement, focusing on the external aspects of a relationship. The commitment is to the conditions of the contract, rather than the actual relationship. A breach of contract from either side can end the relationship.

In contrast, a covenant is about the heart. It is a deep inner commitment of loyalty to the relationship – to protect it and nurture it. Sometimes, there are no clear conditions, like in David's covenant with Jonathan (1 Sam 18:3, etc.). If there are conditions, as in the case of God's covenant with Israel, these simply give additional framework to the relationship.

The goal of a covenant isn't simply to keep the conditions, but to maintain the health of the relationship. If either party violates any of the conditions, that does not automatically cancel the covenant. The relationship can continue, especially if there is willingness to repair the damage. Similarly, if there is rebellion, the other party may choose to pursue the relationship hoping for a change of heart. We see this type of commitment in the father of the Prodigal Son.

God our Father has a covenant commitment to his children, and earthly parents usually have an unspoken covenant pursuit of relationship with their children. A good father doesn't just look for correct behaviour in his children, as if they were simply fulfilling contractual obligations. He looks for a covenant-like desire to pursue the relationship. That requires covenant-faithfulness, which is very different to contract-faithfulness.

Faithfulness to a contract is simply about keeping the conditions, and unfaithfulness occurs when a condition is violated. This is where many Pharisees got it wrong – they treated the covenant like a contract. They thought they were being faithful towards God simply because they stayed within the conditions of the covenant. They focused on hitting the target but they redefined it in terms of a contract.

In contrast, covenant-faithfulness is about continuing to aim at the target of a healthy relationship, even when things go wrong. Any failure to pursue the relationship, or any action that undermines or threatens the relationship, is unfaithfulness. For example, a husband or wife who continually attacks their spouse verbally, undermining their self-esteem, is unfaithful. If a couple reaches a point where they give up on their marriage and only stay together for practical reasons, that too is unfaithfulness.

This is why our heavenly Father has never been interested in those who seek to fulfil the conditions of covenant but don't pursue relationship. This also explains why all the conditions of God's covenant with Israel (the Law) could be summed up as: *Love God with all your heart, soul and mind* (Matt 22:36–40). It has always been about the health of the relationship. Similarly, James says that *faith without deeds is dead* (Jas 2:26). If your declared 'faith' in God is a mere technicality, and you don't act like you trust him, then the relationship lacks life.

The new covenant has different conditions to the old, yet the core commitment is the same: Loyalty to our heavenly Father. We commit to pursue a healthy relationship with him and to avoid deliberately damaging the relationship. We cannot think we have fulfilled the new covenant merely by being 'saved' or having an identity as his child.

RELATIONAL LOYALTY

The importance of covenant loyalty is highlighted by Paul in his letter to the Romans, but it is easy to miss it if we don't understand covenant. At the start of chapter 7, Paul gives the illustration of a marriage covenant being terminated by death. Pay attention, however, as he ends up talking about two different types of death.

Paul's example is of a woman who, after the death of her first husband, is free to marry another (7:1–3). Paul's point is that relationship to the law (being controlled by it) can also end by death, yet it is not the law that needs to die:

So, my brothers and sisters, you also *died to the law* through the body of Christ, that you might *belong to another*, to him who was raised from the dead, in order that we might *bear fruit* for God. (7:4)

There are some important points to note here. Paul is not saying the law is dead and gone, as was the woman's first husband. This time, the original relationship is broken by the believer ("you") dying *to* the law. This isn't a permanent, *physical death* (like the husband's death); it is a *relational death*.

Another example of a relational death is something that can happen in the Middle East, if a son has brought great shame on his family. His father may say,

"You are dead to me. I no longer have a son." In so doing, the father hardens his heart towards his son and 'dies' to him relationally. The father now acts as 'dead' towards the son, being unresponsive to him.

Paul is evidently referring to a similar *relational death* in Romans 7. By embracing Christ, the believer has "died *to* the law". Since that first relationship is dead, the believer is now able to "belong to another". Rather than loyalty only to what had been the *conditions* for the relationship (the law), there should be loyalty to the *relationship* itself. For their relationship with God to be alive and flourishing (that it "might bear fruit"), they must continue to remain voluntarily 'dead' to the law (not controlled by it). To enjoy full richness of life in God, there needs to be a death to other things; some 'pruning' must happen.

DYING TO OTHERS

Even good things can get in the way of our relationship with our heavenly Father, including things given by him. While Paul talks of the need to die to the law, he still has a high view of God's commandments. In the same chapter, he describes the law as "holy, righteous and good" (Rom 7:12). Elsewhere he qualifies, "the law is good *if one uses it properly*" (1 Tim 1:8).

The issue with the law is that any focus on just the *framework* for the relationship undermines and distracts us from the *life* of the relationship. This was one of the problems with the example of the cousin who had a hollow idea of marriage (at the start of this chapter). He was so focused on merely having his 'papers in order' that he didn't pursue the relationship.

Another problem with the cousin was that he thought it didn't matter how he lived, since his wife was so forgiving. Paul had to address this issue amongst believers in Rome who thought similarly about the grace of God.

> What shall we say, then? Shall we go on sinning, so that grace may increase? By no means! We are those who have died to sin; how can we live in it any longer? (Rom 6:1–2)

Paul's "how can we" doesn't question what is possible, but states what is unthinkable. When I stood at the altar and said *yes* to my wife, I virtually said *no* to every other romantic attachment. If you saw me flirting with someone else,

> *We have a relational obligation to stay loyal to the relationship.*

you could rightly ask, "How can you do that?" Similarly, we have said *yes* to God and *no* to sin; how can we deliberately keep pursuing other things that damage the relationship?

Loyalty is the issue. We have a relational obligation to stay loyal to the relationship and keep it healthy. That means more than just following a system – we are obliged to pursue the relationship.

A NEW AIM

"Hey, wait a minute," you may protest. "Aren't we done with all this 'obligation' business in the new covenant?" Well, not according to Paul:

> Therefore, brothers and sisters, we have an obligation – but it is not to the flesh, to live according to it. For if you live according to the flesh, you will die; but if by the Spirit you put to death the misdeeds of the body, you will live. For those who are led by the Spirit of God are the children of God. (Rom 8:12–14)

This is not a *legal* obligation; it is a *relational* obligation. When Paul starts with 'therefore', he is building on what he said prior to this. That included mention of *the Spirit living in you* (v. 11). How did the Spirit get to be living in you? You invited him in; you said *yes* to relationship. When you invite someone into your home, you have an obligation to hang out with them and not go off and do your own thing. Similarly, you have a relational obligation to live by the Spirit, not the flesh.

Let's see how Paul describes the Spirit in the previous verse. You may even recall seeing this in Chapter 1:

> And if the Spirit of him who *raised* Jesus from the dead is *living in you*, he who raised Christ from the dead will also *give life to your mortal bodies* because of his Spirit who *lives in you*. (Rom 8:11)

This resurrection life, here and now, is available to all who keep saying *yes* to God, allowing his Spirit to lead. Being led by the Spirit shows that we are "children of God" (v. 14).

SYSTEM OR RELATIONSHIP?

Being clear about the difference between *contract* and *covenant* is important for making sense of the Bible. We can also speak of this in terms of *system* and *relationship*. Growing out of system-thinking (focusing on the frameworks for life) and into relational-thinking (focusing on life, within a framework) is one of the keys to Father-life.

We need this relational mindset for our relationship with God to be more than a hollow framework. As we read the Bible, particularly Paul's teaching, a relational perspective is essential for getting the message. Paul does not simply promote a *system* for getting people 'saved'. When talking about what we must turn *from*, his emphasis is always on *who* we turn to. Paul is passionate about us coming into the fullness of all that the Father has for us – a dynamic relationship of resurrection-life in his Spirit.

HEALTHY RELATIONSHIPS IMPART LIFE

Living in tune with the Father of Life will also shape our relationships with others. Relationships are the very fabric of life. At school, I learned about how society was made up of different people fulfilling different roles – teachers, doctors, police officers, and such. That is a simple model for children, yet society is more than a system with different functions. Relationships are what knit us all together, and the quality of a society is only as good as the quality of the relationships.

What factors promote a good and long life? Previously, research into longevity focused on physical factors like climate, diet, exercise or genetics. Yet these things are simply part of the framework for life. Recent research has highlighted relational factors, such as the number of people we interact with, and the number of close relationships with people we know we can count on. These things enrich and prolong life more than any other factor.[8]

Another example is found in the area of genetics, which was previously thought of as a fixed system of coding that determined our development. Recent studies in epigenetics have shown how other factors regulate the effect of our genes. One of the key factors, particularly in young children, is relationships. The more we are surrounded by healthy, supportive relationships, the positive potential of our genes is correspondingly released and negative elements suppressed.[9] Good relationships are life.

Relationships are part of the fabric of life at the core of our being, impacting our identity and sense of worth, so healthy relationships are vital. As Christians, knowing God as our Father, and knowing we can always count on him, gives us the best basis for fully living – and can even heal damage from broken relationships or poor genes. How to pursue this type of dynamic, life-giving relationship with God is our next topic.

—

KEY POINTS

- Having the right framework for a relationship is not enough; we also need life in the relationship.
- Keeping covenant means being committed to keep investing in the relationship while letting conflicting relationships die.
- Healthy relationships are alive and spread life.

REFLECTION AND RESPONSE

Are there any things or people in your life that are hindering your relationship with the Father, or holding you back from fully pursuing him? It may not even be sin or something doubtful. Sometimes even apparently 'good' or 'innocent' things or relationships can hold us back or undermine our relationship with God. Ask the Father for revelation.

Dying to such things doesn't need to be some heavy or dramatic process. Keep opening yourself to see the beauty of the Father's character and the value of relationship with him. Saying *no* to less valuable things requires gradually less effort as you continue to say *yes* to God. Ask God to remind you of this and help you during the coming weeks.

8

PURSUING RELATIONSHIP

What are the basic elements of a dynamic relationship with the Father? One aspect is to pursue relationship and to actually live in it. A good example of this is found in the life of Brother Lawrence, as told in the book, *The Practice of the Presence of God*.[10]

LIVING IN HIS PRESENCE

For much of his life, Brother Lawrence served in seclusion in the kitchen of a monastery in Paris, yet his simple approach to life with God has been a great inspiration to many. He did not differentiate between 'spiritual' and 'secular' matters. He knew God's presence and peace just as much in the noise and clatter of the kitchen as when kneeling at communion or in a time of prayer.

His simple approach was to have an awareness of God's presence, continually turning to him – whether it be for assistance, guidance or blessing for the task at hand, or to give thanks when the task was done. His relationship with God was dynamic and fresh.[11]

After reading his book, I was inspired to pursue relationship with God in all of life. That started a long process of learning to know the Father's presence in new ways. In time, he taught me many more things about relationships and the resurrection-life he has for us.

RELATIONAL DYNAMICS

Meaningful relationships are dynamic; they have a continuing sequence of events, a story. All ongoing relationships have a past, a present, and a future – and the all-important present includes active dynamics and interaction. Meaningful relationships have ongoing *life*.

Many passages in the New Testament look back at what has happened in salvation and tell us who we *have become*. Yet such vital facts – including what God has done through the Cross and the Resurrection – are often presented as the backdrop or framework for our relationship with God. The emphasis is on how we should live *now* as we embrace the process of who we *are becoming*. For example, "Since, then, you have been raised with Christ, set your hearts on things above" (Col 3:1).

Similarly, in another passage, Paul repeats the phrase "how much more" as he transitions through three progressively more significant levels of God's work in our lives (Rom 5: 9–11). His basic level is the foundation that we *have been* "justified by his blood" (v. 9). His most significant level refers to the present relational dynamics of "his life" in us and the reconciliation we *now* have (v. 10–11).[12]

Yet, how many of our worship songs focus on the past, as we repeatedly thank him for having saved us? We should certainly celebrate that critical event, yet not let it blind us to the rich, ongoing dynamics of Father-life. Imagine a woman who keeps thanking her husband for having married her, yet rarely expresses what she appreciates about him today.

Relationship with God, like marriage, is partly about who we *have become*, but also about who we *are becoming* as we live out the adventure of that relationship. The same is true for childhood and parenthood. The wedding or the birth gives us the *objective*, historical, non-negotiable, hard facts that provide a framework for the relationship. But then, we need to pour life into that framework; we need to put some 'flesh' on the 'bones' of the structure. We do this in marriage as we *subjectively* respond to our spouse and take initiative to strengthen the relationship. Parents interact *subjectively* with their children, and the relationship deepens and grows.

All deep and lasting relationships are formed in the interactive chemistry of these *objective* and *subjective* components working together – subjective life within an objective framework. The process can't be reduced to a system. Legalism gives us a system of 'who we should be,' emphasising our need to put *subjective* effort into *becoming*. Liberalism encourages us to passively 'rest' in all that is done and finished, giving us a system of *objective* facts about who we *have become*. Yet these views are incomplete and shallow. They both lack relational dynamics.

The primary thing that makes relationships work is the commitment to both honour and pursue the relationship. Sometimes, it's about the *objectivity* to stand by your commitment even when you don't feel like it. Other times, it's about the responsive *subjectivity* of your choices, attitudes, values, and desires as you take risks, pursue the relationship, and enjoy the other.

Relationships are like living things. Like a garden, we need to maintain the boundaries and remove dead wood. We also need to nurture the relationship, water it, and provide the best conditions for growth. If a relationship isn't growing and thriving, it is probably fading or even dying.

GROWTH AND MATURITY

The Song of Songs gives us a vivid description of a deep and dynamic relationship. Some view this purely as inspiration for human marriage. For others, it is a rich allegory of God's relationship with his people, either collectively or individually.[13] Whichever view you hold, it contains insights about how our relationship with God can deepen and develop.

In the early stages of the relationship, the woman proclaims, "My beloved is mine and I am his" (Song 2:16). She thinks firstly of her claim on him and only secondarily of his claim on her. This is similar to a teenager in love, focused on what they get out of the relationship. Likewise, young Christians can be preoccupied with what God has done for *me* and what he means to *me*.

As the relationship develops, the woman later declares, "I am my beloved's and my beloved is mine" (6:3). Now the order is reversed, and his claim on her is foremost. This shows an awakened sense of commitment and perhaps an awareness of the relational obligation to pursue the relationship. As a young Christian, I thought of Jesus mostly as *my* saviour, emphasising what I gained. Fresh life came into the relationship when I finally learnt to know him as Lord and to give myself more fully to him. (The Bible refers to Jesus as 'saviour' only 16 times, yet over 600 times as 'Lord'.)

Finally, we see the relationship deepen when the woman asserts, "I belong to my beloved, and his desire is for me" (7:10). She is fully focused on his claim on her, and she can view the relationship from his perspective. As we become more aware of how much we truly belong to God, the Father of Life, and how he desires that we trust him, we can grow even closer to him.

TRANSLATING DESIRE TO RESPONSE

Do you desire to be closer to God? That is good, but desire is not an end in itself. We may sing of our longing for more of God and speak of our desire to know his presence, but those words are empty if they don't translate into action.

King David expressed a clear desire for closeness with God:

> One thing I ask from the LORD, this only do I seek: that I may dwell in the house of the LORD all the days of my life, to gaze on the beauty of the LORD and to seek him in his temple. (Ps 27:4)

Yet that one desire did not translate to only one form of action; he didn't just sit in the temple all day. David gave himself wholeheartedly to God's calling on his life as king of Israel. He also wrote many psalms to help others grow closer to God. However, the temple in Jerusalem was not even built until after his death. Therefore, David's desire to "seek him in his temple" is figurative. Perhaps David's idea of 'temple' was an abiding awareness of God's presence and a continual conversation with him, like Brother Lawrence.

Similarly, the desire for intimacy expressed in the Song of Songs is not limited to private togetherness. She also desires to be with him as he tends his flocks and looks for growth in the vineyards (Song 1:7; 7:12). There is a special aspect of intimacy that develops as we engage in what the other is doing. We saw that with the father and child gardening together.

At times, our desire to pursue closeness with God means we initiate something to invest in the relationship. On other occasions, God may take the initiative, leaving us to respond. Any inappropriate response, however, can break the intimacy of a close relationship.

Let's say my wife and I are on our couch one evening sharing an intimate time of togetherness and conversation. If she asked me to scratch her back, I wouldn't just ignore her or ask, "Why should I?" If I did, then the intimacy of the moment would be lost. Knowing she likes me to scratch her back, I might even do it without her asking. If I saw her twist her shoulders slightly, I would take the hint and quickly respond with a scratch. Intimacy is maintained by responding to whispers and subtle signals.

There is a sad passage in the Song of Songs where the woman chooses to ignore the call of her lover because it doesn't suit her. When she is finally ready to respond, he is gone, so she goes in search of him (5:2–8). They are only reunited after she starts to acknowledge his claim on her: "I am my beloved's" (6:3).

I remember a specific incident when I was about eight years old. I was playing outside when my mother called me in for dinner. I barely heard her calling, and it didn't suit me just then, so I pretended I had not heard her. That moment of deceit has, unfortunately, been replicated many times over in my relationship with my heavenly Father. The fact that his whispers are often very subtle makes it easy to ignore them.

THE WHISPERS OF INTIMACY

So why doesn't God speak more clearly to us? Why doesn't he speak clearly to unbelievers so that they have no choice but to believe in him? God, the Father of all humanity, wants his children to desire him and to trust him. That can't be achieved by leaving us with no choice. He desires intimacy with his children, so he whispers rather than shouts. By whispering, he tests our heart. Are we willing? Do we trust him? Do we desire relationship?

Young Christians, in their insecurity, often want God to speak loud and clear; they want 'writing on the wall'. That, however, was for a stubborn, rebellious king (Daniel 5). It is not the Father's preferred way of talking to his children.

God can speak to us in many ways: through a Bible verse that suddenly comes alive, through wise words from a godly friend or leader, through circumstances that come together in a special way, or through the confirmation of a 'fleece' (Jdg 6:36–40). Take note of the word 'through' in all these examples. Each of these channels is simply an outer *framework* God may use in speaking to us. We need more than that. When God speaks to us there is always an inner *life* – a witness in our spirit, a discernible *yes* within. Without that inner witness, these various outer forms can become empty methods, or even lead us astray.

This inner witness will typically have a degree of deep peace *which transcends understanding* (Phil 4:7), even in the midst of uncertainty. Another clue to know if the Spirit is prompting us: Does it promote life in some way? Will it bring good fruit? Whatever you are sensing should be clearly in line with God's character, as revealed in the Bible. Let peace, good fruit and the Bible be your guide as you listen to the Spirit.

According to Jesus, it isn't difficult for us to know these inner whispers of the Spirit. He explained that his 'sheep' *listen to his voice* and follow him because they *know his voice* (John 10:3–4). A friend of mine was one of the last professional shepherds in Norway. He spent many weeks each summer in the mountains with the sheep. He has confirmed to me that sheep can easily recognise the voice of the shepherd, and they don't need to be particularly clever to do so. Hearing God speak is not limited by our ability to hear. He is able to make himself heard. What is up to us is our desire to listen and our willingness to respond. In the gardening scene (Chapter 1), we saw the gentle guidance of the father and the child's willingness to learn.

LEARNING TO LISTEN

Perhaps this idea of listening to the Spirit of God is new to you. Or maybe, like me, you have ignored what you have heard, at times. Either way, I offer a few tips to help you listen better as you learn to know his voice.

Firstly, continue to develop a good biblical understanding of the character of God. Knowing him as a good Father is a secure framework for recognising the sort of things he would likely say. Eventually, as we continue to listen to God, we will learn to know him better. The Spirit of the Father is the Spirit of Life. So, whenever your

> **❝ It is not about our ability to hear but our willingness to respond.**

spirit is stirred to move away from whatever destroys relationships and towards what promotes true Father-life, you know his Spirit is at work in you.

Don't start by coming to God with big questions about what choice you should make in specific situations. We can't treat the Father like some crystal ball when it suits us. Rather, develop the habit of responding to his whispers when he takes the initiative. That will make it easier to recognise how he is speaking to you when you come with a big question.

Sometimes, God will speak to us in a way that is 'crystal clear', but often, His messages are more like thoughts crystallising in our mind or a deep sense of clarity in our heart. This may happen suddenly or over time.

I had a habit of always listening to music, often worship, while driving alone. Then one day, I unexpectedly sensed a subtle stirring in my spirit, like an invitation: "Leave the music off and spend time with me in prayer." Listening to worship music is certainly not wrong, yet sometimes even good things can undermine our relationship with the Father if we cling to them. I still sometimes listen to music in the car, but I have learnt to value those unscheduled prayer times – both when the Spirit prompts and when I just want to pray.

From time to time, the Spirit will gently convict, like when I was in Greece and needed help to see how my attitudes and actions were not in line with the Father (Chapter 2). At first, I didn't even sense actual words; it was like an inner illumination bringing clarity, helping me to see from God's perspective. Conviction from the Father is never a dull sense of condemnation. He brings clarity regarding the problem *and* the solution.

At times, God may prompt us to act on his behalf. For example, perhaps you are with a group of people and your attention is suddenly drawn to someone across the room. You immediately sense they are lonely and need a specific word of encouragement. Now, particularly if you don't normally have such thoughts, wouldn't you suspect that the Spirit was prompting you to share Father-life?

With simple things like that, which are clearly in line with the Father's character, there is no great risk. So, don't look for three confirmations before you confront your fear of man and step out. As you learn to hear the whispers of the Spirit, respond with the simple trust of a child learning to walk. Don't be afraid of occasionally stumbling; the Father is able to intervene if you are approaching danger. Remember, we can't trust our skill in hearing, but we can trust in God's ability to speak and guide us. When he makes himself clear, our willingness becomes the issue.

A GROWING RELATIONSHIP

I could say many things about listening to the whispers of the Spirit, but I would rather not. This is about relationship, not following a system. We are all unique, and the way that the Father relates to each of us is also unique. As we, like Brother Lawrence, learn to respond to the Spirit's impulses, our relationship with the Father will grow and flourish with unique expressions of Father-life.

Understanding the type of relationship God desires gives us a foundation for growth. Next, we will explore the Father's hopes and dreams for His children, which will give us a direction for growth.

—

KEY POINTS

- Relationships are like a garden; we need to maintain the framework *and* stimulate life within the framework.
- The Spirit will often whisper to us; intimacy depends on our willingness to respond.
- Knowing the Father helps us as we learn to listen to his Spirit, and listening helps us to know the Father.

APPLICATION

Take a short break from the book now and do something to invest in your relationship with your heavenly Father. Do whatever you feel inspired to do, anything that is intended to enrich the relationship or help you express your desire for relationship.

You might, for example, sing worship songs, prayerfully reflect on this chapter, meditate on the richness of the Father's goodness, go for a walk to talk with your Father, draw a picture, write a poem or even do some household chores while praying (like Brother Lawrence). Do anything you find meaningful, for as long as you choose. Your conscious *aim* to invest in the relationship is more important than what you do or how 'effective' it seems to be afterwards.

9

THE HOPES OF THE FATHER

Let's revisit the scene of the father and child working in the garden . Previously, we said that it was about more than just the beauty of the moment. While not immediately obvious, there is growth, both in the child and the relationship with their father. In time, through the father's patience and gentle correction, the child slowly learns the skills and values of the father, and the relationship deepens as they gradually become more in tune with one another.

ASPIRATIONS

There is something less visible, however, driving and directing the growth process: The father has hopes and dreams for his child and their relationship. While there is total acceptance, there are also high ideals that keep the relationship moving in a certain direction. Another good word here is *aspirations*. The father aspires for his child to value the things he values, that there may be greater harmony and oneness in their relationship.

The aspirations of the child are just as important. The son or daughter aspires to be just like their father, sharing his character, values, skills, and abilities. They

aspire to be with the father, doing whatever he is doing. These aspirations motivate the child to engage in the activity and the relationship – and help to keep their heart receptive and teachable.

The word 'aspiration' is quite interesting. Its Latin origin gives it the meaning: to breathe into or blow upon. The idea is that an aspiration is not a hollow dream but something you act upon. You take steps in that direction to breathe life into the dream, so it may become reality. If a child aspires to be a football star, they don't just lie in bed dreaming about it. They get a ball and breathe life into the vision by developing their skills. Aspirations are like the way we continue to carefully breathe upon a tiny spark or glowing ember as we help a sustainable fire develop and come alive.

In the garden scene, these invisible aspirations also serve another purpose. They ensure there is never any tension between being and doing. Since the child's aspirations are in harmony with the father's aspirations, what the child does will always be in harmony with who they are. While the Western mind is convinced there will always be tension between being and doing, seeing how they can work together is vital for a healthy, growing relationship with our heavenly Father, and for knowing his heart.

BEING AND DOING

I have seen many books and heard a lot of teaching about 'the father-heart of God'. Typical images associated with such teaching are of a father holding a baby in his arms or lifting a toddler in the air. The messages often emphasise that the Father loves and accepts us just the way we are, our need to just rest in him, and the importance of *being* rather than *doing*.

There are some important, foundational perspectives here regarding our understanding of God as our Father. We need the right foundation; we must know our heavenly Father's love and acceptance. Those who are in a rut of legalistic *doing* need to discover the foundation of *being*. Foundations are vital, yet the foundation is only the first phase of a building project. How can we move on to build on the foundational teaching? What more is there for us to learn about God as our Father?

I am a father, with three children of my own. I can relate to the image of the infant child that is totally accepted, and the message about just *being*. I have gazed at my infant child asleep in my arms, and it was all about being, not doing. Nevertheless, in that moment of total acceptance, my heart also carried aspirations of how the child may grow and hopes of being able to do many things together.

There is no conflict between the complete acceptance of who they *are* and the very different vision and high ideals of who they may *become*. I'm sure most parents can relate to this ideal. Yet, while earthly parents may often struggle to keep those two aspects integrated, *total acceptance* and *high ideals* are always in perfect harmony in our heavenly Father's heart.

For a newborn, life is only about *being*. Yet even in the early stages of a healthy parent-child relationship, as the infant starts to respond, perhaps with a smile, what they *do* adds value to the relationship. In time, as the relationship develops and becomes more interactive, the child also develops aspirations. They want to be with the parent; they want to be like them, *doing* what they are doing.

Jesus lived in a Middle Eastern culture where it was normal for a son to learn his father's trade. If he was a carpenter, the son would start hanging around the workshop, eventually helping out. If the father was a farmer, the son would start following him around the farm and would eventually try his hand at farming. The son would typically look forward to the day when he would eventually be fully involved in the family business.

These aspirations of the child are natural and usually touch a father's heart. This is part of what a father would hope to see in his child.

DOING WHAT THE FATHER IS DOING

We don't know a lot about Jesus' childhood years, but we get a fascinating glimpse from when he was 12 years old. You may be familiar with the story of how Mary and Joseph found Jesus in the temple, but do you know what explanation Jesus gave?

Many of the more literal translations interpret the text as: "I must be about my Father's *business*" (Luke 2:49 KJV). This is clearly not about a commercial business but affairs or 'business' in the broadest sense. (Such as when we say: "Mind your own business.")

The Greek word order is different, and the text here seems to be missing a word. Jesus literally explains: "I must be in my Father's". When the text doesn't specify anything in particular, then the implication is *anything* and *everything* to do with the Father.[14]

I think this is a wonderful picture of Jesus' boyhood desire to be involved in whatever his heavenly Father is up to. More than just desire, he says "must", as if driven by an inner compulsion, as if saying, "Of course, it's just natural. A son *must* be involved with his father. That's what sons do."

To me, this scene of Jesus in the temple is just like the child eagerly wanting to help his father in the garden. Or perhaps it's more like a son or daughter on a farm finally getting to drive the tractor for the first time. They're nowhere near ready to run the farm, but they are itching to get involved.

Much later, after Jesus had been baptised and launched into his public ministry, he was still focused on being actively involved in the Father's business. He even declared, "The Son can do nothing by himself; he can do only what he sees his Father doing, because whatever the Father does the Son also does" (John 5:19).

While this refers to the specific relationship between Jesus and the Father, it is also a comment on how a healthy father-son relationship was understood at that time. Jesus, however, took it to a whole new level by living totally in sync with the Father: "The words I say to you I do not speak on my own authority. Rather, it is the Father, *living in me*, who is doing his work." (John 14:10)

Jesus' whole life grew out of intimacy with the Father as he tapped into the Father and lived in step with him, embracing the Father's business. The Father was "living in" him. Jesus fully lived the Father-life.

DOING THE FATHER'S WILL

God the Father wants to live in and through us. This is not about being just slaves, servants or 'instruments' in his hand. He is looking for sons and daughters who embrace the 'family business' and enter into that active relationship with him as we engage in what he is doing. Jesus spells this out for us: "For whoever does the will of my Father in heaven is my brother and sister and mother." (Matt 12:50)

In other words: Those who are looking to the Father to see how they can be involved in the 'family business', they are the ones who are truly a part of the family in an active relational sense. This verse about *doing his will* conflicts with those who would claim it is all about *being*, not *doing*. Even more challenging perhaps is this verse: "But I tell you, love your enemies and pray for those who persecute you, *that you may be* children of your Father in heaven." (Matt 5:44–45a)

What is this? Is Jesus saying we should *do* something in order to *be* children of our Father? The image of the father gazing at his baby doesn't help us at this point. Staying a helpless baby is not the whole of the Father's hopes and dreams for our lives. As we grow, especially as we grow in sharing his heart, what we *do* becomes an important part of the whole relationship.

Dynamic relationships involve both being and doing; you can't separate them. For me to *be* a husband, I need to '*do* husband'. Similarly, to fully *be* a father, I have to *do* some father stuff. I must actively father my children in daily life, not just father them at the time of conception.

For us to fully enter into the relationship of being sons and daughters, we must embrace the relationship and do stuff *with* our Father. Firstly, let God be involved in the things you do. Whatever you do – whether it's going for a walk, reading a book, shopping or talking to a friend – seek to do it with God, in an awareness of his presence and remaining open and responsive to his Spirit (just like Brother Lawrence). Secondly, develop an awareness of what your Father is up to. Listen to the whispers of his Spirit and have a desire to be involved with him.

As we seek to keep *being* and *doing* together, however, a word of caution: Don't let what you *do* define who you *are*; let who you *are* define what you *do*. Let the Father first tell you who you are, then let that core identity shape the things you choose to do (and not do). As mentioned earlier, having our aspirations focused on the Father is what helps us to grow into his aspirations for us. If our aspirations are weak or misguided, there will be little growth.

NO GROWTH OR ASPIRATIONS

Imagine a young couple with their first baby. They have waited expectantly, and now they are finally able to hold their precious child. They gaze with love and acceptance at their baby and look forward to getting to know their child as the relationship develops.

Yet as the weeks and months pass, they see no development, no sign of responsiveness in the face of their child. Doctors confirm their worst suspicions; something is tragically wrong with the child's DNA. As the months become years, they continue to care for and love their child unconditionally. Yet, deep inside, they feel a sense of loss and grief, as they accept that many of their hopes, dreams, and aspirations for the child will never be realised.

The greater tragedy is that many of us have something wrong with the spiritual 'DNA' of our hearts and minds. As we came into the Father's Kingdom, only part of his truth was imparted to us. Perhaps we were encouraged to focus on his acceptance and operate in a passive mode of just *being*. There seems to be little or no responsiveness to his Spirit and few signs of growth. We lack a desire to be involved with the Father in what he is doing, and we don't really aspire to be like him.

This is the tragedy when we focus more on the warm side of God's character – his love, compassion and acceptance – and less on the firmness of his holiness, justice and high ideals. We then have a shallow understanding of grace, seeing only some aspects of it, and we have a rather static spirituality with little development. The Father grieves over us, his children, when we don't develop; when we don't aspire to be with him and like him. He grieves the loss of what could have been.[15]

> **❝** *Don't let what you do define who you are;*
> *let who you are define what you do.*

MISGUIDED ASPIRATIONS

Now imagine another child who is apparently healthy and growing, physically and mentally, yet something is missing. This child lacks a sense of love and acceptance. They constantly struggle with their identity and have low self-esteem. They feel they must prove themself to be accepted.

In human families, this can often happen as a result of real rejection by parents. There are many heart-rending stories of children experiencing physical or emotional rejection. Yet even in good families, children can have a 'short-circuit' in their hearts and minds that causes them to feel rejected and not trust in their parent's love and affirmation.

How many of us have struggled at some point to accept the love of our heavenly Father? We all too easily doubt what he says about us and struggle to feel accepted. Where there is little trust, there is little depth of relationship and our aspirations become more about performance. We focus on who we *should be*, while being ignorant of who we *are*. The Father grieves over sons and daughters like this. He grieves the loss of deep and meaningful relationship.[16]

THE FATHER'S DREAM

The hope of our heavenly Father is that we become who he created us to be. God wants us to be one with him and one with each other as he builds his family (John 17). Earthly fathers in our day may dream of their children growing up to be independent and finding their own path in life. In contrast, God our Father dreams of us growing closer to him, becoming like him and joining him in doing what he is doing.

We cannot simply reduce this to a system or checklist. Having a right framework for life is only a starting point. We must have life in the framework. Our Father desires a real relationship, based on trust and with oneness of heart and purpose.

It is only as we grasp his aspirations for us and embrace the Father-life he gives that we discover who we really are. Part of the Father's dream for us is that we become his heirs. Find out more about our 'inheritance' and 'adoption' – and the connection between them – in the next chapter.

—

KEY POINTS

- Like all deep relationships, the Father-life is about both *being* <u>and</u> *doing*.
- In a healthy father-child relationship, it is natural for the child to want to *be like* the father and *doing what he is doing*.
- Problems arise if we don't understand who we *have become* and already *are* in the Father, or if we fail to grasp the Father's desires and process for who we *are becoming*.

REFLECTION AND RESPONSE

Have you drawn back from being involved in the Father's affairs? What has held you back? Have you been afraid it would lead you into striving in your own strength? Have you thought the Father's plans for you may be hard or unpleasant? Are there things you are not willing to let go?

Ask the Holy Spirit to reveal to you the relational richness, beauty and joy of being involved with the Father in the things *he* is doing in *his* world. Somewhere, deep within you, is a desire to be involved with your Father in what he is doing. Open your heart to embrace the amazing adventure of discovery that awaits those who enter into their calling as a son or daughter of the Living God.

10

OUR INHERITANCE IN THE FATHER

W hat does it mean for us to be God's heirs and 'adopted' as his children? Is it simply about having our 'papers' in order? To explore that question, let's explore what happens when children grow up.

A GROWN-UP SON

Come with me on a trip to London. We are now walking down Paddington Street, in one of the older districts. There, we find a quaint shoemaker's shop dating from 1857, and we look up at the bold sign: "James Taylor & Son". Can you imagine the original James Taylor standing proudly in front of the shop as the sign was installed? What is he telling the world by adding "son" to the sign?

Obviously, "son" tells us James Taylor had a male offspring. Yet that is not the meaning of the sign. It isn't so much a birth announcement as a proclamation that the son has grown up. The word "son" on the sign means there is an adult son who has embraced the father's aspirations and has an active role in the father's business.

Similarly, we could consider a farmer and his son. I found a great photo once of a farmer and his grown-up son standing proudly together in a field. A combine harvester and a truckload of grain were in the background. The satisfaction on their faces appeared to reflect the joy of working together in fulfilling their dreams. It was easy to imagine the son growing up on the farm and dreaming about this day. Now it was a reality; he had become an active heir with his father.

This specific idea of a grown-up son who aspires to be like his father and doing what he is doing appears a lot throughout the Greek text of the New Testament. Yet that meaning is lost in our English translations. When we read verses about us being God's "son" or "child" we imagine being a helpless baby or a small child. Our Western values of independence and individualism add to the confusion. To better understand what the Bible says to us about our inheritance as God's grown-up children, let's have a quick lesson in New Testament Greek.

THE IMPORTANCE OF BEING *HUIOS*

One of the Greek words for child is *teknon*, referring to offspring by birth. As humans, we are all God's 'offspring' in a physical sense – he is the source of life; he knit us together in the womb. As believers, we are also his offspring in a spiritual sense through new birth. This gives us a framework for the relationship.

Another Greek word, *huios*[17], speaks of a son who has reached adulthood and now carries the responsibility of an heir. In the Greek, Roman, and Jewish cultures of the day, this was when the son would start having an active role in the father's affairs and be entrusted with adult responsibility. Yet, even in adulthood and after marriage, the father would continue to develop maturity in his son. A Jewish son was not considered to have reached 'maturity' until he was thirty.[18] This is quite unlike Western cultures today, which emphasise the individual and promote independence at adulthood.

So, *huios* is more than just a technical word for an adult son. It has the implied meaning of one who bears the *likeness* of their father by sharing his character, values, and behaviour. Therefore, *huios* was also used metaphorically of an apprentice, who became the 'son' of his master, as he aspired to be like him, and acquired his skills and values. Similarly, a disciple became the 'son' of his rabbi as he embraced his views, ideas, and worldview.[19]

BEING AND DOING

In the previous chapter, we looked at *being* and *doing*. In one sense, being God's son or daughter is just about *being*. Once we are born again, nothing we do changes the truth of what happened. That is the *objective*, factual side of being God's child, his offspring, his *teknon*. It provides an important framework for the relationship.

We also need the *subjective*, relational side of things. This is where *huios* comes in. This is about us being a 'son' (or daughter[20]) who is mature enough to be meaningfully involved with the father. We *subjectively* choose to embrace the Father's purposes, character, and values. We aspire to be like our Father and to be with him, so we trust him and voluntarily enter into the ongoing relational role he has for us. To be *huios* brings life into the relationship – it is about both *being* and *doing*.

Many people believe there is an inherent tension between *being* and *doing*, as though these work against each other. I don't see any signs of this tension in the life of Jesus, and I know we can follow in his footsteps. The key is to embrace the Father's aspirations for us, as we enter into our *role* and *calling* as his sons and daughters.

We should not think we can *become* God's children by what we *do*; we are not born again by our own efforts. This is the clear message of gaining righteousness by faith and not by works. (See Romans 4, etc.) But once we have *become* God's children, then who we *are* should be reflected in the way we live. This is the message of being alive in Christ and living by the Spirit. (See Romans 6 and 8, Galatians 5, and many other passages.) If who we *are* does not impact how we *live*, then our faith is "dead". (See James 2.)

The following summary contrasts these two concepts:

teknon	*huios*
Typical translation: "child"	Typical translation: "son"/"child"[21]
Meaning: offspring	Meaning: adult son/heir
Physical likeness (likeness in 'nature')	Likeness in character, values and activity – oneness
Being	Being and doing
The present facts of a past event	Ongoing, voluntary, relational role
Purely objective (a statement of reality)	Mostly subjective (builds on desire and trust)
A framework for life	Life in the framework

LIKE FATHER, LIKE SON

In light of this understanding of *huios*, let's go back to that verse from Matthew we looked at in the last chapter:

> But I tell you, love your enemies and pray for those who persecute you,
> that you may be children [*huios*] of your Father in heaven. He causes
> his sun to rise on the evil and the good, and sends rain on the righteous
> and the unrighteous. (Matt 5:44–45)

Now the message is clearer. We should love our enemies so that we may truly be *huios* – grown-up sons (and daughters) who reflect the character and values of our Father. He loves his enemies (giving sun and rain to both good and evil), and desires that we share and reflect his character. This is about the aspirations of the Father for his children, that we, in turn, may aspire to be like him.

We find a negative example of this when Jesus says of the Pharisees: "You belong to your father, the devil, and you want to carry out your father's desires" (John 8:44). They are not the devil's offspring literally, but they are his 'sons' by character. The devil is their 'father' because they are about his business and aspire to his character and values.

The statement that Jesus is the 'Son of God' is often based on *huios*. More than just a family relationship, it tells of involvement, likeness, and being a true representative. For example, "The Son [*huios*] is the radiance of God's glory and the exact representation of his being" (Heb 1:3a). This verse is partly about the uniqueness of Christ, but it is also a statement about the implied meaning of *huios* – one who reflects their father.

A MAN HAD TWO SONS …

In one of his most well-known parables, Jesus starts with the words: "A man had two sons" (see Luke 15:11–32). Guess what the word is for sons? It's *huios* (though in a plural form). In other words, "A man had two adult heirs."

We call it the story of the 'Prodigal Son', and it is commonly viewed as a story of forgiveness. But perhaps we tend to look at it from *our* perspective. We identify with the son, so we make him the main character. The central figure, however, is the father, a father who is just like God. Let's take a fresh look at this from his perspective. As you read this, re-focus on the father and notice how his total acceptance and high ideals are evident. In particular, keep in mind his *dreams and aspirations* for his sons and his desire for relationship.

THE FATHER WHO IS JUST LIKE GOD

Imagine you are a Jewish father living in the Middle East at the time of Jesus. You are a rich farmer with two sons who love to follow you around the farm. It is a proud day when you finally celebrate the *Bar Mitzvah*[22] of your first son. You formally recognise him as an adult heir as he becomes legally accountable for his actions.

A couple of years later you proudly affirm your second son in a similar way. As the years pass, each of them becomes more actively involved in what you are doing, and you gradually give them more authority and responsibility.

Lately, however, you have been concerned about your second son; his heart seems to have grown cold. Still, you are shocked the day he says, "Dad, I want out. I'm not interested in farming, and I don't want to hang around here waiting for you to die. Just give me my share of things now, and I'll be on my way."

You are heartbroken. You have always loved and accepted this son, even while longing for a deeper relationship. Now, even in his rejection of you, you still accept him. You also accept the reality of the situation and release your son, even giving him his share of the wealth when he goes.

As your son slowly fades from view, the relationship dies. You grieve over the hopes, dreams, and aspirations that dissipate like mist. He thinks he has taken his inheritance, but that was just the financial part of it. He has walked away from his role as an heir and so much more. Having a relationship with you did not fit into his visions for his life, and he has rejected all that you were willing to invest in him.

Yet the hope in your heart never fully dies, and years of absence have not diminished your desire for relationship. You quietly cling to your hope and find yourself often gazing into the distance, wondering, longing.

Unknown to you, the son is still alive but in a desperate state. He has hit rock bottom and has nowhere to turn. He has thought of going back home but can't bring himself to do so. He knows your character, that you don't carry grudges, so he knows he will be forgiven. He had already felt that forgiveness when you released him and gave him his share of the wealth. The great weight in his heart is *shame*. How can he ever face you again? He has brought shame on the whole family. He knows things can never be as they once were. Yet one day he realises that things don't need to be the same; he could be a servant on the farm instead. At least then he would have a place to stay, with some real food, and a good employer.

One ordinary day, your whole world suddenly changes. You see your son approaching. You drop everything and rush to meet him.

The son has been dreading this moment; he has been rehearsing and polishing his speech during the whole journey. He can't bear to look you in the eye. He drops to his knees on the dusty road and starts blurting out his lines. He acknowledges the biological relationship by addressing you as "father" (he is still your offspring, *teknon*). Yet he admits the lack of a practical relationship, declaring he is no longer worthy to be your son (*huios*).

You interrupt his shame-filled words and kneel to meet him in the dust. You lift his face, kiss him, then pull him to his feet. "Servant? What nonsense! You are my son," you declare as you give him your robe. The fine robe is a physical expression of the dignity you have granted by calling him your '*huios*'. "You are my son," you repeat as you put a ring on his finger, reinstating him to the authority of an heir. He wasted his wealth, and things can never be exactly as they were, but he is back in the family business. The relationship was dead, your son (*huios*) was 'dead', but now he is alive!

THE RICH INHERITANCE OF RELATIONSHIP

The father's response goes far beyond the forgiveness the son expected. He is overwhelmed by the outpouring of grace as the father engages in his mess, bringing restoration. The father restores relationship, authority, and the role as an heir. Most of all, the father removes shame as he restores honour, dignity, and identity.

Our richest inheritance in the Father is found in our relationship with him. Yet we can so easily miss it. Just like the younger son in this story, we too can be more interested in the blessings of our inheritance than the relational role with the Father or our identity in him. We may know the Father's acceptance as his *teknon*, yet be indifferent to his high ideals or aspirations for us as his *huios*. That robs us of relationship.

Sometimes, like the older son, we can be unsure of who we are. He thinks he needs to earn the father's acceptance and blessing. That robs him of the intimacy he could have in sharing the father's heart and purposes. His criticism of his brother and father shows that he is totally out of touch with the father's character and values. His relationship with the father is shallow. He is living the life of a servant rather than a son and heir. He only thinks of the future aspect of inheritance: everything that is to become his one day.

OUR ADOPTION AS HEIRS

To go even deeper in our understanding of inheritance, there is one more important aspect of *huios* we need to explore. The Greek word *huiothesia* appears only five times in the New Testament and only in Paul's letters. It literally means 'son placing' (being instated as *huios*), yet it is usually translated as 'adoption'.

What comes to mind when you hear 'adoption'? Do you picture infants or small children? In our day, adoption is something that happens to orphans. *Young children without a family, gain a family.*

It was very different in the Greco-Roman world of the New Testament. There, adoption meant that *a household without an heir, gained an heir*. Households needed an heir, and the one being 'adopted' was typically an adult and not an orphan.[23, 24]

The story of *Ben-Hur* gives us an example.[25] Judah Ben-Hur is betrayed into slavery and serves on a Roman galley. There, he gains the trust of a Roman commander, Quintus Arrius, and they develop a close bond. Since Arrius' only son has been killed and his household is without an heir, he adopts Ben-Hur as his heir. This automatically releases Ben-Hur from slavery, giving him Roman citizenship – and new responsibilities.

Someone adopted in this way was cut free from all former ties. Therefore, 'adoption' was a way of escape for an adult son due to inherit a large debt (thereby being a 'slave to debt'). If the son could find a family in need of an heir, he could be *released* from the impending debt. However, he was now *bound* to allegiance to the new father and the responsibilities of the new household.[26]

This radical change of status and allegiance seems to be why Paul chose to use 'adoption' as a metaphor for our new relationship to the Father (see Romans 8 and Galatians 4). Paul's initial readers would have naturally assumed he was referring to adult adoption. They would have easily understood the message of our new status and allegiance as God's grown-up heirs.

THE SPIRIT OF SONSHIP

In Galatians, Paul tells of God's purpose to "redeem those under the law, that we might receive *adoption to sonship* [*huiothesia*: instatement as sons/heirs]" (Gal 4:5). Notice that this 'adoption' doesn't imply we were ever orphans – that is a Western cultural assumption. This 'adoption' is more like how the Prodigal

> **❝** *The one being 'adopted' was typically an adult and not an orphan.*

Son is reinstated into right relationship as an heir after his period of 'slavery'. Paul goes on to declare: "So you are no longer a slave, but God's *child* [*huios*: grown-up son/heir]" (4:7).

However, this is more than just a change of status from slave to free. Paul explains how the Father has given us the "Spirit of the Son [the *Huios*]" (4:6). It is this '*huios*-Spirit', this 'Spirit of sonship', that enables us to enter into our new lifestyle, with a new loyalty to the Father. Paul gives a similar message in Romans:

> For those who are led by the Spirit of God are the *children* [*huios*] of God.
>
> ... the Spirit you received brought about your *adoption to sonship* [*huiothesia*].
>
> ... Now if we are *children* [*huios*], then we are heirs – heirs of God and co-heirs with Christ, if indeed we share in his sufferings in order that we may also share in his glory. (Rom 8:14, 15b, 17)

Being led by the Spirit is what enables us to be mature 'sons' that reflect the character and values of the Father. When we receive his Spirit, God can pronounce, "You are my *huios*" (as he said when Jesus was baptised). Having his Spirit makes us the Father's heirs. Allowing ourselves to be led by the Spirit is what keeps us as his heir. Keeping "in step with the Spirit" (Gal 5:25) shows our allegiance to our true Father.

BEING AN HEIR

Being an heir doesn't mean that we take over the farm when God dies; it is about an active relationship *with* the Father. Our role as 'sons' is not something that just automatically happens. We need to actively embrace the role of representing his interests and sharing his blessings. This will sometimes mean enduring hardship or dying to our own desires as we "share in his sufferings" (Rom 8:17). But that is the only way to come into the fullness of the inheritance the Father has for us.

Our 'adoption' in Paul's teaching is about dying to the influence of all previous 'fathers' (including our self-made targets) and choosing our heavenly Father as the target and focus for our lives. It is about following the Spirit within that cries, "Father," while focusing on him and aspiring to be like him.

As I started to grasp these perspectives, I found that it had far-reaching consequences for how I lived. As I listened to the voice of the Spirit within, who continually called my attention to 'Abba, Father', it became easier to make good decisions in line with his will and values. Soon, Father-life was flowing in and through me in fresh ways.

There was one important foundation in my life, however, that made this growth possible. Years earlier, the Father had already given me some key perspectives on faith. As God taught me to embrace his aspirations for my life, this foundation of faith became more important than ever. That will be our next topic.

—

KEY POINTS

- God's desire for his children is that we grow in bearing his likeness – showing his character and carrying the family values.
- Part of our privilege as heirs of God is the relational role of being involved with the Father in what he is doing.
- Biblical passages about our 'adoption' never imply that we were once orphans but refer to our role as adult heirs of God while allowing his Spirit to lead us.

REFLECTION AND APPLICATION

What has impacted you most in these last two chapters about sonship and inheritance? (Reflect on that first or discuss it.)

Now, who can you share this with? One of the most important aspects of entering into our inheritance as sons and daughters is to engage with the Father in what he is doing in the lives of others. Let the Father expand your vision for his family. Ask him now to reveal who you can encourage by sharing something you have learnt. Perhaps you could even send a message or make a call straight away. Be willing to spread Father-life.

11

FAITH IS FOUNDATIONAL

The Bible makes it clear that faith is essential for our relationship with our heavenly Father. After all, we are saved by grace through faith. Abraham was considered righteous in God's eyes on the basis of faith, and the same applies to us. Furthermore, "everything that does not come from faith is sin" (Rom 14:23). Yet what is *faith*? What does it mean to have faith in the Father, and how does he help us to have faith?

MAKING SENSE OF FAITH

As a young Christian, I wanted to know how to grow in faith, but I struggled to make sense of it. Some people even warned, "Don't try to figure it out; just believe." Yet even in trying to 'just believe', I could never find which 'muscles' to use to 'exercise' faith.

As I looked to the Bible for clarity, the fragments of insight I gathered seemed disjointed. For example: "Faith is a gift of God,"[27] and "We all have a measure of faith."[28] This seems to say that if you don't have much faith, then it isn't your fault;

that's all God has given you. Did I even need more? We are told that even faith as small as a mustard seed is enough to move a mountain (Matt 17:20). Yet I certainly had not done much 'earthmoving'.

Reading about the heroes of faith – both in the Scriptures and in various biographies – didn't help much either. They were too far ahead. I gained little understanding of how they got to where they were in faith or how I could follow in their footsteps.

In time, my walk with the Father – actually my whole life – became deeper and more real, with a greater sense of liberty, when I got a fresh view of faith. God revealed a few simple keys that tie everything together in a wonderful way. I had tried to understand faith as a system. But a relational view of faith made all the difference.

DEFINING FAITH

The word 'faith' doesn't seem to be clearly defined in the Bible – perhaps because it was a common word that didn't need much defining. But somehow, in our day and age, 'faith' has a mystical ring. It is a word that belongs in the church, not on the street. It is a word that an 'enlightened' scientist may scoff at or call irrelevant. Faith, for many people, is something quite intangible and abstract. Yet the truth is that faith is concrete and practical; it is very much a part of people's everyday lives without them being aware of it.

Each time you deposit money into a bank account, you exercise faith in the bank, in the financial institutions, and in the judicial system that keeps them all honest. When you drive across a bridge, you exercise faith in the engineers and builders of the bridge and those responsible for the ongoing maintenance. Despite not consciously thinking in these terms, your actions are an expression of your faith – your trust and confidence – in these systems and structures.

The most foundational definition of faith is simply: *trust*. This is true in Greek, Hebrew, English, Norwegian, and many other languages. When words like 'faith' and 'believe' are used in the Bible, the core idea is trust. Trust is a relational word. It is also a very practical word. You might claim to trust a person, but if you don't step out and display your trust in action, your words are empty. Let me illustrate this with a story inspired by real events.

TRUST IN ACTION

A famous tightrope walker had just crossed over Niagara Falls on a rope and the crowd were duly impressed. Yet they were hungry for more – and he was ready. This time he carefully went across and back with a wheelbarrow. Everyone was amazed, yet he continued to up the game.

"Now, how about I put this sack of potatoes in the wheelbarrow?" he asked. "Do you believe I can do it? Do you have faith in me?"

"Yes, we believe in you," they replied. "Do it!"

So, boosted by their declaration of faith in him, the tightrope walker made his way across and back again. The crowd were ecstatic; they had never seen anything like this.

"Now, let's replace the sack of potatoes with a person," he suggested. "Do you still believe in me?"

A buzz of excitement spread through the crowd. "Yes," they cheered. "We believe in you! Do it!"

Gesturing to the crowd, he waited for them to settle before asking, "Then who will volunteer?"

Only the background roar of the waterfall could be heard as silence fell on the crowd. They 'believed' in him, yet who was willing to put their faith into action? Nobody moved.

Finally, a young girl stepped forward. "I will," she said confidently. She alone had faith in the tightrope walker. Her belief was not just words. She proved her trust as she climbed into the wheelbarrow. She was, in fact, the daughter of the tightrope walker. Perhaps only a daughter or son is able to show that kind of trust.[29]

BELIEVING IN GOD

I used to think that believing *in* God was just a matter of believing some facts *about* God or things that Jesus had done. Perhaps I was influenced by reciting creeds or by reading 'statements of faith'. What we believe *about* God is important, yet it is easily overemphasised. Our beliefs about God only give us a framework for the relationship.

Remember our basic model of a garden – *life in a framework*. For us to have life in our relationship with God, we need the life-dynamics of really believing *in* God – being willing to put our trust *in* him. Believing that God is our Father includes actively trusting him.

In Chapter 8, we looked at contract and covenant. Contract-thinking will leave us simply believing the right things *about* God. Covenant commitment leads us to faithfully pursue the relationship within that framework. Do you want a mere *system* of belief or a living *relationship*?

THE FAITH OF ABRAHAM

Abraham is often called the 'father of faith'. His faith is foundational to the New Testament teaching about justification by faith. Evidently, he knew how to 'get in the wheelbarrow' with God.

One passage that describes Abraham's faith is found in Romans chapter 4. Earlier in the chapter, Paul lays down a clear foundation for justification by faith. He concludes by describing in more detail the faith of Abraham and how it can apply to us. Let's go through this verse by verse, starting with verse 18.

> Against all hope, Abraham in hope believed and so became the father of
> many nations, just as it had been said to him, "So shall your offspring be."

The first thing we see is that Abraham's faith was *not dependent on his circumstances*. His situation gave no grounds for hope. He was childless, so how could he become 'the father of many nations'?

> ... Without weakening in his faith, he faced the fact that his body was as good as dead – since he was about a hundred years old – and that Sarah's womb was also dead. (v. 19)

Not only did he not need encouraging circumstances to feed his faith, his *negative circumstances could not undermine his faith*. If you are sick and praying for healing, you don't need to deny you are sick in order to have faith. I like the way Paul expresses it here: "he faced the fact". When we have faith, we can look negative circumstances in the eye without being shaken.

This is like when the twelve spies went into the Promised Land (Numbers 13 and 14). Two of them came back with a good report, yet they did not deny the challenges. They explained that, yes, there were giants in the land and fortified cities. But, so what? God had spoken!

Similarly, we see in the next verse that Abraham based his faith on what God had spoken:

> ... Yet he did not waver through unbelief *regarding the promise of God*, but was strengthened in his faith and gave glory to God, ... (v. 20)

Here, we get a glimpse of the foundation of Abraham's faith. He was able to 'face the facts' and still find hope because his focus was on God himself and the promise He had given.

How could Abraham be so sure God could be trusted? Well, many Bible translations end verse 20 with a comma. Verse 21 continues with further explanation:

> ... being fully persuaded that God had power to do what he had promised. (v. 21)

The fact that Abraham was "fully persuaded" is given as the reason why he "did not waver through unbelief." In a moment, we'll look more closely at what it means to be fully persuaded and what Abraham was persuaded about. For now, take note of how central this is in Paul's presentation of Abraham's faith. The next sentence adds even more significance to Abraham's "being fully persuaded":

> ... This is why "it was credited to him as righteousness." (v. 22)

Wow. This must be an important key. If you want to have the type of faith that does not waver, the type of faith that God credits as righteousness, then you have to get a hold of Abraham's "being fully persuaded". Paul makes it clear that this is something we too can take hold of and enter into. Abraham is not out of reach; we can walk in his footsteps:

> ... The words "it was credited to him" were written not for him alone, but also for us, to whom God will credit righteousness – for us who believe in him who raised Jesus our Lord from the dead. (vv. 23–24)

Notice again that we are to "believe in him who raised Jesus". As mentioned in Chapter 1, we are to believe in Jesus, but just as importantly, we are called to trust in the One who gives life, the Father of Life. He was also the focus of Abraham's faith.

THE SOURCE OF ABRAHAM'S FAITH

Abraham was not simply persuaded about the outcome. Neither was he focused on how it was going to happen. In fact, other passages make it clear that he was, at times, rather uncertain about the details of what would happen and how (e.g. Heb 11:19). Abraham was fully persuaded *that God had power to do what he had promised.*" God himself was the focus of Abraham's faith. Yes, it was often connected to a particular outcome – in this case, having a son. But his faith was in God, not the son.

Faith is a *relational* word. Faith can't exist in isolation or simply in connection with a desired outcome. Faith needs a basis for trusting; it needs to be directed towards something or someone trustworthy. Because faith is relational it is also about consistency. Our faith in our heavenly Father must be an expression of our ongoing pursuit of relationship with him. We can't just trust him in certain 'spiritual' matters. We must trust him daily and in *all* of life.

I used to think of faith as some kind of mystical substance I needed from time to time. Paul writes in Romans 12 of a "measure of faith" given by God.

> **" Abraham didn't just have faith**
> **he had faith in God.**

I imagined I had a cup with just a few drops of faith. I struggled to understand how or where I could get enough of this mysterious stuff for whatever challenge I was facing.

Abraham didn't 'have' faith in that sense; it wasn't some stuff he had to find whenever he had a need. Abraham didn't just have *faith*; he had *faith in God*. Abraham only had to look to God – to his almighty nature and his faithful character – in order to have faith. Once he was fully persuaded that God was both able to do what he said and trustworthy enough to keep his word, he had all the faith he needed.

While we can rightly look up to Abraham with great admiration, we can also think of him being like the child digging in the garden with his father (Chapter 1). Abraham didn't have a perfect track record in trusting God and knowing his ways. He sometimes 'missed the mark' or had faulty theology. At times, he 'dug' in the wrong places. There is, however, a childlike beauty in Abraham's trust in God. Into the basic framework of his relationship with God, he poured a living willingness to trust. Our heavenly Father is more interested in our current heart attitudes and willingness to trust than our past performance or right beliefs about Him.

BEING FULLY PERSUADED

So, how did Abraham get to be *fully persuaded*? I have been pondering this passage and seeking to live it out for well over 30 years, and I can still only come up with two basic ingredients.

Let's use this book as an example. Through it, I am trying to persuade you of certain views concerning God the Father. What does it take for you to be persuaded? Firstly, I need to present *evidence*. I need to lay before you certain facts and present them in a trustworthy and convincing way. Yet is that all it takes for you to be persuaded?

Have you ever tried to persuade someone without succeeding? You may have had good evidence and presented it well, but they weren't convinced. What was missing? Why weren't they persuaded? Perhaps they were not *persuadable*.

To be persuaded, a person needs to be *willing*. They need to have an open heart and mind, with a willingness to look at the evidence and consider the reasoning. There also needs to be a willingness to step out in trust on the basis of the evidence. Furthermore, if there are questions, there needs to be a willingness to look into them.

For Abraham to be fully persuaded that God could be trusted, two things needed to happen: God needed to present some convincing evidence of his power and trustworthiness, and Abraham needed to be open to consider the evidence. We could formulate it like this:

Evidence + Persuadability = Faith

- *Evidence*: God gives more than enough evidence of his trustworthiness.
- *Persuadability*: We are open to receive that evidence, willing to be persuaded, willing to trust.
- *Faith*: We become fully persuaded of his trustworthiness, thereby faithfully trusting him.

THE GIFT OF RELATIONSHIP

The Father freely gives us more than enough evidence for us to 'get in the wheelbarrow' and enjoy relationship with him. We only need to be open to *receive* his evidence and let him convince us of his goodness. Truly, faith is a gift; relationship is a gift. Seeing the relational dynamics of faith is essential for fully living in Father-life.

The relational perspective also helps us to make sense of faith. For example, the words, "everything that does not come from faith is sin" (Rom 14:23) tell us that, *whenever we are unwilling to trust God, we damage the relationship.* Deep and meaningful relationships need a foundation of trust. Similarly, the statement, "Without faith it is impossible to please God" (Heb 11:6), simply means God is looking for relationship, therefore he values our willingness to trust him higher than all else.

Knowing God as our Father gives us a good foundation for trusting him. It is one of the most natural things for a son or daughter to trust their Father when they see the goodness of his character, and they desire to be like him. The more we learn to trust him, the more we will gain confidence in him and can give ourselves faithfully to the relationship.

—

KEY POINTS

- Faith is essentially about trust and is a natural part of life.
- The Father gives us evidence of his trustworthiness, helping us to take steps of trust.
- Our Father is able to persuade us of his trustworthiness if we are willing to receive the evidence he gives and are open to being persuaded.

APPLICATION

Take a moment to look up some Bible verses about faith or believing, and reflect on their meaning in light of this relational view of faith. Choose a few familiar verses, or try some of these suggestions: Matthew 21:21, John 7:38, Galatians 2:20, Hebrews 11:1, Hebrews 11:6, 1 Peter 1:21.

Finding synonyms for *faith* and *belief* may help demystify these terms and give you a fresh, relational perspective. Depending on the context, you may be able to substitute the word faith with *trust* or *dependence*, sometimes even *faithful trust* or *confident trust*. Some verses, however, are about the *willingness to trust*. Yet other verses speak of faith in terms of the position of faith, the place of *confidence*, when one is *fully persuaded* that God can be trusted.

Consider your chosen verses one at a time. Try to identify which synonyms or equivalent terms for faith or belief fit the context, and make your own paraphrase. Read your adaptation aloud, and consider if other synonyms might fit better. In prayer, invite the Father to bring clarity, and to expand your willingness to faithfully trust him.

12

CONFIDENT FAITH

Would you like to have confident faith in God? Our ability to fully trust him is dependent on how we handle the evidence of his trustworthiness. Let's consider how evidence is handled in a court of law.

CAN GOD BE TRUSTED?

Put yourself in the position of a judge in a courtroom. This courtroom represents your life, and there is an important case: God has been accused of not being trustworthy. Your aim as the judge is to have a fair trial and to be *fully persuaded* about the outcome. You may not end up being 'certain', but you aim to be *confident* in your decision.

In this decisive case, God is representing himself as the defence. Therefore, he presents the evidence. As the judge, you don't need to find the evidence, but you must consider it carefully.

The evidence that the Father is able to present includes:

- The *documentary* evidence of Scripture.

- The *testimonial* evidence of witnesses – those you have met personally and those you have encountered throughout the Bible and church history. These witnesses can testify to their own experience of God's faithfulness.
- The *circumstantial* evidence we find in creation. Creation points to a Creator. Paul says that this sort of evidence leaves people without excuse for not recognising God's existence and putting their trust in him (Rom 1:18–21).
- Finally, God can remind you of your *own experience* of his goodness and faithfulness.

EVIDENCE AND ACCUSATIONS

Now, let's consider the prosecution. It is his job to present evidence that the Father cannot be trusted. What sort of evidence can he bring? What is his case against God?

The Bible refers to him as the accuser (Rev 12:10). He is not just the accuser of God's sons and daughters, he also accuses the Father. Accusation is one of his main tactics; he started in the garden, accusing God of deceiving Adam and Eve. Be aware, however, that he is quite skilled at making a toxic mix of facts and accusation, designed to deceive and instil fear. His primary aim is to undermine our trust in the Father.

For example, "No, you can't trust God. What about Aunt Mary who died of cancer? You prayed for her and God didn't heal her. You can't trust God."

"No, don't trust God with your finances. What if he doesn't provide for you? You have to be responsible and make sure you have enough for your own needs."

One of your most important roles as judge is to sort out the empty accusations from the hard facts. You must be willing to look *at* the evidence and to look *into* the accusations.

Be aware, however, that questions and doubts are not enemies of faith. They can even be a doorway to faith – *if* you are willing to look into them. The real enemy of faith is fear. Fear undermines faith by attacking our willingness to trust. The accuser's goal is to raise questions in a way that makes us draw back in fear, unwilling to pursue the matter. If you do that during this important trial, then you have lost your impartiality and are not a good judge.

Any unresolved questions about the Father's trustworthiness are just that, unresolved. They are not hard evidence that God cannot be trusted. Court cases often end with some questions still unanswered. Remember, you don't need to be 'certain', just confident. Faith is not about everything making perfect sense, but about enough things making enough sense.

YOU BE THE JUDGE

How is the evidence stacking up? The defence has a good case with all sorts of credible evidence. The prosecution, however, hasn't presented any firm evidence yet, just lots of accusations and insinuations. The case is starting to look clear cut, but how can you be *fully* persuaded while there are so many unresolved questions?

How about getting out of the courtroom and testing some of the accusations against God? Ultimately, the only way to find out if someone can be trusted is to trust them. We have to be willing to climb into the 'wheelbarrow' with the Father if we are to find out more about his trustworthiness.

Our repeated steps of faith will, in time, resolve some of our questions. Whenever that happens, the case of the accuser is weakened and we gain new evidence that the Father can be fully trusted. That really tips the scales.

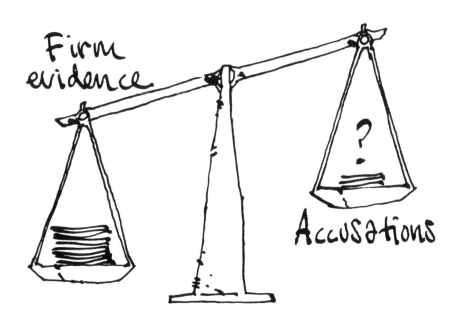

We will never find answers to all of our questions, especially regarding the future. True faith will always have at least some unanswered questions. Faith is about being willing to trust even when things are not one hundred percent clear or 'certain'.

Eventually, as we keep stepping out in trust, more and more accusations will be proven false. Soon, the weight of the evidence becomes overwhelming, and we reach a firm conclusion. "Case closed."

We, like Abraham, can be *fully persuaded* in our heart and mind that the Father can be trusted. This is not the end of our faith being put to the test, but it does mean that we now live from a position of trust, that our inclination is to trust, and that trusting the Father will come naturally. It means we will no longer need to go back and forth about whether to trust God every time we face a challenge.

RECEIVING THE GIFT OF FAITH

Coming to a place of being fully persuaded of God's faithfulness is a pure gift. As mentioned in the last chapter, we only need to be willing to receive the evidence he gives and allow him to convince us of his goodness. This willingness is so essential that we must maintain it throughout the whole process. We must first be willing to receive the evidence, then willing to consider and accept the evidence, and finally, be willing to act on it. That requires both an open heart and an open mind.

Jesus made it clear that evidence alone isn't enough. Those with a closed heart will not be persuaded, even by strong evidence, such as someone being raised from the dead (Luke 16:31).

We cannot even have an open heart, however, without the Father's help. It is God who "works in you to will and to act" (Phil 2:13). How does he do that? Well, he doesn't just override our will. The Father reveals his true goodness to us. It is the revelation of his "kindness" that helps you to open your heart "to lead you to repentance" (Rom 2:4).

Ultimately, we must be *willing* to be willing. The Father doesn't require us to throw the door of our heart wide open. If you open the door of your heart just enough to let a little of his light come through, he will help you be willing to open it more. Even if your willingness is "as small as a mustard seed" (Matt 17:20), he can help that grow into confident faith. Truly, faith is totally a gift.

FAITH AND REASON

Can our mind get in the way of faith? Well, a *closed* mind can certainly be a problem. But the issue is not the mind; pride and stubbornness cause the mind to be closed. Paul expresses it this way: "The mind governed by the flesh is death, but the mind governed by the Spirit is life and peace" (Rom 8:6). When pride rules our minds we demand answers that satisfy our sense of reason. Rather, we must learn to think and ask good, open, life-giving questions in a way that seeks to be in tune with the Spirit.

Having an *open* mind is important in the process of faith. We need to use our mind to consider, reflect upon, and come to reasonable conclusions about the evidence of God's trustworthiness. Earlier, we looked at how relationships have objective and subjective elements working together (Chapter 8). When it comes to faith, we need both the *objective* consideration of the evidence and the *subjective* willingness to accept it and respond to it. We see both these elements in Abraham's faith.

Abraham surely had many questions in mind when God challenged him to sacrifice Isaac. He apparently struggled to understand how everything was going to work out practically. But by *reasoning* through the evidence, he found faith. His reasoning led him to at least one scenario that helped him to trust God. Even though the solution he imagined was not what happened, it reminded him that God can do all things, and this gave him hope. This open-minded reasoning process is mentioned as part of Abraham's faith journey in the great faith chapter, Hebrews 11:

> Abraham *reasoned* that God could even raise the dead, and so in a manner of speaking he did receive Isaac back from death. (v. 19)

Don't be fooled into believing that thinking and using your mind undermines faith. Having a *closed* mind, or even a *closed* heart, does that. Loving the Father with all your heart, soul, mind, and strength means keeping an *open* heart and mind towards him, willing to trust him and give him the last word – in all aspects of life. Engage your heart and mind, but don't let your feelings or your reason have the last word. Rather, we must let God be God. Remember, he isn't just our Father, he is God, Lord of the universe. Always be willing to let God have the last word.

WILLING TO LET GO

Perhaps you have heard the story of 'Bruchko'. (If not, I highly recommend the book by that name.) At only 19, Bruce Olson went alone to live with the isolated Motilone tribe in the jungles of Colombia. At first, Bruce found it hard to fully rest in the hammocks the tribe used for sleeping in their communal hut. He tended to keep one foot on the ground, but his friend challenged him to trust the ropes and allow himself to be fully suspended in the hammock.

Years later, Bruce used this as a metaphor for faith when his friend asked how he could "walk on Jesus' trail". Bruce had previously wondered how he could describe faith, as he found no word for it in the tribal language. Now, to explain following Jesus, he told his friend, "You have to tie your hammock strings into Him and be suspended in God."[30]

Imagine visiting this tribe and being given a hammock to sleep in. One of your hosts helps you tie your hammock into the rafters. What happens next? You climb into the hammock and start lowering yourself into it. Soon, your whole body weight is resting in the hammock – almost. You still have one foot on the ground or one

Are you willing to 'tie your hammock' into the Father?

hand holding firmly to the rafters. Will the ropes hold? There is only one way to find out: *Let go.* Yet even after you let go, one question remains. Will you fully *rest* in your hammock, or will you lie awake all night wondering if it will hold?

Are you willing to put your faith in Father God? Are you willing to 'tie your hammock' into the Father? Or more importantly, are you confident enough in the 'knot' and the 'hammock' to fully rest in it and let it hold you?

LETTING GO

When I first knew God was calling me to be a part of mobilising Norwegians to missions, I had many questions. Norway was the last place I could imagine serving God. I had ended up in Norway for some months but was eager to move on. I had earlier felt the Father calling me to foreign mission work, and had imagined being somewhere like the Himalayas, the Amazon, or Timbuktu. Yet the sense of clarity with which Father God now communicated was undeniable; it was like pieces of a jigsaw puzzle falling into place. I just knew God had something more for me in Norway.

One of my biggest questions was about finances. I had little funds left and no regular income or support. I was about to head home to Australia, partly to work on finances. How could I stay in Norway as an unpaid volunteer with Youth With A Mission? How would I cover my expenses?

"I'm not asking you about finances," I sensed the Father saying. "I'm asking if you are willing to stay."

God had been teaching me about Abraham and about being fully persuaded. I understood that my willingness to trust him as my Father was essential, so I decided to stay, even though I had many unanswered questions. I did, after all, have plenty of evidence of his trustworthiness.

Just a few days later, God challenged me to give away most of what I had. The Spirit had spoken so clearly about the person I should give to and the amount. "But God, I don't even have enough to cover my first month here," I protested.

"Even if you keep the money, you don't have enough. Either way, you are dependent on me. Are you willing to trust me?"

I was willing, but it took a couple of days before I could get the cash, find the person and hand it over. Within minutes, a young couple approached me. They were leaving the mission to get married and had an uncertain financial situation, but God had laid it on their hearts to give me regular monthly support for a period. The amount they committed to give was just enough for my monthly expenses. The Father certainly took care of the finances. He has continued to do so for over 30 years.

It is only as we are willing to let go, and then actually do so, that we get to experience how much we can trust the Father.

CONFIDENCE AND FAITHFULNESS

Experiences such as that helped strengthen my confidence in God. Confidence, which has been mentioned throughout this chapter, is one important aspect of faith I wish to highlight. The word comes from Latin, where the root meaning was 'have full trust'. Confidence is like a living plant. As we continue to be willing to trust God, we nurture our faith in him, and it flourishes into confident faith. In time, this produces good fruit in our lives. We find it easier to trust God, we have more peace and less anxiety, and we become more confident in our identity as sons and daughters of the Father. Having confidence in God is a "blessed" state (Jer 17:7 NIV).

A second key aspect of faith is our faithfulness. This helps to provide part of the framework in which our confident faith can grow. Faithfulness will sometimes require objectivity as we choose to stand by our covenant commitment even when we would rather not. In the Hebrew language and worldview, *faith* and *faithfulness* are inseparably connected, and both build on the concept of firmness. A person who has faith has come to a *firm* position, like Abraham who was *fully persuaded* that God could be trusted. The person with true faith will also remain *firm* in that trust, not wavering but *faithfully trusting*.

I believe that faithfulness is one of the most foundational aspects of God's character, and therefore it is something he looks for in us. As your relationship with the Father gradually becomes more *firm*, your experience of Father-life will deepen.

Having a relational view of faith gives a firm foundation for our next topic, which is closely connected with faith: righteousness. My relationship with God has been revitalised in recent years as he has transformed my understanding of what the Bible reveals to us about righteousness. Gaining a relational view of righteousness has been a game changer.

—

KEY POINTS

- In looking at the evidence of the Father's trustworthiness, we need to be aware of how the enemy seeks to undermine our trust with fear and accusations.
- Unresolved questions are not a threat to faith, and reasoning with an open mind can help faith to grow.
- Based on the evidence we have, we need to be willing to let go and let our Father have the last word.

REFLECTION AND RESPONSE

How can you grow in your confidence in the Father? Are there any challenging steps of faith he is leading you to take? Start meditating regularly on the *evidence* you have of his nature and character, and your confidence will grow. You could also make a list of some of the evidence you have of God's faithfulness in your own life.

How can you grow in your faithfulness towards the Father? You don't need to strive and discipline yourself in your own strength. Your *willingness* to be faithful is vital. Invite him to help you to be more willing, and to receive the evidence he gives you of his goodness.

PART THREE

ALIGNING WITH THE FATHER

Our trust in the Father opens the way for us to live in right relationship with him. A word the Bible often uses to describe our right relationship with God is 'righteousness', yet this term is easily misunderstood. It is partly about right 'legal' standing, yet also about right living – both aspects are in the teaching of Jesus and the early apostles. What, however, is right living? What is the right way for us to be human? And what does it mean that God is righteous? Be ready for some extra portions of 'meat' in these chapters.

The LORD is righteous in all his ways
and faithful in all he does.
Psalm 145:17

13

JESUS THE GAME CHANGER

Jesus clearly ushered in a new era, and the new covenant gives us a fresh basis for being righteous in God's eyes. Yet what has actually changed from the old covenant to the new? What are the new 'rules of play'?

THE GAME CHANGE

Picture yourself at a soccer game where your team is battling to win the championship. No goals have been scored yet, and it is now the final minute. Suddenly, your team gains an opening and shoots for the goal. The goalkeeper manages to deflect the ball slightly, but it sails into the upper corner of the net. It's a goal!

Elation quickly turns to dismay as you hear the referee's ruling: the goal is not recognised. A new rule has been introduced. If the goal-keeper is at least able to deflect the ball, then it is considered a save. How would you feel about this unexpected change in the rules?

What if you were a Jew at the time of Jesus? You grew up believing in God and have earnestly sought to love him with all your heart, faithfully following his Law. Then one day, you hear of this incredible teacher called Jesus. You follow the crowds up to a hillside and listen in amazement to his words of wisdom, in what is later known as the Sermon on the Mount. How would you feel as you hear these shocking words?

> For I tell you that unless your righteousness surpasses that of the Pharisees and the teachers of the law, you will certainly not enter the kingdom of heaven.

> You have heard that it was said to the people long ago, 'You shall not murder, and anyone who murders will be subject to judgment.' But I tell you that anyone who is angry with a brother or sister will be subject to judgment. Again, anyone who says to a brother or sister, 'Raca,' is answerable to the court. And anyone who says, 'You fool!' will be in danger of the fire of hell. (Matt 5:20–22)

What! Did Jesus just change the game? Did he 'move the goalposts' or 'raise the bar'? Are we to be even better than the Pharisees? In what way is our righteousness to surpass that of the Pharisees?

A HOLLOW FORM OF RIGHTEOUSNESS

What if Jesus is not just upping the game? What if Jesus is redefining the goal, the rules of play, and the whole game? What if it is like going onto a field, ready to play soccer, only to discover you are in a game of golf?

What was wrong with the 'game' of the Pharisees and their view of righteousness? Partly, they thought they could attain righteousness by their own efforts. Yet the real problem lay in their idea of what they should attain. It was their 'righteousness' – their concept of what it meant to be right with God, of what they were aiming at – Jesus was against.

The Pharisees, being experts in the Law, approached life from a legal perspective. To them, righteousness was a matter of legal perfection or moral purity, as though being in right relationship with God was simply about following a system. In reality, their 'relationship' with God only had a framework but lacked relational life. They focused on the outside; their righteousness was hollow.

Significantly, the Pharisees thought from the outside in; they thought that right behaviour is what *made* them righteous. In contrast, Jesus turned everything inside out.

THE INSIDE·OUT KINGDOM

One day, Jesus had a heated exchange with the Pharisees about ritual cleansing. He then turned to the crowds and explained, "What goes into someone's mouth does not defile them, but what comes out of their mouth, that is what defiles them" (Matt 15:11).

The issue of ritual purity may not concern us. What Jesus is talking about here, however, is two fundamentally different views about being right with God. Tim Keller, an insightful pastor and author, refers to these views as *outside-in cleansing* and *inside-out cleansing*.[31] We could also call the results *outside-in righteousness* and *inside-out righteousness*. Jesus highlights the fact that true spiritual life, like all forms of life, is something internal that grows outward. Inner life leads to outer growth.

The Pharisees, with their worldly outside-in perspective, had fallen for one of the oldest lies around: that we can simply *do* something in order to *become* someone. At the dawn of time, Adam and Eve were sold the idea that by eating the forbidden fruit, they could become like God (Gen 3:5).

The Pharisees thought that doing the right things made them clean and righteous, thereby acceptable to God. The Father, however, doesn't accept us based on what we do; he accepts us because of *who we are*. We are already his; he is our Creator; we come from him. As we approach our Father, the only thing he looks to is our heart. Do we approach him with the humility of offspring who acknowledge him as our Source, our Creator, our God? Do we admit we need a Saviour? There is always grace for the humble (Jas 4:6, etc.). Not recognising that we belong to him can cause us to either approach him with pride in our achievements, or hold ourselves back in shame over not being 'good enough'. This can happen if we think our 'adoption' means we are not his natural children.

The issue here is identity. The world thinks: *I do, therefore I am.* (What I do defines me and gives me status and acceptance.) True sons and daughters think: *I am, therefore I do.* (I know who I belong to, and that shapes the things I do and don't do.) This is why I want to love as my Father loves, and why I aim to not call my brother a fool or even think that in my heart. Not because doing or not doing such things makes me anybody. Rather, they are ways of expressing who I am. My understanding of who I am, however, will be shaped by my view of righteousness.

A RICHER VIEW OF RIGHTEOUSNESS

Righteousness is probably one of the most important and most misunderstood words regarding the Father's vision for our lives. For years I thought its meaning was quite specific and only related to certain 'legal' technicalities about being right with God. Yet it was also a vague and mysterious word, an obscure religious term that didn't relate to daily life. In my shallow understanding of faith-righteousness, I had taken care to avoid the trap of the Pharisees' works-righteousness, but I still thought it was all about legal perfection. Like the Pharisees, I thought I attained righteousness simply by fulfilling the conditions of the covenant. In my case, the new covenant seemed to only require me to *repent, confess and believe* – then I was 'legally perfect' in God's eyes. I thought that fulfilling those conditions was all there was to it.

Grasping that God declares us to be righteous based on faith, not works, is a crucial foundation, but we must see the bigger picture. Our right relationship with God *starts* with having the right framework, but then it needs *life* in the framework. If we are satisfied with just fulfilling the legal conditions of the new covenant, without pursuing the core relationship, perhaps we are 'new covenant Pharisees'.

It was an eye-opener for me to discover that both the Old and New Testaments present a rich, multifaceted view of righteousness, with a lot of emphasis on how we live. Look at how strongly John stresses this point as he connects righteous living with love: "it is evident who are the children of God, and who are the children of the devil: whoever does not practice righteousness is not of God, nor is the one who does not love his brother" (1 John 3:10 ESV).[32] Righteousness is about much more than mere formalities; it is about an overflow of life and love. Let's explore what the Pharisees had misunderstood about the original game.

REDISCOVERING THE ORIGINAL GAME

While Jesus is clearly against the game of the Pharisees, we must be careful to see the difference between the Pharisees and the old covenant. The Pharisees are not, as I had often thought, the 'poster boys' of old covenant righteousness. Before Paul experienced the radical game change of Jesus, he was a Pharisee.[33] Yet when he teaches on righteousness by faith, he uses Old Testament texts as his foundation. There is no indication that he is trying to redefine the old covenant view, yet he is clearly opposed to the worldly outside-in view he once held as a Pharisee.

Many of Paul's references to the Old Testament make a clear connection between righteousness and faith.[34] Yet they don't tell us much else about righteousness. One passage that is particularly helpful in understanding righteousness is easily missed because the message is somewhat hidden. In Romans 4, Paul calls on David to support what he is saying, yet it appears as though Paul misquotes David and puts words into his mouth. Pay attention as you read Paul's words, including his quote from David:

> David says the same thing when he speaks of the blessedness of the one to whom God credits righteousness apart from works:
>> 'Blessed are those whose transgressions are forgiven, whose sins are covered. Blessed is the one whose sin the Lord will never count against them.' (Rom 4:6–8)

Why does Paul say that David is talking about righteousness being credited? Paul's quote from David does not even mention righteousness. This is part of a key passage in Paul's writings about righteousness by faith, yet he seems to be on thin ice by quoting David like this.

HIDDEN IN PLAIN SIGHT

To understand what is going on here, remember that Paul knew the Scriptures very well, as did most other devout Jews in his day. Also, they didn't have chapter and verse numbers as we do. A simple way to reference a whole passage was to quote a key snippet or opening line. For example, saying, "The Lord is my Shepherd," can work as a reference to the whole of Psalm 23 – even in our day.

In Romans 4, Paul quotes only the opening lines of Psalm 32, yet he clearly has the whole psalm in mind. The blessed ones Paul refers to are only called "righteous" in the final line of the psalm. A careful reading of the whole psalm gives us insight into King David's – and Paul's – understanding of faith-based righteousness.

David contrasts the righteous and the unrighteous, even putting himself in both of those categories. Two key themes emerge that define the righteous. Firstly, *the confession of sins*: "When I kept silent ... your hand was heavy on me ... Then I acknowledged my sin ... and you forgave" (vv. 3–5). Secondly, *the need to let God lead*: "Do not be like the horse or the mule, which ... must be controlled ... or they will not come" (v. 9). Both these themes are expressions of *trust*, which is mentioned directly in the closing lines:

> ... the LORD's unfailing love surrounds the one who trusts in him.
> Rejoice in the LORD and be glad, you righteous;
>> sing, all you who are upright in heart! (Ps 32:10b–11)

David clearly connects righteousness with trust (also known as 'faith'). We find no trace here of the outside-in, works-based righteousness of the Pharisees. There is no mention of law, and not even a hint of legalism or 'sinless perfection'. Rather, this psalm reflects the new covenant emphasis on faith, repentance, and lordship, which is probably why Paul quotes David.

Elsewhere, when David chooses to focus on the Law in Psalm 119 (his longest psalm), there is still no hint of legalism. Rather, David is totally in awe of the beauty of God's character, revealed in his law. He is so in tune with God that he values the things God values, as a true son would (see Chapter 9). David continually says things like, "Your statutes are my delight; they are my counsellors" (v. 24). Significantly, he repeatedly refers to God's laws as being "righteous".[35] If laws can be described as righteous, then righteousness is more than simply complying with law.

In another psalm, David tells us, "The wicked borrow and do not repay, but the righteous give generously" (Ps 37:21). Notice that the righteous go beyond the simple framework of paying debts and doing what is 'right'. Similarly, when Paul says that those who have been stealing should no longer steal, his point is that they should learn to "share with those in need" (Eph 4:28). The truly righteous

> ❝ *David gives us a much clearer lens for understanding the heart of the old covenant.*

don't just follow checklists and 'balance the books'; they stimulate life in others by being a blessing and sharing freely.

For many years, I thought the Pharisees gave us a lens for understanding the old covenant. Yet they had it all wrong; they treated it as a contract; they had the framework but not the life. David gives us a much clearer lens for understanding the heart of the old covenant, especially concerning righteousness. What hinders us from grasping this?

OLD COVENANT RIGHTEOUSNESS

The more I research, the more I see that the idea of 'righteousness' in the Old Testament is an entirely Hebraic concept, far removed from our Western thinking and the views of Greek philosophers. Our failure to understand the Hebraic perspective is perhaps the main reason why the old covenant is viewed as legalistic and nothing like the grace of the new covenant.[36]

How can we hope to grasp this foreign concept? Fortunately, you don't need a degree in Hebrew to do so. The many sections of poetry in the Old Testament, particularly in the Psalms and many of the Prophets, help us see the meanings associated with righteousness.

Hebrew poetry builds strongly on couplets (pairs of lines). Often, the couplets use *synonymous parallelism*, where the same idea is repeated, but phrased differently (using synonyms). In some cases, the synonyms for righteousness relate to 'firm' aspects, such as integrity, uprightness, justice and even wrath.[37] More commonly, however, the synonyms are 'warm' and relational. Words like love, faithfulness, salvation, and peace regularly appear. For example:

I do not hide your righteousness in my heart;
    I speak of your faithfulness and your saving help.
I do not conceal your love and your faithfulness
    from the great assembly. (Ps 40:10)

Love and faithfulness meet together;
  righteousness and peace kiss each other.
Faithfulness springs forth from the earth,
  and righteousness looks down from heaven. (Ps 85:10–11)

There is a rich complexity to the Hebraic concept of righteousness, encompassing a whole range of meanings. This could be confusing, except that we have already learnt that 'warmth' and 'firmness' don't need to be in tension (Chapter 5). Also, in the context of a right relationship, both are necessary. Together they stimulate the growth of relational life. All the various meanings connected with 'righteousness' centre on the foundational concept of *right relationship*. Pursuing that sort of righteousness means treating relationships like a garden, maintaining and nurturing them.

This relational view of righteousness is clear in many passages. For example, Isaiah describes a "righteous nation" as "the nation that keeps faith … those whose minds are steadfast, because they trust in you" (Is 26:2–3).

MUTATIONS

This ideal concept of righteousness, however, has many worldly mutations, leading to various *types* of righteousness. This is why Jesus challenged the Pharisees about their righteousness, not just their way of trying to get there. Paul, with his Hebraic view of righteousness, contrasts "the righteousness that is by the law" with "the righteousness that is by faith" (Rom 10:5–6). He isn't comparing the old covenant with the new. Rather, he is contrasting a mutation with the real thing. Simply aiming to fulfil the conditions of a covenant is a very different type of righteousness compared to one that pursues covenant relationship.

Where does that leave us? Jesus rejected the law-righteousness of the Pharisees, yet he clearly affirmed the faith-righteousness that we find throughout the Old Testament. Has anything actually changed? The answer is yes and no.

JESUS CHANGES 'EVERYTHING'

Jesus is the ultimate game changer; he is the 'before-and-after One' of world history. Jesus changes everything, even as we acknowledge that many things are still the same.

A friend who came to faith as an adult describes how 'everything' was different. The deep change in his core worldview even made the grass and the telephone poles seem different. People who knew him could describe him as a 'new' person, despite recognising him as the same one. This 'new' person was not a replacement of the old one but a new and more dynamic version, with a new degree of being alive.

Similarly, the new covenant isn't a total replacement for the old one. As mentioned previously (Chapter 7), the essential core of the covenant commitment is the same: to love God and neighbour wholeheartedly. Yet the new covenant gives us a new framework and a fresh basis for loving God and neighbour. For example, the Old Testament Scriptures reveal God as the Father of Israel and, indeed, of all humanity, every individual. Through Jesus, however, we gain a fresh and deeper revelation of his father-heart towards us and others.

The same is true of righteousness. The fact that God is righteous and desires us to be in right relationship with him remains unchanged. Yet the life, death, and resurrection of Jesus bring an explosive freshness to these concepts.

Figures such as Abraham and David give us limited models of being righteous with God; they had their bad days and were only shadows of the ideal. Jesus is the ideal, and he gives us a much clearer model of what it can mean to live daily in right relationship with the Father. Jesus also became the new "once for all" sacrifice (Heb 10:10). We are even told that Jesus' sacrifice is relevant for "sins committed under the first covenant" (Heb 9:15).

This gives us a fresh, dynamic basis for approaching the Father with confidence. The blood of Jesus is the ultimate proof that the Father, in his pure, saving, faithful righteousness, has done everything to have right relationship with us. This blood is now the only valid basis for being righteous before God. Furthermore, the Spirit has been given that we may live in Christ and him in us, allowing his righteousness to permeate our lives and impact our world in a whole new way.

Yes, Jesus changes everything. Yet, God is the same, yesterday, today, and forever. His own righteousness is unchanged, and the type of right relationship he desires with us is the same. Furthermore, the call for his people to *live righteously* continues in the new covenant. John even connects it with having God as our Father: "everyone who practices righteousness has been born of him" (1 John 2:29 ESV).[38] Only by the Spirit of the Son within can we know the freedom of practising righteousness as his sons and daughters.

Gaining a richer view of righteousness, in both the Old and New Testaments, has been one of the biggest game changers in my life in recent years. It has brought freshness into my relationships with both God and others; it has revitalised my understanding of Father-life. In the next few chapters, we will continue to explore righteousness, starting with the Father's righteousness.

—

KEY POINTS

- The Pharisees had a wrong idea of how to become righteous because their whole concept of righteousness was faulty.
- The mindset of outside-in righteousness simply seeks to fulfil the conditions for covenant relationship; inside-out righteousness pursues life within the relationship.
- The New Testament perspective on righteousness builds firmly on the Old Testament foundations of faith-righteousness.

REFLECTION AND RESPONSE

Take a moment to prayerfully read Psalm 32, which Paul refers to in Romans 4. Note the contrast between those who trust God and those who don't. We read of the blessedness of those who confess their sins, allow God to teach them, and put their trust in God – they are considered 'righteous'. What else do you see?

Next, read Romans 4:1–8 (while keeping Psalm 32 in mind) to gain some context of how Paul weaves the psalm in with his message.

For added insight, review Chapter 11, specifically regarding the faith of Abraham. (See the *Key Points* at the end of the chapter to refresh your memory). Then, read Romans 4:18–25.

Do you need a game change regarding righteousness? Conclude with your own prayerful response to your heavenly Father.

14

OUR RIGHTEOUS FATHER

Jesus is quoted as addressing God as: "Righteous Father" (John 17:25). What does it mean when we describe God as righteous? I've had to learn that many of our assumptions about what is 'right' reflect system-thinking and are at odds with Father-righteousness.

THE FATHER'S HEART

I walked through a dining hall one day and saw some dirty dishes lying around. "That's not right. They shouldn't be there," I thought to myself, as I carelessly judged someone for not following 'the system'.

Immediately, I sensed the Spirit of the Father gently challenging me. "If you truly believe they shouldn't be there, then why aren't you willing to do something about it?"

Now, I am not saying we should always tidy up after others. However, the Father had rightly identified an inconsistency in my response. I wasn't as concerned about where the dishes should be as I was that someone had not followed the system. I was making them look bad, and myself look good – in my own eyes. I was a self-appointed referee in the game of life, yet my knowledge of what was 'right' was far from the Father's heart.

THE FINGER OF THE PHARISEES

The Pharisees had a similar system-based understanding of what was right, and Jesus was openly critical of their self-righteousness attitude:

> They tie up heavy, cumbersome loads and put them on other people's shoulders, but they themselves are not willing to lift a finger to move them. (Matt 23:4)

Perhaps the Pharisees pictured God like a strict father wagging his finger and saying, "You should! You shouldn't!" By highlighting their unwillingness to even "lift a finger", Jesus was saying indirectly, "I'm not like that; the Father is not like that."

Our heavenly Father is 'firm' and has the right to expect certain things of us. Yet his righteousness is also 'warm' – he is "gracious and righteous ... full of compassion" (Ps 116:5). That means he engages himself in the relationship. Whatever

the Father requires of us, he is also willing to help us with. In dealing with man's sin, God didn't just wag his finger from a distance. Neither did he simply "lift a finger" to give a little help. Our righteous Father got involved in our human mess and got his hands dirty – God got his hands bloody while doing everything he could to make things right.

Please note, however, that Jesus did not criticise the Pharisees for aiming to keep the Law. In this same passage, Jesus had just told his Jewish audience that they should listen to the Pharisees, who were leaders in the community, and "be careful to do everything they tell you" (v. 3). The issue, for Jesus, is about their attitudes, their motives and the inconsistency in their lives – "they do not practise what they preach". Furthermore, they put "heavy loads" on people's shoulders, yet are unwilling "to lift a finger" to help.

They emphasised the framework of *doing* what was right, but didn't have a right *heart*. They were specialists on God's holiness and justice purely from a legal point of view, yet were completely out of touch with the Father's life-giving mercy and compassion. They were not *rightly aligned* with his heart and incapable of relating to God as a person.

BEING RIGHTLY ALIGNED

Our relational alignment towards our heavenly Father (our trust in him) is essential for being in right relationship with him. Yet he is also in right relationship with himself. To say God is 'righteous' means that everything about him is in right alignment – his nature, character, motives, words and actions all line up perfectly.

There is an intense beauty to God. He is not just 'flawless' in a technical sense (always following the rules); he is flawless in every way. Everything about him fits together perfectly; his 'warmth' and his 'firmness' are in perfect harmony; he is good! This inner alignment and consistency of character is expressed in the way he is rightly aligned in all relationships. In other words, God is *relationally consistent*. He always does what he can to have the best relationship possible with as many as possible. We see this most clearly in his covenant faithfulness.[39] Indeed, faithfulness is one of the most common synonyms for righteousness in the Old Testament poetry.

These concepts of alignment and consistency are implicit in our English word 'righteous'. The word 'right' comes from the Latin *rectus*, meaning 'straight'. The form 'righteous' was originally 'rightwise', meaning 'right-ways'.[40] The *right-ways-ness* of God means that He is straight and consistent in all his ways. In all his dealings with others, he is always consistent with his character and within the relationship. "The LORD is righteous in all his ways and faithful in all he does" (Ps 145:17).

In going back to the original Hebraic concept of righteousness, we find the verb *tsadaq* (to be righteous). This ancient Hebrew root meant to be straight or stiff.[41] The literal meaning, when applied to people, gave the abstract concept of being *righteous* or *just* – in other words, being 'straight' or 'stiff' (unwavering/consistent) in character and relationships. We find a hint of this meaning of straightness when David says, "Lead me, LORD, in your righteousness ... make your way straight before me" (Ps 5:8). David is confidently asking for God's merciful help, that he too may walk in *right-ways-ness*. This aspect of straightness is also expressed in the New Testament.[42]

THE RIGHT REFERENCE POINT

Understanding that righteousness is a matter of alignment can be helpful, and not understanding this can be a source of great confusion. Misunderstandings arise because there are subconscious assumptions about the *reference point* for right alignment. Just recall the things we said about faith: you can't just have faith; faith is a relational word; it needs to be directed towards something or someone (Chapter 11). Similarly, you can't just have righteousness. The word 'righteous' points somewhere, and that reference point defines what *type* of righteousness it is.

If we are sons and daughters who aspire to be like our Father, then he is our reference point and 'referee' – we aim for Father-righteousness and he is the one to declare us righteous. In contrast, the Pharisees simply aimed for law-righteousness – the Law was their reference point and, in their role as 'experts in the Law', they were the self-appointed 'referees'. Similarly, we can have a certain theology or doctrine as our reference point, thinking that if we just believe the right things, then we are 'right' with God.

Having God as our reference point and referee means aiming to be like him and to reflect his consistency of character and relational faithfulness. It isn't about achieving 'perfect' alignment; it's about our willingness to trust him and let him lead us. When he sees that sort of trusting faith, as he saw in Abraham, he calls it 'righteousness' – being in right relationship with him.

The alternative to aligning with God as our 'target' is that we end up defining our 'own targets' (see Chapter 4). To break out of that, we need the game change that Jesus brings. He doesn't just change the rules a little; he redefines the whole game, giving us a new goal and a new referee. Let me paraphrase how he does this in the Sermon on the Mount:

You say you are righteous because you are rightly aligned with the law – "I have not killed; I have not committed adultery". But I tell you that if your heart is not rightly aligned with the Father's heart – you haven't killed but you wish your brother was dead; you haven't committed adultery but you are full of lustful thoughts – then you are not in right relationship with him.

DRIVING LESSONS

I was driving to town one day when another driver pulled out of a side street just in front of me. I was irritated: "He should have waited; I have the right of way!"

What happened next was a subtle form of road rage. I didn't hoot my horn, shout, or use hand gestures. I just hit the brakes hard enough to send a signal that I had been inconvenienced: "You got in my way! You owe me an apology."

Immediately, I sensed the Spirit of the Father whisper to my heart, "What was that?"

I knew I had deliberately overreacted, though I wanted to make it look like the other driver had caused it. So, I started to justify my actions while focusing on legal technicalities: "He shouldn't have done that. I haven't done anything wrong. I have a right to be offended."

The Father, of course, saw straight through my pretences. The stirring in my spirit was gentle yet clear: "I am your Father who loves to forgive, who remembers that you are dust. Will you embrace my heart and my values and align your heart with mine? Extend forgiveness; don't be so quick to judge. You have no idea of their circumstances or why they did what they did."

My 'righteous indignation' was definitely not Father-righteousness. I had been thinking only in terms of what was *'correct'*, of claiming *my rights*, and of being *in the right*. That is system-righteousness, being in right alignment with a system. God wanted me to be rightly aligned with his heart and his values, choosing him as my reference point and trusting him as my referee. In his grace, he gave me an opportunity to realign my heart, that I might grow to be more like him. Perhaps we could add the following to a contemporary version of the Sermon on the Mount:

You say that road-rage is wrong, but I say that even if you grumble under your breath or carry offence in your heart, then you have not understood my character or my Kingdom.

USING GREEK GLASSES

Even as we earnestly seek to be in right alignment with our Father, we need to be aware of how different 'glasses' will colour our concept of righteousness. For example, the Greek language and worldview give their own twist to 'righteousness'.

For us, gaining insight into the Greek perspective often helps in understanding the New Testament. We must remember, however, that its writers did not have a Greek mindset, despite writing in Greek. Sometimes, the writers of the New Testament have clearly played on the Greek worldview in their word choice.[43] On other occasions, they have used Greek words to convey Hebraic concepts that go against the worldly thinking of Greek society.[44]

This is particularly relevant regarding the concept of righteousness; wearing 'Greek glasses' can bring in worldly assumptions that distort our view of the Father. For example, it may be helpful to know that a court case in the Greco-Roman world could end with the accused being 'justified' by being declared 'righteous' ('not guilty'). But if that leaves us with the impression that right relationship with God is *only* a matter of legal status, our relationship will have little depth (like the cousin in Chapter 7).

The Hebraic concept of righteousness, shaped by godly revelation, reveals a rich and dynamic understanding of 'right relationship'. In contrast, the worldly view sees righteousness more in terms of complying with a system. This is what we find in Greek culture and philosophy.

Greek society in New Testament times was built around the concept of *nomos*. This word refers to 'law' in all its expressions, including customs, obligations, and legal norms. Significantly, a person was considered 'righteous' if they conformed to the system of *nomos*.[45] In other words, righteousness was simply a matter of right alignment with a static system. The accompanying table contrasts the godly and worldly views of righteousness.

Someone influenced by this Greek mindset might assume that the statement, "God is righteous," simply means he is 'legally perfect' and always acts 'by the book'. While there is a clear element of correctness about God's behaviour, his righteousness is about much more than alignment with a defined system.

Godly View of Righteousness (biblical Hebraic mindset)	Worldly View of Righteousness (typical Greek mindset)
Right relationship (in every sense)	Simply right behaviour/right standing
Being figuratively **'straight'** in character and relationships	**'Correctness'** in a technical/legal sense ('straight' in relation to a system)
Relationship-based	System-based
Dynamic	Static status
Heart alignment with the person and character of God	Behavioural alignment with a system of what is 'correct' (*nomos*)
Inner consistency and relational faithfulness (which includes honour and respect for those who give laws)	Simply conforming to laws, norms, customs, virtues, obligations, expectations, etc.
Inside-out: Inner righteousness will be expressed in righteous living	Outside-in: Living righteously earns the status of being 'righteous'
Life within a framework	Only a framework, lacks life
Promotes and releases *life*!	Aims for *order* and *correctness*

THE RIGHTEOUSNESS OF GOD

I have often heard it said that Jesus was righteous *because* he didn't sin. Yet, Jesus did not just follow a system of right behaviour and thereby attain 'righteousness' as a legal status or some kind of 'Diploma of Achievement'. He did not earn outside-in righteousness. No, Jesus' whole life was centred on the Father as his reference point and referee. He was always right with God and his right life flowed out of that right relationship. He was righteous, therefore he didn't sin.

The righteousness of God – Father, Son and Spirit – is a core quality that permeates all other character traits. He is always rightly aligned within himself through consistency of character, and he is always faithful in pursuing healthy relationships. We occasionally see his righteousness expressed in wrath or judgement, because he is opposed to all that damages life and undermines relationships, yet it is mostly about promoting life. As mentioned earlier, the righteousness of God means that he does what he can to have the best relationship possible with as many as possible.

When Paul refers to the 'righteousness of God', it is often in connection with God's work of salvation through Jesus. For example, "in the gospel the righteousness of God is revealed" (Rom 1:17). Does this 'righteousness of God' simply refer to God's 'legal correctness' as he gets Jesus to address important legal matters on our behalf? It is valid to consider the 'firm' legal aspects of salvation, and Paul likely had that in mind. Yet there's much more here. In the Gospel, we also see the warm, compassionate, forgiving, life-giving, relationship-pursuing righteousness of the Father as he seeks to save sons and daughters who have gone astray. Just recall the relational faithfulness we see in the father of the Prodigal Son; God is a righteous father in a similar way.

As you read these words of Paul, remember the Old Testament perspectives he is building on. Keep in mind the synonyms for 'righteousness' such as love, faithfulness, mercy, and salvation.

> But now apart from the law the [*merciful, forgiving*] righteousness
> of God has been made known … This [*generous*] righteousness is
> given through the *faithfulness* of Jesus Christ to all who believe. … all
> have sinned and fall short of the glory of God, and all are justified

> *He doesn't just seek to make us 'correct'*
> *he desires to win our trust.*

[*restored* to right relationship] freely by his *grace* through the *redemption* that came by Christ Jesus. ... He did this to demonstrate his [*loving, patient*] righteousness, because in his *forbearance* he had left the sins committed beforehand *unpunished* – he did it to demonstrate his [*faithful*] righteousness at the present time, so as to be just [the Righteous One] and the one who justifies [*restores* relationship with] those who have *faith* in Jesus. (Rom 3:21–26)

The life-giving, relationship-pursuing righteousness of the Father that is "given" to us is much more than just a new legal status. In his compassionate 'right-ways-ness' towards us, he left former sins unpunished. Now, this same faithful and merciful 'righteousness of God' gives us grace, forgiveness, reconciliation, resurrection life, and everything else we need to live in alignment with him. Paul uses this term 'righteousness of God' to speak of how God's judgement and grace are joined together, as he extends forgiveness and draws us into his Kingdom.[46] This is much richer than just legal correctness. Truly, "The LORD is gracious and righteous; our God is full of compassion" (Ps 116:5).

LESSONS FROM A GARDEN

Recall the image of the father and young child working together in the garden (Chapter 1). The son or daughter sometimes makes mistakes, so not everything is 'correct'. Yet in the father's eyes, the whole situation is just perfect; everything is as it should be; the child is in right relationship. The father isn't looking for faultless performance but a *pure heart*. He looks for trust, cooperation and a desire for togetherness.

If the child were to be deliberately rebellious, the father may need to be firm. As it is, there is openness and trust in the relationship. We see the father's relational righteousness in the way that he corrects his child gently and sometimes chooses to not intervene. The child's righteousness is seen in his trust as he accepts his mistakes and allows the father to lead him – just like David's description of righteousness in Psalm 32 (see Chapter 13).

We could compare this garden scene with Abraham's experience. In a sense, God invited Abraham to come and work with him in his 'garden', the world. God promised to bless Abraham and shared his vision of wanting to bless others through him. All Abraham did was accept the invitation. He said yes to God; he put his trust in him: "Abraham believed God, and it was credited to him as righteousness" (Rom 4:3, Gen 15:6).

In God's eyes, trust is the most essential ingredient in the type of covenant relationship he wanted with Abraham – and desires with us. In contrast, worldly 'righteousness' doesn't build on trust; you simply do what is required and behave 'correctly', perhaps even motivated by fear or shame. The type of right relationship the Father is looking for, however, requires a right heart – it needs life in the framework.

The skills for pursuing right relationships are like the skills of a gardener. We need to know when to prune and when to nourish. As I look back on my early years of parenting, I can see many situations where I was too focused on the 'pruning' (correcting my children's behaviour) and not so skilled in nurturing the heart relationship.

Our righteous Father has high ideals for his children and will occasionally 'prune' us. Yet he doesn't just seek to make us 'correct'; he desires to win our trust. That is why his great forbearance is also an expression of his righteousness (Rom 3:25). It is also why love and gentleness are listed together with righteousness as things that Paul tells his 'son' Timothy to pursue (1 Tim 6:11).

I have had to learn that worldly 'correctness' only teaches us about how things 'should' be. When things are not as they should be, it seems right to react in judgement or attempt to 'correct' the situation – often damaging relationships in the process.

Father-righteousness, however, gives us the wisdom to respond in a good way, in true relational *right-ways-ness*. The more we learn to align ourselves with the Father's heart in that way, the more we become an extension of his righteousness in the world. That is our next topic.

—

KEY POINTS

- The Father is in alignment within himself and is consistent in all relationships; he calls us to align with his heart and character.
- If we are to live in Father-righteousness, then he must be our reference point and referee.
- The worldly mindset of 'correctness' can distort our view of the Father and how he calls us to live in right relationship with him and others.

REFLECTION AND RESPONSE

Take a moment to read the following passages: Psalm 36:5–10; Psalm 71:15–19; Isaiah 51:4–6. Meditate on the richness of the Father's righteousness as you read.

Father-righteousness is something we can pursue and grow in. Paul exhorts Timothy, "Flee the evil desires of youth and pursue righteousness, faith, love and peace, along with those who call on the Lord out of a pure heart" (2 Tim 2:22).

Do you desire to pursue righteousness with a pure heart? Ask the Father to help you be more aligned with him and to grow in reflecting his consistency of character and relational faithfulness.

15

BECOMING THE RIGHTEOUSNESS OF GOD

Part of the Father's aspirations for his children is that we engage with him in what he is doing. To understand our role, we must understand God's ultimate vision for humans. What will heaven be like? I don't just mean the environment (streets of gold, gemstones, mansions) or the things that are not there (sickness, pain, suffering). What about the relationships? What will it be like to live in a sinless world?

A PERFECT WORLD

Try to imagine life when every relationship is an expression of God's goodness. Even in our wildest dreams, I don't think we can come close to knowing what it will be like to only be met with, love, respect, honour, truthfulness, faithfulness, generosity, encouragement, blessing – and every other good and pure attitude, motive, and way of acting. That will be, quite literally, a divine experience.

Now, instead of imagining what it would be like to experience those things, imagine being that way yourself. What would it be like for you to only ever express love, respect, honour, truthfulness, faithfulness, generosity, encouragement, blessing, and every other good and pure thing? Wouldn't that also be a divine experience of peace, harmony and wholeness as Father-life flows and gains expression through you?

The first description, of how you would experience pure goodness in everyone else, is still out of reach. We will have to wait until the Father has made "everything new" (Rev 21:5). But the second description, of how you can express his goodness to others, is part of the Father's vision for his sons and daughters in the here and now.

We will never fully attain it in this life, but we can embrace the vision and keep aiming at the Father's high ideals and aspirations for us. As we increasingly reflect more and more of our heavenly Father's character and values, we reveal to others his right ways of being and relating. The Father desires that we, in this life, actually "become the righteousness of God" (2 Cor 5:21). To better grasp what Paul means by that, let's explore the whole passage from the beginning.

AN ACTIVE LONGING

At the start of 2 Corinthians 5, Paul talks about the limitations of our "earthly tent" and our longing to be in our "heavenly dwelling" (v. 1–4). In describing this future hope, he comments that we were "fashioned for this very purpose" (v. 5). Paul then turns his attention to the here and now and the need for us to live well while we are "at home in the body" (v. 6–9). How we live in this period of longing is so important that we will be judged "for the things done while in the body, whether good or bad" (v. 10).

According to Paul, we do not just have a future purpose; we have a purpose in this life. Part of our purpose is to "try to persuade others" (v. 11). Presumably, we are to persuade others about the immense goodness of God, as we reflect his goodness. This is not simply a command for us to obey. Rather, our persuasion of others is to be driven by an inner life-force: "Christ's love compels us" (v. 14). Because he "died for all", we should no longer live for ourselves but "for him who died … and was raised again" (v. 15).

Next, Paul starts to go into detail about the Father's purpose for his sons and daughters and how we can live for him in this period of longing for fullness.

We are to be agents who bring Father-life into his world. To be that, our view of others must align with the Father's view; we are to "regard no one from a worldly point of view" (v. 16). We must also realise that what we long for in the future is now available to us; we can already live the new resurrection life: "If anyone is in Christ, the new creation has come: the old has gone, the new is here!" (v.17).

AGENTS OF RIGHTEOUSNESS

What is this new life all about? What does it mean to no longer live for ourselves? Paul next uses three different ways to describe our role in God's purposes. Each shows how our Father wants us to become an *extension* of what he is doing. Keep in mind the Father's aspirations for his children as you read these verses:

All this is from God, who reconciled us to himself through Christ and gave us *the ministry of reconciliation*. [promoting healthy relationships] ...

We are therefore Christ's *ambassadors*, as though God were making his appeal *through us*. [like an adult heir who can act on behalf of their father] ...

God made him who had no sin to be sin for us, so that *in him* we might *become* the righteousness of God. (2 Cor 5:18, 20a, 21)

Do you see what these verses tell us? The righteous Father pursues relationship, providing a way for us to be reconciled to him. Now he invites us to become his relationship-pursuing righteousness in the world, as we grow in reflecting his character, drawing others into right relationship with him. This is only possible through Jesus, the Prince of Righteousness. It is only as we live "in him" that we can "become" the very righteousness of the Father.[47]

The thrust of Pauls' message in this whole passage in 2 Corinthians 5 is not our initial justification or the legal framework for our relationship with God. Rather, Paul presents how we can build on the foundation of being in Christ, engaging with God as we long to see his vision fulfilled.

SLAVES TO RIGHTEOUSNESS

This way of giving ourselves over to God's vision for righteous living is also referred to as being "an instrument of righteousness" (Rom 6:13) and "slaves to righteousness" (v. 18). As Paul describes this way of life, he repeatedly contrasts *before* and *after* salvation (Rom 6:15–23). For example: "Just as you *used to* offer yourselves as slaves to impurity ... so *now* offer yourselves as slaves to righteousness" (v. 19). Paul goes on to describe the "benefits" of these contrasting ways of life (v. 21–22) and concludes by contrasting the results: "For the wages of sin is death, but the gift of God is eternal life in Christ Jesus our Lord" (v. 23).

The way Paul expresses this in terms of 'death' and 'life' reflects an interesting aspect of the Hebraic worldview: the righteous are seen as being 'alive', both in this life and the next, while the wicked are 'dead', even in this life.[48] Therefore, the resulting 'wages' of sin includes 'death' in this life. That means: a lack of fruitfulness; not being fully alive as God intended; not being connected with the true source of life; shallow relationships; a non-life. God's gift of eternal life, however, starts here and now. This includes: being fully 'alive' and in tune with God's vision for humanity; drawing on his Father-life; living righteously; knowing fruitfulness; having deep and meaningful relationships; and abundant life. When Father-life is 'abundant', it spills over and touches those around us.

As we 'idolise' our righteous Father, we become 'slaves' to righteousness and Father-life. This will be evident in righteous living, showing we truly are children of God: "If you know that he is righteous, you may be sure that everyone who practices righteousness has been born of him" (1 John 2:29 ESV). Jesus also spoke of identifying the righteous and the unrighteous based on what they did or didn't do (Matt 25:31–46).

WORKS OF RIGHTEOUSNESS

Is all this talk of what we 'do' starting to sound a bit too much like 'works'? Aren't we supposed to be saved by faith and not works? Yes, but remember, faith without works is dead (Jas 2:14–26). There may appear to be a tension between these two messages, but only if we equate 'works' with doing what is 'correct'.

'Works' simply refers to what we *do*. It can refer to things we do to gain something or the things we do as an outflow of who we are. Can we become righteous through our own 'works'? No, that is *outside-in works*. However, if we truly are righteous and the Spirit is alive in us, should that be evident in what

> **" The righteous are seen as being 'alive',
> while the wicked are 'dead'.**

we do? Yes! God is good and his Spirit prompts us to do 'good works'. Now we are talking about *inside-out works*, which are a natural fruit of Father-life. Like dandelions pushing through asphalt, Father-life presses out.

Paul mentions these two types of 'works' in his letter to Titus. He emphasises that God saves us "not because of righteous *things we had done*, but because of his mercy." God's purpose, however, is that we "might become *heirs*" and be those who are "careful to devote themselves to *doing what is good*" (Tit 3:5–8). As mature 'heirs' of the Living God – those who reflect his character and act on his behalf – his life in us should impact society around us.

Godly righteousness is not only a matter of behaving well and avoiding doing anything bad. In the Hebraic view, living righteously requires "positive deeds".[49] David saw the need for both: "Turn from evil *and* do good" (Ps 34:14). Peter affirms this as still applying in the new covenant (1 Pet 3:11).

Doing good means anything that promotes life rather than death. This is why David says, "The wicked borrow and do not repay, but the righteous give generously" (Ps 37:21). It isn't enough for us to stay out of trouble and meet our obligations – that is contractual living, which is 'dead'. If all we manage to do in life is fulfil our obligations, pay our debts, and balance the books, then the sum total of our life is zero. That is not life. Simply aiming for balance is "neither hot nor cold" (Rev 3:15–16). In contrast, Father-righteousness takes us beyond the framework of what we should or shouldn't do and brings an overflow of life into relationships.

A woman I know was surprised one day when the manager of her local grocery store gave her a bouquet of flowers. He was impressed by how she had consistently been so friendly, positive, and encouraging with the staff. She had gotten to know many of them and would often stop to chat briefly. She was so 'alive', even as she did her shopping, that people noticed. Perhaps you are not as outgoing, but there are countless ways for Father-life to flow through us and touch those around us.

GARDENING RIGHTEOUSNESS

Life produces life, and righteous living causes an overflow of life. David even speaks of generous righteousness having eternal fruit: "They have freely scattered their gifts to the poor, their righteousness endures forever" (Ps 112:9). Paul quotes and builds on this as he writes to the Corinthians (2 Cor 9:7–11). There, he speaks of God's ability to bless us abundantly, that we may "abound in every good work" (v. 9). He uses terms such as 'sow' and 'harvest' to emphasise the fruitfulness of godly righteousness (v. 10). He also stresses that generosity needs to come from the heart (v. 7).

True generosity isn't something that can be legislated. The fruit of the Spirit need to come from the heart, in an organic way. Expressions of Father-life such as love, joy, peace, forbearance, kindness and goodness don't come from following rules or a system of 'correct' behaviour. All of these, in their purest form, will always be inside-out expressions, growing organically from a right heart.

Father-righteousness is *Father-life!* It grows and bears fruit, promoting life, growth, and fruitfulness wherever it is. The poetic imagery of the Psalms tells us, "The righteous will flourish like a palm tree, they will grow like a cedar of Lebanon" (Ps 92:12). Isaiah describes God's life-giving righteousness as showers of rain that cause righteousness to flourish among men (Is 45:8). Similarly, Hosea challenges us to garden righteousness:

> Sow righteousness for yourselves,
>   reap the fruit of unfailing love,
> and break up your unploughed ground;
>   for it is time to seek the LORD,
> until he comes
>   and showers his righteousness on you. (Hos 10:12)

How can we garden righteousness? The two tasks assigned to man in the Garden of Eden were to "work it and take care of it" (Gen 2:15). The two verbs in the Hebrew text are literally: *serve* and *keep*. To serve, in this context, means to cultivate (develop and nourish). To keep means to maintain order (weed, prune and remove dead wood). The calling was to nurture life within the framework and to maintain the framework for the life.

As we grow in Father-righteousness, we learn to nurture and promote life in relationships and individuals around us. We also show respect for the frameworks of society by honouring earthly authorities while staying within God's moral framework. Father-righteousness addresses both the right heart of 'social justice' and the right boundaries of 'legal justice'.

THE FRUIT OF RIGHTEOUSNESS

As we seek to live this way, what fruit can we hope to see? Part of the Hebraic understanding is that righteous living brings *shalom* into the community.[50] This is expressed in Isaiah, where we are told, "the work/fruit/effect/result of righteousness will be *shalom*" (Is 32:17, various translations).

The Hebrew word, *shalom*, can be rightly translated as 'peace', yet it is an active peace, full of life. Worldly concepts of peace can be passive, such as silence, calm, or a lack of conflict. Some Eastern religions view peace as a state of perfect 'balance' or emptiness, with no desires. In contrast, God's idea of peace is abundant life, as he intended. Rather than silence, it is like a symphony orchestra making beautiful, uplifting music in perfect harmony. Instead of having no desires, it means to passionately desire all that is good. *Shalom* means fullness, wholeness, well-being, health, harmony, prosperity, good relationships, good desires, and being satisfied by all that is truly good.

This was central to all the hopes and dreams Israel had for their Messiah. He was to be the "Prince of Peace" (Is 9:6) and would reign in righteousness (Is 9:7, 11:5, etc.). In other words, he would maintain a secure *framework* for peace (no war or conflict) and promote the *life* of peace (fullness, wholeness and harmony). Yet, the Messiah has already come and is still here in the form of the 'Body of Christ'. We are his agents of reconciliation, righteousness, and peace. We are to live in such a way that Father-life flows through us and bears fruit, bringing wholeness into relationships with God and fellow man, ultimately impacting all of society.

The Norwegian revival preacher, Hans Nielsen Hauge, travelled extensively around Norway from 1797 to 1804. He planted hundreds of prayer groups and promoted moral reform. At the same time, he helped start numerous small businesses and taught people to grow potatoes, leading many out of poverty and malnutrition and bringing widespread social transformation. The positive influence of Hauge's ministry brought so much *shalom* into Norwegian society that the impact is still evident over 200 years later.

A simpler example is found in the testimony of a young graduate who ended up working with a notoriously difficult boss. After a few weeks, her colleagues were amazed at how she wasn't bothered by his grumpy, demanding, and insensitive behaviour. He even seemed to be less difficult when she was around. Her only 'secret' was to bring Father-righteousness into her workplace. She didn't live by worldly thoughts about what is 'right' – it wasn't about whether he *deserved* to be treated well, or whether she had a *right* to be offended. Rather, she aligned with her righteous Father, who is gracious and full of compassion (Ps 116:5). If her boss was grumpy, she responded with joy. When he was demanding, she was gracious, and when his words were hurtful, she forgave. She brought Father-life into her workplace and became a living testimony to the character of God. This is something we all can do.

DRIVEN BY A VISION

Just imagine the combined effect if every Christian lived like this. The New Testament teaches us how we should be 'salt' and 'light' that impact the world around us. I once heard the explanation that salt in the saltshaker has no influence – it is only as it is spread and becomes invisible that its impact is felt and tasted.[51]

Similarly, the Church cannot fulfil its role when gathered in the 'salt shaker'. While most of our understanding of church focuses on the 'the church gathered', we need to understand our role and calling to be 'the church scattered'. Salt makes a difference. Wherever we are – at work, at school, at the sports club or at church – should be a better place because we are there.

In other words, our 'works of righteousness' should lead to the fruit of *shalom*. Similarly, when our goal is righteous living, we will sow *shalom* wherever we are: "a harvest of righteousness is sown in peace by those who make peace" (Jas 3:18 ESV). Becoming the righteousness of God is our calling, even as we long for that day when we shall dwell in God's perfect righteousness and *shalom*. If we truly value his righteousness, we will seek to live it now.

Peter, in a chapter about the coming 'Day of the Lord', raises a question about the present: "What kind of people ought you to be? You ought to live holy and godly lives as you look forward to the day of God and speed its coming." (2 Pet 3:11–12) Our lives are to reflect our righteous Father as we value his ways and his vision for humanity. We do this, Peter goes on to explain, while "looking forward to a new heaven and a new earth, where righteousness dwells" (2 Pet 3:13).

Another thing we can look forward to is "the wedding of the Lamb" (Rev 19:6–9). As John describes his vision of this event, he tells of the bride being "clothed in fine linen", which "stands for the righteous acts of God's holy people" (v. 8). Everything done in true Father-righteousness has lasting fruit and eternal value. This is a vision worth living for.

Yet, learning to live in such a way that we 'become the righteousness of God' is dependent on really grasping Jesus' game change. The next chapter will explore what that means.

—

KEY POINTS

- As sons and daughters of God, we have a role and a calling to live righteously in this life, and promote his vision for human relationships, as we look forward to the day we can fully experience that vision.
- Living righteously goes beyond simply avoiding evil; it brings life into relationships through doing what is truly good, not just 'correct'.
- The fruit of righteous living is *shalom* in the community around us – peace, wholeness, well-being, healthy relationships, prosperity, and more.

REFLECTION AND RESPONSE

One of the most basic commands of God is: "Do to others as you would have them do to you" (Luke 6:31). Take a moment to reflect on that in relation to the question at the start of this chapter: What would it be like to live in a perfect world?

If you can imagine life at its best, then you know what to aim for in this life. Yet we can only start to achieve that as we live "in him" and allow Father-life to gain expression in our lives. If that is your desire, take a moment to pray.

16

GRASPING THE GAME CHANGE

What needs to change for us to grow in Father-righteousness? What can hinder us or distort our understanding of God's vision for our lives? We need to have the right focus to see the vision clearly.

RECOGNISING PATTERNS

As humans, we are wired to recognise patterns. From the moment we are born, we instinctively identify patterns around us – patterns of sound, form, and behaviour. In time, as patterns repeat, we make subconscious assumptions about what is 'normal', 'good', 'right', and 'true'.

Significantly, as we grow, any new experience or information is subconsciously filtered through our established assumptions. When we encounter something that we find easy to relate to, and it fits well with our existing views, then we will automatically feel positive about it and are less likely to reflect on or question it. This aspect of human behaviour is referred to as *cognitive ease*.[52]

Even as Christians, if we hear teaching that seems to fit the pattern of our existing views, we often accept it without looking into it. For example, I used to be certain that 'Abba' was Aramaic baby talk for 'Daddy' and was a way for us to address God as a small child would. I had heard this repeatedly in sermons, and it fit nicely into the patterns of my warm ideas about God the Father. Yet there is no basis for this view. When I later looked into it, I discovered that the theologian who originally promoted this view in the 1960s quickly tried to correct his error.[53] Yet the myth lives on.

This teaching may not be heresy, and Christians need to know that sort of closeness with God. However, if relating to God as *Daddy* limits us to think *only* in terms of being immature children, then that hinders us from fully living as his sons and daughters. Having a simple, childish approach to life is not always good.

Our subconscious desire for life to fit into certain patterns influences the expectations we carry into relationships. We want people and circumstances to fit our patterns of what is 'right' or 'supposed' to happen. We expect our spouse, friends, boss or even God to act in certain ways. The power of our expectations is so strong that we can end up trying to change people and circumstances to fit our patterns, rather than adjusting our expectations to reality.

Father-life calls us to maturity. We need to grow out of the childish limitations of pattern-thinking and system-righteousness. Yet shifting our focus to the Father and everything he values won't always be easy.

LOOKING BEYOND PATTERNS

A similar shift of focus is needed to see the hidden 3D image in a *stereogram*. Stereograms are a special type of picture – they look like a pattern but carry a hidden 3D image. If you stare at the stereogram long enough and manage to shift your focus, suddenly you can see a new image with three-dimensional depth. Yet if you allow your focus to slip back to the original 2D pattern, then the 3D image disappears.

I used to struggle to see these hidden images and had given up on stereograms. All I saw was patterns in two dimensions. Yet, while working on this chapter, I felt the Spirit prompting me to give it another go.

It took a while to slowly adjust my focus without snapping back to the 2D pattern. After much re-focusing, suddenly I could see it. A new and very different image appeared. I thought it would be easy to do a second stereogram once I had

cracked the first one, but I found I still had to concentrate. I gradually got quicker with each new image, but it still took effort to not stay locked on the 2D pattern.

This is similar to how my view of the Bible has changed. I was convinced the Bible was God's Word to us and was something we should build our lives on. Yet I realise now that I was subconsciously just looking for instructions to follow or patterns to conform to. That gave me a shallow 2D view of the Father's heart and character, as though he was only interested in having us conforming to a pattern of 'correct' behaviour.

Gradually, I learned to not let the details and patterns be my focal point as I looked at the Bible. Rather, God himself was to be my focus. Suddenly, the Father started to come alive with 3D clarity. My spirit was awakened as a fresh sense of liberty and the relational richness of Father-life came into focus. Yet, as with the stereograms, this ability to view the Bible from another focal point takes some getting used to and is an area for ongoing growth. We naturally think in terms of system-righteousness and need help to grow in Father-righteousness. Fortunately, the Spirit is here to help us.

WE NEED A CHANGE OF VIEW

You are probably familiar with the verse about the Spirit convicting us of sin, righteousness and judgement (John 16:8). It is easy to understand why we need to be convicted of sin, but why righteousness? Here is how the NIV translation renders the passage:

> But very truly I tell you, it is for your good that I am going away. Unless I go away, the Advocate will not come to you; but if I go, I will send him to you. When he comes, *he will prove the world to be in the wrong about sin and righteousness and judgment.* (John 16:7–8)

So why is it good for the Spirit to convict or "prove the world to be in the wrong" about these things? Perhaps because the worldly human way of viewing them is distorted and needs correction. One commentary explains that, regarding sin, righteousness, and judgement, "new ideas are to be borne in upon the human mind by the spirit".[54] Jesus explains why we need the Spirit to bring these new ideas and a change of view:

About sin, because people do not believe in me. (v. 9) – The world views sin as breaking the rules or going 'too far'. The Father tells us that all that isn't of faith is sin. The real sin is that we don't 'believe in' God – we are not pursuing a faithful, trusting relationship with him, letting him be our reference point and referee. We need a fresh view of sin, shifting from a system view to a relational view.

About righteousness, because I am going to the Father, where you can see me no longer. (v. 10) – The world views righteousness as keeping the rules or being rightly aligned with norms (system-righteousness). True righteousness is about being rightly aligned with the Father, remaining focused on him. When Jesus was here on earth, he was a living example of Father-righteousness. Now, we need the Spirit to reveal this to us and guide us in it.

About judgment, because the prince of this world now stands condemned. (v. 11) – Knowing that the enemy is defeated is an important aspect of fully trusting the Father. We also need to trust God as judge, and avoid judging others based on our system-based view of right and wrong.

The Spirit of the Father desires to help us make the necessary changes of view. That is exactly what I experienced after my 'road rage' and when I was concerned about dirty dishes (Chapter 14). I was preoccupied with the 'right' patterns of behaviour and the way things 'should' be. The Spirit helped me to change my perspective and to focus on the Father. Then his Father-righteousness snapped into view with 3D richness.

A FRESH WAY OF LIVING

Embracing this game change – as we shift our focus away from the 'patterns of this world' to the Father – leads us into a whole new way of living. It is more than just turning from sin, selfishness, fleshly desires, and everything negative. The Father-life is not just about repenting from unrighteousness, but also from the world's way of viewing righteousness and what is 'right'. This is not limited to 'spiritual' matters – it affects all of life and our views and assumptions about 'good', 'normal' or 'acceptable' behaviour.

As we embrace this game change, some interesting misunderstandings may occur. Father-righteousness is so foreign to most people, that even acts of kindness can cause confusion because of our 'abnormal' behaviour. I once heard author Erwin McManus give a good example of this.

He was at a checkout and overheard an older couple who did not have enough money to complete their purchase. Erwin felt led to get involved, so he turned to the cashier and said, "Excuse me. I'd like to buy that for them."

Erwin was not following the system of 'normal' behaviour, so the cashier reacted, "I'm sorry sir; you're not allowed to do that."

Erwin tried to clarify, "No, you don't understand. I would like to buy this *for* them."

The cashier still didn't get the point, and called across to the next cashier, "He's not allowed to do that, right? He can't just buy this other customer's item."

The cashier was focused on the *system*. Erwin was focused on the Father. He honoured the system of payment but didn't follow the assumed patterns of how it should happen or who should pay. Instead, he allowed the Spirit to lead him in expressing the Father's caring, generous righteousness in that situation. He 'broke the rules' in a generous way, going beyond rules and seeking to bless and impart life. This is Father-life!

GALATIANS REVISITED

Paul wanted the Galatians to embrace this same game change. I used to think that Paul's letter to the Galatians was all about turning from the Law of Moses – or in my case, from religious legalism – and embracing the Father's grace. Martin Luther seems to have connected 'law' in Galatians with the religious legalism he saw in the Catholic church of his day. I now see a much broader message in

Galatians that addresses every form of 'system-thinking', not just religious legalism. It relates to all of life, not only 'spiritual' issues.

The Galatian believers were not Jews. However, when they start turning to the Law of Moses for the very first time, Paul accuses them of turning *back* to something "weak" (Gal 4:9). Whatever they are turning back to is not the Law of Moses. Rather it is the way they relate to it. They were returning to the weak and childish life of following patterns of behaviour and conforming to systems, rather than being led by the Spirit. Previously, they had followed the patterns they had grown up with – they observed the customs of their culture, including idol worship. Now, as new believers, some Judaizers had convinced them that, to be good Christians, they should carefully follow Jewish customs and patterns of worship. Challenging this false teaching is the whole point of Paul's letter.

A key word in Galatians is *law*, which in the Greek text is *nomos*.[55] We mentioned earlier how the Greek view of righteousness was based on conformity to *nomos* (Chapter 14). This important Greek word refers to "what is proper" and it could apply broadly to "any norm, rule, custom, usage or tradition".[56] Essentially, it defines a pattern of 'right' behaviour. Within any group, their *nomos* defines the standard of how a 'good' person is expected to live. This then becomes the reference point for their concept of 'righteousness' (i.e. system-righteousness).

MANY FORMS OF *NOMOS*

Every grouping – every culture, club, workplace, congregation, etc. – has its own *nomos*-systems, its own expected patterns of behaviour. Sometimes they are written; sometimes they are just assumed. When patterns of behaviour become so normal that they are assumed, people are expected to conform to them. What is merely *normal* then becomes as *law*.[57] (This is why Erwin caused such a stir at the checkout with his *abnormal* behaviour.)

The Jews had a clear, written standard for what was right: the Torah. In the Greek texts, this was translated as 'the *nomos*' (the law). Yet, as mentioned, *nomos* has a range of meanings far beyond Torah and even broader than just 'law'. Paul was clearly aware of this and played on these various meanings, particularly in his letter to the Galatians.[58]

Many theologians seem to have missed this point, assuming that *nomos* refers only to Torah and Paul is simply contrasting the Law of Moses and grace. Rather,

> *“ Simply following a system can never bring life.*

Paul's message to the Galatians (and us) relates to all forms of 'law' (*nomos*). He contrasts the childish patterns of system-righteousness with the mature life of focusing on the Father and being led by his Spirit.

THE SOURCE OF LIFE

Paul makes an important claim, which we miss if we have wrong assumptions:

For if *a law* [*any nomos*] had been given that could *impart life*, then righteousness would certainly have come by the law [*that particular nomos*]. (Gal 3:21b adapted by author)

This means that no system of behaviour exists that is capable of giving *life*. In other words, *any nomos*-system – whether a set of rules, norms, guidelines, expectations, virtues or whatever – is just a basic *framework* for life. Simply following a system can never bring life. It can even bring 'death' and damage relationships.

For much of my life, I focused more on the way things 'should be' than on the relationships or the people involved. I thought that to grow spiritually, I needed to *do* more of *this* and less of *that*. Yet merely conforming to a pattern can never bring lasting growth. Even the most biblical *nomos*, the God-given Torah, was a static framework for living well.

Where does the life come from? Life comes from those who are alive. Ultimately, there is only one true source of life: the Father. We find life in him, not in any system. Being *under nomos*, focusing our attention on any *pattern of this world*, will blind us from seeing the richness of the Father and will hinder us from the Father-life. When we trust him and respond to him more than to our own *nomos*-assumptions (our own targets), then we really start to experience life!

A CALL TO ADULTHOOD

Paul calls us to grow out of the childish ways of a *nomos*-based life. He claims that before the coming of faith, all of us – Jews and Gentiles[59] – "were held in custody under *nomos*[60]" (Gal 3:23). Being *under nomos*, can be equated with young children being under a "guardian" (4:2) or even a slave master (4:3). Being *under* a system means that *it* becomes our definition for what is good, continually influencing our lives, our choices, and our identity.

Paul does not call the Jews to abandon the Law of Moses. Elsewhere, he refutes such accusations (e.g. Acts 21:21). Paul affirms the Law as holy, righteous, good, and spiritual (Rom 7:12–14). It is a good framework for Jewish society. Neither does he call the Galatians to disregard the norms and rules of their society. Believers are told to honour and respect all governing authorities (e.g. Rom 13:1–7).

It is not a question of whether we have structures, rules, and norms; it is whether we are *under* them, finding our identity and sense of 'correctness' in them. The Galatians had not previously been under the Law of Moses, yet they had their own rules to live by, their *nomos*. Paul tells them that God sent his Son *to redeem those under nomos*. Why? That they might no longer serve a set of norms but *might receive 'adoption'* – instated as 'huios', his adult heirs and representatives. "Because we are his *huios*, God sent the Spirit of his *Huios* into our hearts, the Spirit who calls out 'Abba, Father'" (adapted from Gal 4:4–6).

The '*Abba*' cry here represents the reverence and respect of a mature Spirit-led son or daughter who longs to be like their Father and do what he is doing. This means turning away from the childish ways of focusing on 'normal' or 'correct' patterns of behaviour. When we live the Father-life, we focus on bringing life into those *nomos*-frameworks. Then we will often be 'abnormal' as we bring Father-life into our interaction with others in unexpected ways (like Erwin at the checkout).

THE SPIRIT HELPS US CHANGE OUR VIEW

A key element in the first passage we looked at in this chapter (John 16:7–11) was that the Spirit helps us change our view. There is a similar message in Paul's letter to the Galatians. Having addressed our need for a new perspective in Galatians 4, he then transitions into the topic of life in the Spirit. I failed to see that when I thought Galatians was all about freedom from bondage. I focused on what we are saved *from*, and not what we are saved *to*. Paul doesn't just want us 'saved'. He talks in terms of being set free *from* the bondage of being system-focused children, and set free *to* being Father-focused adult heirs. Galatians is about a change of focus leading to a change of allegiance and identity.

Being led by the Spirit is vital for growing in this Father-life. "If you are led by the Spirit," Paul claims, "you are not under *nomos-systems*" (adapted from Gal 5:18). He concludes his letter by explaining life in the Spirit (Gal 5–6). His examples are very down-to-earth and practical. They have a lot to do with how we live our daily lives with others. That will be our focus in the final part of this book.

—

KEY POINTS

- Changing our 'point of focus' is essential for seeing the Father for who he is and entering into the Father-life.
- *Nomos*-systems (norms, rules, expectations) are all around us and can give us a *framework* for good relationships. Being *within* nomos is fine; being *under* it is to be avoided.
- The Spirit of the Father helps us to change our perspective and focus on the Father.

APPLICATION

Consider taking a break from this book to prayerfully read Galatians 5:13–6:10. This passage emphasises life in the Spirit, the main thrust of Paul's solution to the Galatian problem. Notice how life in the Spirit isn't presented as a high-flying 'spiritual' matter. Paul's idea of spiritual adulthood is very practical and a part of everyday life. For us, even everyday situations – at a checkout, finding dirty dishes, or while driving – can come into fresh focus.

After reflecting on that passage, respond in prayer and prepare your heart to be increasingly led by the Spirit during the coming days and weeks.

OPTIONAL ACTIVITY

If you haven't yet tried seeing the 3D image in a stereogram, search online for 'How to view 3D Stereograms'. Then search for 'easy stereograms' and give it a try. This may even help you to embrace the challenge of shifting your focus away from patterns of 'correct' behaviour and to the Father himself.

PART FOUR

THE FATHER-CENTRED LIFE

The Bible makes it clear that knowing about the truth is not enough – we need to put it into practice.[61] These final chapters will cover a variety of topics regarding how to 'practice righteousness'. Father-righteousness represents a new way of being that is foreign to most people, including many Christians. It all centres on the Father and the life that flows from him. To be human as God intended means to live in harmony with him, his heart, and his values. As more of God's sons and daughters learn the art of being fully alive, many others will get a taste of Father-life, and the fruit of righteousness will spread.

In him was life, and that life was
the light of all mankind.

John 1:4

17

FROM FENCES TO WELLS

Living in Father-righteousness will affect the way we relate to others. One particular way of viewing the world, which seems very normal and 'right', will have to change. It is about how we define who is 'in' and who is 'out'. We must learn the art of focusing on the Father.

BEING IN THE RIGHT PLACE

At the time of creation, God specifically placed Adam and Eve in the garden he had planted. Even so, they were not 'in the right place' by simply being in the garden. Once they were no longer pursuing relationship with the Father of Life, they were no longer in the right place with him.

Similarly, the beautiful scene of the father and child gardening together (Chapter 1) is all about their relationship and the shared activity. If the child just wanders around the garden doing their own thing, they aren't really 'in the garden with their father'. Even if the child is right beside their father yet preoccupied in their own world, they aren't really with the father.

For us then, being in the right place with God is not so much about right standing as right walking. This is another important aspect of the game change as we transition from system-thinking to relational living – or from focusing on patterns to focusing on the Father. Making this change can have a profound effect on how we view others and interact with them.

THE BOUNDARY OR THE CENTRE

Another way to understand this is by considering 'bounded sets' and 'centred sets', which is two different ways of defining groups. Missiologists and church-planters have found these terms useful in describing good discipleship and church dynamics.[62] While the Bible is more about centred sets, we tend to read it in terms of bounded sets.

Bounded sets dominate Western thought. Groups are typically defined by membership criteria and boundaries, emphasising who is in or out. Being a Christian, then, and being in 'right relationship' with God is easily thought of in terms of a checklist. Conversion is paramount and is seen as crossing the line between 'outsiders' and 'insiders'. Once we are 'in', it is easy to think we have arrived. This view will always seem 'right' to a Westerner.

A very different approach is found in centred sets, which are defined by the centre. The issue is whether you are moving towards the centre or away from

it. As Christians, then, the real issue isn't about how far we have come, but the direction we are heading. Are we focused on the Father and growing closer to him? Accordingly, conversion is about a change of allegiance to a new 'centre', which is an ongoing journey. We turn from 'our own targets' to 'the Father's target' – from worshipping and valuing other things to worshipping the Father and growing closer to him.

I like to describe this contrast in terms of 'fences' and 'wells', which can evoke some clear imagery. In Australia, farmers have two very different ways of looking after their cattle. A normal approach is to set up fences. Yet in the vast, dry areas of the inland, where properties can cover thousands of square kilometres, it is easier to just dig wells. Since there is no other water, the cattle will not wander more than a day's walk away from the well. They know what gives life.

HOW FAR CAN I GO?

As Christians, we can easily focus on boundaries and want to know what is 'OK' and 'not OK'. The aim is to stay within the fence, though the fence easily becomes the focus. Have you ever seen a horse in a fenced yard? Where is the grass most worn? Isn't it just inside the fence? The horse is drawn to the boundary and spends time by the fence, looking out.

I have met many young Christians who have questions about how far is OK. For example, boy meets girl and they believe it is wrong to have sex before marriage. Yet how far can they go? How much touching is too much? What's OK?

I don't like to answer that sort of question directly. It is a misleading question that will always lead to a bad answer because that way of thinking is not helpful. Defining what is 'OK' puts the focus on the fence.

I would rather raise a new question: What are you aiming at? Are you aiming at the Father's highest for you, avoiding anything that may undermine your relationship with him? Do you seek to go as far as you can in trusting him and pursuing him? Or are you aiming at how far you can have your own way and stretch the relationship without going too far? Instead of aiming at Father-righteousness are you simply aiming at 'OK'? If all you want is an OK life, with an OK wife (or husband), and an OK relationship with God, then you will have to figure out for yourself what is 'OK'. I would rather aim for God's highest than settle for 'OK'.

ALL THINGS ARE LAWFUL BUT …

Paul seems to have faced some of the same issues as he discipled new believers. They wanted him to define the limits: "How far can we go? Is it OK to eat food that has been offered to idols? What about sex? What's OK?" They wanted the childish simplicity of a *nomos*-system.

While addressing these issues, Paul says, "All things are lawful" (1 Cor 6:12 and 10:23 KJV). If we think in terms of fences, that sounds like saying there are no fences – that we are no longer under law, so anything goes. Yet that is clearly not his point.

The next word Paul uses is "but", which indicates a shift in focus. Paul wants his readers to shift from the childish simplicity of focusing on defined boundaries and systems of behaviour. The new focus is to be the Father himself; the aim is to bring his character and values into our behaviour, as we love God and neighbour. That will require awareness of the people around us and the inner workings of our heart. We need to learn how to think in a new way. We should not be under slavery to rules or to 'freedom'.

> 'I have the right to do anything,' you say – but not everything is beneficial. 'I have the right to do anything'– but I will not be mastered by anything. (1 Cor 6:12)

> 'I have the right to do anything'– but not everything is constructive. No one should seek their own good, but the good of others. (1 Cor 10:23b–24)

Do you see how Paul shifts the focus from the 'fence' to the 'well'? Paul wants us to focus on *life* itself, not just a framework for life. We need to think in terms of what brings good fruit in our lives and the lives of those around us.

CONSIDERING OTHERS

The childish view defines what is good by drawing a line, and godliness is defined by criteria. This is driven by our rebellious desire to eat from the *Tree of Knowledge of Good and Evil*, and it feeds a subtle sense of pride. Judging others makes us feel 'godly'. Yet our focus on outer behaviour is hollow and leads to deception.

The mature view is that goodness is defined by the Father. His *Tree of Life* teaches us that goodness is defined by what brings life, not a simple checklist. Godliness is similarly defined by God himself, so it is both firm and warm. It is about being 'Godlike' in character and values, which includes desiring the best for others, as the Father would.

When fences colour our view of the world, we can become indifferent to others. In doing what is 'right' or what we have a 'right' to do, we easily hurt others. Our fences also give us a judgemental view of those who are on the 'outside'.

Staying right with God has to include consideration of others and having his heart towards them. As we learn to think in terms of the well, we consider what will bring life into relationships and build people up. This will include learning to accept others as they are, instead of building fences that define who is acceptable and who is not.

GO AND DO LIKEWISE

Jesus also taught that godliness includes treating others well. He was once asked, "What must I do to inherit eternal life?" In other words, how can I be in the right place with God? His answer, through the parable of the Good Samaritan (Luke 10:25–37), challenges the way we view and relate to others – particularly 'outsiders'.

In terms of fence-thinking, the priest and the Levite had good reason for not getting involved. If they helped the beaten man, they might touch blood, making them ritually unclean and unable to perform their duties. No, they needed to stay within the 'fence' of ritual purity. In their focus on the upright aspect of God's righteousness, they had lost touch with his mercy and compassion – just like the Pharisees who wouldn't even lift a finger to help (see Chapter 14).

A surprising twist comes at the end of the parable when Jesus asks who the neighbour of the beaten man was. While it is easy to see that the Samaritan modelled true neighbourly love, the shock is that the Samaritan (a despised 'outsider') was identified as the Jewish man's neighbour, whom he should love. This is a radical call to show boundary-breaking love across lines of enmity, ethnicity, and theology.

But the greatest challenge for us comes as Jesus concludes: "Go and *do* likewise." Father-life will lead us to leave our comfort zones as we express Father-love to those who are not within our definition of 'right'. Loving 'outsiders' and accepting others as they are is part of what it means for us to *become* an extension of the Father's merciful righteousness in the world (see chapter 15).

LOVE YOUR ENEMY

Have you ever tried to love someone you see as your enemy? I have not yet found a way to do that. We need to put aside our judgements and be willing to accept people as they are if we are to start having a heart of love towards them.

I am impressed by the story of Daryl Davis, an African-American who reached out with openness and respect to high-ranking leaders of the Ku Klux Klan. Understanding, trust, and friendship gradually grew, even while they held very different values and views. Daryl's willingness to cross the fence and his openness to engage were essential. In the end, many members ended up leaving the Klan.[63]

It was quite a different story with the prophet Jonah. He viewed the world as 'us' and 'them', and the Assyrians of Nineveh were definitely the enemy. As long as he viewed them as 'the enemy', he struggled to represent God's heart.

I used to see Muslims as the enemy and had little compassion for them. I had heard all sorts of Christian teaching that strengthened negative stereotypes. Yet I had never gotten to know a Muslim and had no interest in doing so. That started to change as I prepared to go to a Muslim country for the first time. As the Father taught me to love Muslims, I needed to stop seeing them as 'the enemy'. Before I was ready to have dialog with Ahmet in eastern Turkey, I had to put aside my presuppositions and have a heart that was ready to listen. I needed to take down the fence I had built in my heart.

I have been on a similar journey in relation to homosexuals. I grew up in a time when homosexuality was not widely accepted or even talked about. I was in my twenties when homosexuality gained a lot of negative press as the HIV/AIDS epidemic hit the headlines in the 1980's. While the liberal theology of some Christians emphasised social justice and the need for compassion, I was influenced by conservative evangelical views, with an emphasis on legal justice and moral absolutes. That made it easy to build a fence between right and wrong, defining who was 'in' and who was 'out'.

Today, we still see tension and suspicion between the LGBT+ movement and many evangelical Christians. Yet it seems to me that the roots of enmity

> ❝ *People need to believe that you value them before they can value what you believe.*

go back to the judgemental fences in the hearts of many Christians decades ago. We must dismantle our fences and break free from judgementalism if we are to truly love our 'enemy'.

HAVING A RIGHT HEART

When we focus on a 'fence' and think in terms of a standard for what is OK or not OK, it affects our ability to fully accept others. We imagine we are 'OK' simply because we do certain things, believe certain things or have prayed a certain prayer. We have misunderstood the Father's heart and we will likely judge others who are not 'OK' by our standard.

The Father's acceptance of us has nothing to do with standards and being OK. The Father demonstrated his unconditional love and desire for relationship "while we were still sinners" (Rom 5:8). Our value in the Father's eyes is not because we are 'OK' but because we are *his*, made in his image. Every human belongs to God, whether they know it or not. "The earth is the LORD's, and everything in it, the world, and all who live in it" (Ps 24:1).

That needs to be our basis for accepting others who are outside our 'fence'. Such acceptance does not compromise the Father's high ideals. The Father's ideals are intended for *us* to aim at. (Remember the Father's target in Chapter 3.) His ideals are not suited as a measuring stick of our performance and certainly not the performance of others. Showing acceptance towards others who are 'not up to standard' should not weaken my aim to be like my Father. Rather, to have a heart that reflects his values, I need to learn to accept others as being valuable in his eyes just for who they are. If I judge others by a standard, then I have failed to understand the Father's target for my own heart.

At the same time, we have to recognise that people in the world still think of acceptance in terms of a standard. If I just tell an unbeliever about my high ideals, they may assume I judge them and do not accept them. If, however, I repeatedly show compassion and acceptance, then eventually, they may be ready to accept my high ideals without feeling judged. To put it another way: People need to believe that you value them before they can value what you believe.

CHURCH STANDARDS

Within the Body of Christ, however, there is a place for maintaining some moral standards. It is normal for any group with a defined purpose to have some membership criteria. Like good gardeners, pastors need the skills to nurture growth and healthy relationships while maintaining boundaries and order.

If a church member is on a collision course with Kingdom values, church leaders need wisdom to disciple them with love. Sometimes, when all else has been tried, leaders may need to exercise tough love.[64] The situation is more serious if a member's actions are in danger of giving the church – and God – a bad name in the community.

This is part of Paul's concern as he chastises the Corinthian believers for tolerating immorality in the church. There is behaviour "of a kind that even pagans do not tolerate" (1 Cor 5:1). Yet we are not to become the 'morality police' and judge outsiders in the same way. Paul makes a clear distinction regarding unbelievers:

> I wrote to you in my letter not to associate with sexually immoral
> people – not at all meaning the people of this world who are immoral,
> or the greedy and swindlers, or idolaters. In that case you would have
> to leave this world. ... What business is it of mine to judge those outside
> the church? (1 Cor 5:9–12a)

The biggest problem with a sinner is not that they have 'crossed a line', but that they are *out of line* with God. To get right with God, people must learn to trust him. We must help them to discover the 'well' – the Father of Life – and to drink from him. Yet it is hard for outsiders to know and trust the Father when we, his children, are known only as judgemental moralists who build fences.

Paul cautions the Colossians: "Be wise in the way you act towards outsiders ... Let your conversation be always full of grace" (Col 4:5–6). In the end, kindness leads to repentance (Rom 2:4). There are currently many positive initiatives as Christians reveal the love of the Father to 'outsiders'. Good fruit is being seen as God's children share the living water of Father-life instead of building fences.

EVEN LOW FENCES NEED REMOVING

Perhaps you have never struggled to accept those who are different, and your 'fence' of acceptance is low and wide. Perhaps you have never struggled to know the Father's total acceptance or show it to others. Yet, is your sense of acceptance or your acceptance of others simply based on being 'OK', or being 'good enough'? Have you really understood God's compassion for all who are made in his image? The Father wants your acceptance of others to be based on his view of them.

If there is any 'fence' in our thinking, we may be satisfied to just stay anywhere inside that 'fence', without really aiming at the Father and being shaped by his high ideals. The Father-life is a call to stop living by our 'fences' (and our self-made targets) so that we may live from the One who is Life.

It makes no difference whether we have a legalistic 'high fence' of acceptance or a liberalistic 'low fence' that accepts almost anything. Once we focus only on a certain standard as our reference for life, we are no longer focused on our heavenly Father. We will no longer be able to keep his unconditional acceptance and perfect ideals together. We will emphasise either the Father's acceptance (low fence, wide area) or his high ideals (high fence, small area). You cannot have both if you are thinking in terms of a standard.

For example, if I view smoking or excessive drinking as 'OK', then I will probably find it hard to support someone who is trying to break out of addiction. On the other hand, if I consider these things to be 'not OK' then I can be judgemental. Neither way promotes life nor reflects the Father's heart.

TOTAL ACCEPTANCE AND HIGH IDEALS

As we aim to be like our Father, we need to embrace the fullness of who he is. We need to have in mind *both* his total acceptance *and* his high ideals. We aim to do what is right in the sense of his framework of absolutes for right living. Within that framework, however, we aim to have a right heart that is in line with God's heart. That means seeing the shortcomings of ourselves and others in light of the Father's total acceptance, his unconditional love – even towards sinners.

I thank God that our value in his eyes isn't based on our performance and that he doesn't view us only in relation to an objective standard. Standards are important, but trust is vital. Therefore, at times, we need to keep our standards to ourselves while we focus on building trust with others.

This is one of the biggest points of difference between system-thinking and the Father-life. When we only aim at a standard – what is *right*, what is *normal*, or what we have a *right* to do – then the standard becomes *both* the ideal to aim at *and* the measure of performance. We end up judging ourselves and others, or taking pride in our efforts or our 'freedom'.

On the other hand, the Father's target – living in tune with him, reflecting his character and values – sets the focus on the heart. What we aim at will be more important than our performance, and our identity will not be based on our performance. That frees us to meet others with Father-life.

To stay aligned with the 'well' rather than the 'fence', we have to know who we are in the Father's eyes. Fully grasping how the Father views us in our weakness and poor performance is one of the biggest keys to keeping our identity in him. That is our next topic, as we continue to explore various practical aspects of living the Father-life.

—

KEY POINTS

- 'Living by the fence' can give us a false sense of identity and keep us shallow in our relationships with others and with God.
- 'Living by the well' keeps us focused on the Father, trusting him and drawing our identity from him, as we embrace his character and values.
- We need to grasp *both* the Father's total acceptance *and* his high ideals. However, as we encounter others, it is usually best to start with acceptance and compassion.

REFLECTION AND RESPONSE

What 'fences' have you focused on in your life? How do those fences affect the way you relate to others? Are there any groups of people you find hard to accept? Consider or discuss these questions briefly.

Have you tended to focus more on the Father's high ideals or his total acceptance? Ask the Father to help you keep these connected in your life, and to keep your aim on him and his righteousness.

18

THE FATHER'S EYES OF GRACE

Do you really understand how your heavenly Father views you? Revelation of how God views us in our weakness is vital if we are to view others in the same way. We all need to learn the art of seeing like the Father, having his eyes of grace.

INCREDIBLE GRACE

I once heard the story of young salesman who, following a string of successful deals, was entrusted with securing a major contract worth a million dollars. Things were progressing well, and the deal was as good as done. Yet somewhere in the process he missed an important memo and overlooked a couple of key details in a document. By the time he realised it, the contract was already lost.

He knew it was entirely his fault. It was no surprise, therefore, when the boss called him in. The short walk through the office did not take long, yet it seemed to last an eternity. He knew he had to face the music, yet he wanted somehow to express how sorry he was. He struggled to find words.

His boss welcomed him warmly, catching him off guard. His surprise grew as the boss continued talking positively. He was expecting to be grilled, yet his boss was talking about what a great salesman he was and the potential he saw in him.

"But don't you want to talk about the contract I just blew?" he protested, struggling to get a word in.

"Oh, don't worry about the contract," his boss replied, as though it was only a minor slip. "I'm sure you've learnt your lesson, and I know you are committed to your work. I want to talk about your future with the company."

"What do you mean my future? I messed up big time. Aren't you going to fire me?"

"No, I don't want to fire you. I see a lot of potential in you. Anyway, with the loss of that contract, I've just invested a million dollars in your training. You are now my most valuable employee," his boss quipped with a smile. "I'm certainly not going to fire you!"

THE ESSENCE OF GRACE

I think this is a great illustration of grace. Yet what is it about this story that illustrates grace?

I used to think that grace was primarily about forgiveness – in particular, *undeserved* forgiveness. Forgiveness is evident in this story, yet that is only part of the grace here. Earlier, we talked about how grace goes beyond forgiveness to active involvement, restoration and pursuit of relationship (see Chapters 6 and 10).

One vital element in this story is belief in the value of the person and their potential. This is clear both here and in the story of the Prodigal Son. This belief in the person finds expression in a commitment to the relationship. There is a willingness to invest in the person, to help them grow and reach their potential. Grace is willing to accept a situation that is less than ideal, then respond to it in an ideal way (with a right heart).

Here again, we meet *both* the total acceptance *and* high ideals of the Father. Grace isn't just passive acceptance or lack of caring. No, it accepts others as they are, yet also sees the ideal potential in them and behaves in an ideal way towards them, to help see that potential realised.

FAVOUR

The word grace has a range of meanings, although favour is one of its core ideas. What does it mean to show favour or to act favourably towards someone? You give them some form of *benefit* or something *good*, or you treat them in a *good* way.

What does it mean to view someone favourably? You focus more on the good aspects and the potential you see in them, and less on the not-so-good things that are plainly visible or already history. They say, "love is blind", yet grace is not a matter of blindness. Father-grace sees our faults and failings yet chooses deliberately to focus on other things. True grace views others favourably, emphasizing their value rather than highlighting their shortcomings.

VIEWED AS RIGHTEOUS

An example of viewing someone favourably and choosing what to focus on can be seen in a passage we looked at earlier (Chapter 13). Paul is explaining righteousness by faith:

> David says the same thing when he speaks of the blessedness of
> the one to whom God *credits righteousness* apart from works:
> 'Blessed are those whose transgressions are forgiven,
> whose sins are covered.
> Blessed is the one whose *sin* the Lord will *never count*
> against them.' (Rom 4:6–8)

Do you see how the crediting of righteousness and not counting of sin are two sides of the same 'coin'?

The words *credit* and *count* are both translated from the same Greek word, *logizomai*. This word and its various translations – such as credit, count, reckon, and impute – can all be used in an objective, technical way, such as in accounting. This sort of interpretation is widespread in Western theology.

Yet such terms can also have a subjective, relational usage, in how we choose to view another. For example, you may 'credit' someone as having been a tremendous support to you, or 'count' someone as a close friend.[65] Later in the book of Romans, Paul uses *logizomai* in this way when he speaks of how he *chooses to view* his sufferings as insignificant in light of the glory ahead.[66] This subjective view of the situation, choosing what aspects to emphasize, seems to also be Paul's usage in the passage above. Remember, Father-righteousness is more about heart alignment than technical 'correctness' (chapter 14).

Father-grace teaches us to view people favourably, focusing on the good potential in the relationship and not on the past shortcomings. God sees our sin and "knows our weaknesses". Yet in his grace he "remembers that we are dust" and chooses to focus on other things in his view of us. The Father is interested in the future more than the past, and he looks to the heart more than performance. He looks for *faith* – in other words, a willingness to trust him, to be in relationship, and to let him be the reference point and referee for our lives. If he finds that willingness to trust him, then he lets that define who we are in his eyes. It is his grace that sees our failings yet views us as righteous because of our willingness to trust him.

This passage in Romans is quite problematic if you think of righteousness only as legal perfection (a system-based view), because Paul is not saying God does not see our sin. Rather, he doesn't let it define us; he chooses to focus on something else. This is the heart of the Father. He wants his children to view others in a similar way.

VIEWING FAVOURABLY

Recall the illustration of the father working in the garden with his child (Chapter 1). He did not view his child as technically perfect. Rather, he needed to see the imperfections and mistakes so he could interact with his child while promoting growth. From that relational perspective, it was just 'perfect' and everything was 'right'. He saw his child's heart, trust, and desire to be with him and like him.

Similarly, the boss viewed the young salesman with grace. He saw the potential and commitment. So he chose to focus on those aspects rather than the failings. He focused on the future rather than the past.

God viewed Abraham with grace. Abraham wasn't perfect but he was willing to trust God. As mentioned earlier (Chapter 11), Abraham was "fully persuaded" about God's trustworthiness, and *that* is why God "counted" him (viewed him) as righteous (Rom 4:21–22). Vine's Dictionary explains how this *imputing* (reckoning/counting/crediting) of righteousness is about how God chose to view Abraham, "with a view to" his faith.[67]

> **❝** *Father-grace teaches us to view people favourably,*
> *focusing on the good potential and not the past.*

Father-grace is about viewing others favourably and is closely related to Father-righteousness.

GETTING PRACTICAL

My journey in understanding more of my heavenly Father's grace towards me has been inseparably linked to his teaching me to view others with his eyes of grace. Learning to extend Father-grace to others has enabled me to better grasp and receive grace from the Father. John makes a similar connection regarding love:

> Whoever claims to love God yet hates a brother or sister is a liar. For whoever does not love their brother and sister, whom they have seen, cannot love God, whom they have not seen. (1 Jn 4:20)

If my view of others is influenced by system-righteousness and legal perfection, then I will likely not view them favourably. I will focus more on behaviour and everything that is not up to standard, not 'OK' or not 'correct'. I might see a person and think: "There's that guy who is always messing up and causing trouble."

With Father-grace, I may see the same person and think: "He's the guy who is struggling to know who he is because of an absent father. He has some good leadership potential. How could I help him discover who he is in the Father's eyes?"

The first view focuses on the past and writes off the future. In human eyes, the person is defined by their actions. Father-grace has a broader view. It views the past with empathy and remembers that we are dust. It focuses on the future and is willing to be involved.

God knows our 'God-given potential' and is willing to trust us. Part of the Father-life is learning to see the God-given value and potential in others. Yet, for us to show grace to others, we need to be aware of the contrast between Father-grace and the typically human way of showing favour.

BEING FAVOURABLE OR DOING FAVOURS?

When the New Testament teaches about divine grace it uses the Greek word *charis*. This word, however, could also be used in a very worldly way. For example, "because Felix wanted to grant a favour [*charis*] to the Jews, he left Paul in prison" (Acts 24:27). Interestingly, some translations say that he wanted to *acquire* favours. Both are true when it comes to worldly *charis*. Whenever you *do* a favour then you also *earn* a favour. In ancient Greek society, *charis* worked like a system of accounts with merit and debt. There was always an obligation to return a favour, and failure to do so was a serious offence.[68]

In contrast, the *charis* of God is about the pure-hearted, generous goodness of the Father. Paul teaches us that genuine love "keeps no record of wrongs" (1 Cor 13:5). Neither does it keep careful account of our merits and debts for favours. The Father-life is about true goodness expressed in *acting favourably* towards others, not just *doing favours*. We are even called to act favourably towards those who least deserve it. Why? Because that is what our Father is like. His goodness isn't limited to those who can 'return the favour'.

Take a moment to read the following passage prayerfully. Here, Jesus the game changer contrasts the credit-based system of *doing favours* with the true goodness of Father-grace:

> If you love those who love you, what credit is that to you? Even sinners love those who love them. And if you do good to those who are good to you, what credit is that to you? Even sinners do that. And if you lend to those from whom you expect repayment, what credit is that to you? Even sinners lend to sinners, expecting to be repaid in full. But love your enemies, do good to them, and lend to them without expecting to get anything back. Then your reward will be great, and you will be children [*huios*] of the Most High, because he is kind to the ungrateful and wicked. Be merciful, just as your Father is merciful. (Luke 6:32–36)

We are not to pursue the human system of favours, keeping account of credits and debts, and returning favours. Rather, we are to live the Father-life, treating everyone favourably with generous Father-righteousness. That is "to our credit" in the favourable eyes of the Father.

NON-MERITABLE FAVOUR

Divine grace is often described as 'unmerited favour'. I used to feel uncomfortable about this term. Firstly, there was the word 'unmerited', which reminded me of how undeserving I was. Secondly, the word 'favour' implied that I now 'owed God a favour'. I felt an obligation to be a 'good boy', to prove myself deserving of his unmerited favour.

I see now that Father-grace is not primarily about the one who is undeserving, but about the heart and character of *the one extending grace*. Perhaps it is more helpful to define divine grace as *non-meritable favour*. It has nothing to do with merits or whether we deserve it or not, or with our performance or lack of it. If we think we *owe* God a favour in a technical sort of way, then we have missed the game change and have not yet grasped Father-grace.

The Father's favour is not something we can ever 'repay'. Yet we can respond to his favour with gratitude and appreciation. One of the ways we can show appreciation to the Father for the way he views and treats us is to value his ways above our ways and to desire to be like him. The grace of God has the power to transform our lives and affect the way we view and treat others. The next chapter will explore how we can express Father-grace in the way we give and receive.

—

KEY POINTS

- The Father sees our imperfections and failings, yet focuses on the value and the potential he sees in us.
- The Father desires for us to view others with his eyes of grace and treat them accordingly.
- The world thinks in terms of doing and earning favours; Father-grace is about *being favourable* and *acting favourably* regardless.

REFLECTION AND RESPONSE

Take a moment to reflect on your previous view of grace. How did you understand the Father's grace towards you? How have you expressed grace to others? (Think about or discuss this before proceeding to the next question.)

Are there some specific areas that need to change in your view of grace and your way of treating others? Ask the Spirit to help you grow. (Then look to the next chapter for some tips.)

19

GRACE THAT FLOWS FREELY

What helps us to maintain good relationships? Some simple principles can be valuable, but we need the right ones. We must avoid the 'wisdom' of the world and let Father-righteousness teach us the art of giving and receiving.

MAINTAINING GOOD RELATIONSHIPS

Popular wisdom tells us that good relationships need to be *fair*; they need to build on *give and take*, rather than just taking. This phrase, *give and take*, is so popular that it appears in thousands of song lyrics. Pursuing such equity in relationships, however, typically leads to some form of account keeping. As a system, *give-and-take* ultimately ends up damaging relationships.

In contrast, Father-grace is all about *giving and receiving*. At first glance, this might seem similar, yet it is very different. There is life in giving and receiving. Father-life flows *freely*, with no strings attached: "Freely you have received; freely give" (Matt 10:8).

GIVE AND TAKE

In the system-thinking of the world, a 'good' person is willing to be 'gracious' and extend a favour. Yet after several favours, there is a growing expectation of a return favour, or at least some expression of gratitude. When there is none, they are 'justified' (according to their assessment) in withholding further favours.

Give-and-take is not an exact system of account keeping, but it defines limits. Most people can be loving, forgiving, helpful, gracious, generous, and so on – to a certain point. Then the system-thinking starts to come into play, and ideas of credit and debt appear. We use words like 'deserve' and 'owe':

- "You don't *deserve* any more help."
- "You *owe* me an apology!"
- "I have given long enough; now it is my *turn* to get."
- "I *deserve* better than this!"

The trouble with give-and-take is that it isn't true giving. Whatever is given has 'strings attached' because you are still able to use it to your advantage later. You can always refer to it at any time and claim *credit* for it. Give-and-take works subconsciously like a bank account with deposits and withdrawals. It is a contractual approach to life and relationships.

TAKING

The give-and-take lifestyle ends up destroying life. The inspiration to take comes from another 'father' who wants us to carry out his desires (John 8:44). The 'father' who inspires us to *take* is "the thief" who comes only to *steal, kill and destroy* (John 10:10). Taking can have many forms, yet all of them undermine and weaken relationships. Here are some of the ways we can feel justified to *take* from others:

- Taking revenge (repaying evil with evil, unwilling to forgive)
- Taking the law into our own hands (based on our own view of right and wrong)
- Taking liberties (reinterpreting rules to suit us, as we define our own 'targets')
- Taking advantage (exploiting other's weakness)
- Taking the easy way out (giving as little as possible, sometimes adjusting rules, or exploiting)

- Taking credit for what we've done (ensuring that others know our merit-worthy acts – they owe us recognition)
- Taking credit for what someone else has done (a form of stealing)
- Taking offence (we make the person our debtor: "You *owe* me an apology.")
- Taking something or someone for granted (assuming that others will follow our script or our expectations: "*Of course* they should ...", "*Of course* I have a right to ...")
- Robbing others of dignity (when we view them through negative stereotypes)

At first glance, I would have rejected the idea that these were issues in my life. Yet just as the Father had to show me my subtle form of road rage (Chapter 14), I had to learn that all of the above can have subtle forms or be hidden under layers of pretence.

All these things are contrary to the character and values of our heavenly Father. Jesus highlights the contrast: "The thief comes only to steal and kill and destroy; I have come that they may have *life*, and have it *to the full*" (John 10:10).

BLAMING

There are also many indirect forms of taking, where we give people guilt, blame or shame. In such cases, we *take* their dignity, respect, or sense of worth. We can "kill and destroy" a person's spirit:

- "You *should* know better."
- "You *should* have more respect."
- "You *should* know what I mean."
- "You *should* be more mature."
- "It's entirely your *fault*."
- "Look at the mess *you* have made."

Sometimes, we are so keen to point out faults and shortcomings that we go a step further:

- Waiting to catch someone out, purely to increase their guilt or to shame them.
- Or worse still: Setting a trap to catch someone out, purely to *take* pleasure in it.

The Father is not like that. He doesn't just point at shortcomings like the 'finger of the Pharisees' (chapter 14). He certainly doesn't set traps or wait to catch us out, and he is not quick to judge.

SYSTEM OR RELATIONSHIP

The mindset of give-and-take is system-thinking. When things are not as they 'should' be, it teaches us how to *react*. The point is to do something to balance the books, or at least to blame someone. It trains us to eat from the Tree of Knowledge, which leaves us with a lifeless system.

In contrast, giving-and-receiving is a relational approach to life. It is about bringing Father-life into whatever situation we find ourselves in. When things are not as they should be, Father-life takes us beyond basic knowledge to *wisdom, grace* and all that promotes life. It teaches us how to *respond* in an ideal way, regardless of all that is not ideal.

Our ideal response isn't based on the ideals of a system, or how the situation 'should' be. Rather, our ideal is the Father himself. By looking to him and allowing his Spirit to prompt us, we can respond with ideal motives and attitudes, while considering others as he would. Sometimes, the ideal response is to give people some slack and 'breathing space'. At other times, we may respond by focusing on what can be done to restore and heal, rather than on what just happened or what is wrong. By focusing on the Father of Life and eating from his Tree of Life, relationships grow stronger. We become one with our Father and more in tune with others.

OUR GENEROUS FATHER

The Kingdom of the Father is all about *giving and receiving*. The Father gives without any 'strings attached'. He gives freely and desires that his children give freely to others, thereby becoming an extension of his righteousness and grace. God is generous and gives us "everything we need for a godly life" (2 Pet 1:3). The Father loves to cancel debts and is quick to forgive. Even under the old covenant, he gave numerous guidelines for regularly cancelling debts, offering freedom to slaves, and treating enemies well.

As the Father taught me about the giving-and-receiving nature of his grace, there were two specific areas where I needed growth. One of these was about

> **"** *The Father gives freely and desires that his children give freely to others.*

giving – pure, genuine, releasing, no-strings-attached giving. I thought I had learned to be quite generous, at least at times. Yet generosity was still not my most natural mode of living.

A BIG DEAL OVER SMALL CHANGE

I was on a flight once where snacks were available for purchase. I don't regularly buy snacks for myself when travelling; perhaps I'm a bit of a cheapskate. Yet this time I sensed the Spirit of the Father prompting me to loosen up and be a bit more generous with myself. So I broke with tradition, and ordered one of the cheaper snacks. The flight attendant gave me the snack, took my money, and then went to attend to other passengers.

"Hey, I want my change!" I protested within myself. Suddenly, I was preoccupied with the change owed to me, even though it was less than one dollar. Again, I sensed the Spirit of the Father prompting me to loosen up and just let it go. He wanted me to be generous, just as he is generous. But I struggled with the thought of this multinational airline withholding money that was rightfully mine. It wasn't right!

Well, my heart wasn't right either. It didn't matter whether it was about a beggar or an airline; my heavenly Father was not impressed with my attitude to money. I am ashamed to say I struggled briefly until I was able to release the debt and also release blessing over the flight attendant. Who knows, perhaps he was having a bad day. I certainly didn't need to make it any worse for him by getting agitated about some small change.

Then immediately – as if on cue – the flight attendant turned around and gave me my change. I don't know what had happened – perhaps he had to serve some other passengers before he had the right change. By that point, I didn't even need the change. Yet the perfect timing confirmed the lesson the Father was teaching me about having a generous, releasing heart. I am continuing to learn about being generous like my Father.

TAKING OFFENCE

Another issue I had to work on was being easily offended. This is a form of taking because we make the other person our debtor: "You *owe* me an apology!" It is one thing to recognise that someone is behaving offensively, but when we react by *taking* offence then our heart quickly gets out of line with the Father. He is slow to judge and quick to forgive.

After some months, I thought I had really learnt this lesson. I was increasingly able to stay calm in a variety of potentially offensive situations. I felt more at peace and in tune with the Father.

Then one day, I encountered an unexpected test, as a careless attempt at being funny backfired. Someone I looked up to took offence at my failed humour, and they were upset with me. It felt unjustified; I hadn't meant anything bad by it. "Anyway," I thought to myself, "they are in the wrong. Reacting with offense is not right!" But then I realised – I was taking offence at the fact that they were offended at me!

I thought I had learnt the lesson about not being easily offended. Yet I had learnt it in terms of 'correct' behaviour, not right alignment with the Father's heart. As long as it was 'the right thing to do', then I found myself judging others for not doing it. As the Spirit led me back to right alignment with the Father's heart, I was able to release, ask forgiveness, and bless without offence.

VARIOUS FORMS OF GIVING AND RECEIVING

Here are a few other important examples of giving:

- For*giving* (willing to cancel debts)
- Giving the benefit of the doubt (willing to believe the best, not assume the worst)
- Giving our full attention (especially in a conversation, valuing the other)
- Giving respect (accepting other's authority, and respecting those under us)
- Giving encouragement, comfort or support
- Giving discipleship (investing in the potential of others)
- Giving our best (doing things wholeheartedly, "as unto the Lord" Col 3:23)

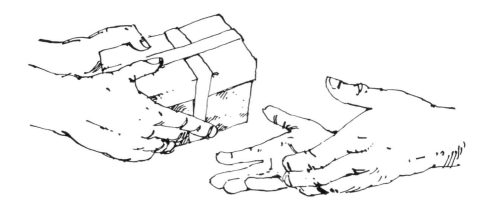

- Giving hospitality (especially to strangers and refugees, Deut 10:18–19)
- Blessing (release blessing, especially when least deserved or expected)

We also need to develop our ability to receive. Here are some areas that are often challenging:

- Receiving advice (graciously, even when not needed or asked for)
- Receiving a compliment (graciously, without pride or false humility)
- Receiving criticism (not *taking* to heart or reacting to unjustified criticism)

ACCEPTANCE AND IDEALS

As God led me deeper into his *giving-and-receiving* way of living, I started to see how it connected with things I had learnt previously about his character. Throughout this book, we have talked about how the Father meets us with both total acceptance and high ideals. That gives us a model for meeting others with a giving-and-receiving heart of grace.

The Father *accepts* us and receives us as we are, with no conditions. We, too, can learn to accept others in the same way. We can view people and value them as the Father does: because they are his; because they come from him; because they are made in his image. Regardless of their level of relationship with him, or lack of relationship, every human is still *his* in a deep, foundational way.

On the other hand, everything the Father says or does or gives is *ideal*; his thoughts, motives, and actions all line up and are always uncorrupted and pure. The more we align ourselves with his righteousness, allowing his Spirit to lead us, the more we will meet others with an ideal heart. We will see the potential in them and be willing to believe the best about them. We will increasingly be able to give "good and perfect gifts from above" (Jas 1:17).

This is also a good model for how we can relate to ourselves. We can learn to *accept* ourselves as we are, with all our limitations and failings, while continually aiming at the Father's *high ideals* and treating ourselves in an *ideal* way (not condemning ourselves, etc.). The point is to be conscious of what to aim for, not assess how well we are performing.

CONTRASTING VIEWS

The give-and-take mindset distorts our understanding of both acceptance and ideals. Firstly, we only want to receive what is good or ideal. Therefore, our acceptance of situations, others, or even ourselves, will be selective – based on being 'good enough'. We will often be unwilling to accept or find it a challenge. Yet what we give may be either good or bad, depending on the situation and what is 'deserved'. Following a give-and-take approach to life ultimately damages relationships and brings death.

In contrast, the Father's giving-and-receiving lifestyle teaches us to accept all sorts of situations and people – including those that are 'bad' or less than ideal. Our giving is to be selective, seeking only to bring what is good into those situations or relationships, responding with an ideal heart. As Father-life is released, relationships are restored and grow healthy.

This simple table highlights the contrast:

MINDSET:	**Give-and-take**	**Giving-and-receiving**
ACCEPTS:	Want to accept only the good. (Selective)	Willing to accept both good and bad. (Even when undeserved)
GIVES:	Give both good and bad. (Often as 'deserved')	Aim to give only what is good. (Selective)
BRINGS:	Death	Life
RESULTS:	Damaged relationships	Healthy relationships

THE FATHER-CHALLENGE

One day, as I was still learning some of these things, a clear challenge crystallised in my mind:

> How far could I go in living out the Father's total acceptance and high ideals? Could I live in such a way that no matter what happened – no matter who got upset with me, offended with me, or let me down; no matter what broke down or didn't work out as expected – could I **start by accepting the situation**? No, not passive resignation to the situation, nor reactionary rejection of the situation, just calm acceptance of the fact that no matter how things 'should' have been, this is how they were. Then, could I **respond in an ideal way**? Could I bring some life into the situation – with good motives and attitudes, with Father-grace, with Father-righteousness, with Father-life?

As I tried to live this out, I soon felt alive in a whole new way. There was peace, joy, and harmony in my life – and a greater sense of living in sync with my heavenly Father. Perhaps Joseph knew this same peace and harmony as he continued to act well, even in slavery and imprisonment (Gen 37–47).

For my part, I was soon enjoying this way of living so much, that a new thought crossed my mind: *Even if I didn't believe in God, I would want to live this giving-and-receiving lifestyle.* Yet here's the catch: it wouldn't work. The fullness of the giving-and-receiving life is only possible through total, faithful trust in the Father. Joseph's righteous living was only possible because of his complete trust in God.

Without God, we will always reach a limit when someone goes too far. It is only through his total acceptance of us that we can fully accept others. It is only because of the value he sees in others that we can also value others unconditionally. Furthermore, it is only because of his empowering grace and righteousness that we can even come close to responding in an ideal way in any situation.

Ultimately, the life of greatest freedom and being fully alive is only possible through total abandonment, trust, and submission to the Father of Life. Finding freedom in submission is a complete riddle for most people. Yet, it is an important key to the Father-life, which we will explore in the next chapter.

—

KEY POINTS

- The system of give-and-take sounds 'right', but it is only a framework and lacks life.
- Father-life gains expression through giving and receiving.
- The Father wants to take us deeper in knowing for ourselves and expressing to others his total acceptance and high ideals.

REFLECTION AND RESPONSE

What aspects of give-and-take thinking or behaviour can you recognise in your life? (Take time to consider/discuss this.)

Prayerfully re-read the challenge in this last section, *The Father-challenge*. Are you ready to take the challenge? The point is not to see how well you can perform. The point is to have this as your *aim* and to consistently look to the Father to lead you as you grow. Invite the Father to expand your capacity to receive and to give. Invite him to teach you more about his total acceptance and high ideals.

20

FINDING FREEDOM IN SUBMISSION

Do the words freedom and submission sound like opposites? Or can you see how they are connected in meaning? We need to grasp this if we are to wholeheartedly submit to the Father as our God and King. It's time for a lesson in the art of letting go.

WORLDLY FREEDOM

In our day and age, there is a lot of emphasis on *freedom of choice* and not having any limitations placed on us by others. The popular concept of personal freedom is: "I do whatever I want to do."

Let's imagine a state of absolute freedom in that sense. You are free to do whatever you want, with no limitations. Now, let's take it all the way and say that this absolute freedom applies not only to you but to everyone else. What would that be like? It would likely be a state of lawlessness and anarchy. How absolute is your freedom then?

In this state of 'absolute freedom' you decide to drive to the shop and buy a cold drink. You go outside and discover that your car has been stolen. Therefore, you set off to the shop on your bicycle. On the way, however, you are attacked and your bike is wrecked. Yet you are still determined to exercise your freedom, so you continue on your way, limping to the shop, only to discover that the shop has been looted and burnt to the ground.

The world's idea of absolute freedom is an illusion. When fallen humans just do whatever they want, we end up with anarchy, chaos, and ultimately, no freedom. Your freedom to choose depends on *predictability*; other people around you need to behave somewhat predictably. If you have a car, your freedom to drive wherever you want is dependent on the other road users behaving predictably and not creating chaos on the roads. Without at least some predictability you cannot have freedom of choice. God's idea of freedom is always within defined, predictable boundaries. He sets us free to flourish within his predictable framework for life.

Our selfish pursuit of doing whatever we want actually leads to bondage – bondage to our desires and bondage to sin. True freedom is when you are also free to *not* exercise your freedom.

A friend of mine, who really likes coffee, insists he isn't addicted: "I'm free to drink coffee whenever I want. Yet sometimes, that freedom comes over me like a rush," he says with a wry smile. Not very convincing.

THE FREEDOM OF JESUS

Jesus wasn't in bondage to 'freedom', or sin, or selfishness, or anything else. Jesus must be the freest person to have ever walked the planet. Yet was he free? He regularly spoke of always doing the Father's will. Is that freedom? And towards the end of his life, he was arrested, taken captive, beaten, and killed. How can that be freedom?

The secret to Jesus' freedom was that he *wanted* to do all those things; he *desired* to do the will of the Father; he *willingly* embraced the Cross.

Yes, we see the agony of Jesus in Gethsemane, yet he never resists the Father's will. It is his choice to go ahead, and he clearly goes willingly when arrested. Jesus' response to the soldiers looking for Him (in the Greek text) is literally, "I am" (John 18:4–6). With that powerful reminder that he is the *I Am* (Yahweh), the whole troop of soldiers is thrown backwards. It is as if Jesus says, "I just want everyone to be clear about who has authority here. Now that's clear, I choose to let you arrest me."

The world's ways are often a distortion of the ways of the Kingdom. The world says freedom is: "*I do whatever I want to do.*" In the Kingdom of the Father, freedom is: "*I want to do whatever I do.*" They sound very similar but there is a night-and-day difference. The world focuses on the outer behaviour of choosing what to do. God focuses on the inner issues of motivation and having a willing heart. We are to willingly embrace his loving boundaries and guidelines for life, having him as our reference point and referee (Chapter 14).

When the Son sets us "free indeed" (John 8:36) he does not set us free to do whatever we want. "Free indeed" does not mean free from all rules and submission. The Son sets us free to willingly and wholeheartedly love God and neighbour as we live the Father-life. Any 'freedom' we think we have that is outside of that framework is not the freedom he gives. When we take liberty for ourselves or define our own freedom, we are not "free indeed". True freedom cannot be taken; it can only be received. The one who gives freedom also defines the limits of that freedom. The important question is: Are we *willing* to accept those limits?

The biggest key to true freedom is a *willing* heart. It all comes down to our willingness to *trust* the Father and give him the last word in all things as we align with his heart.

UNDERSTANDING SUBMISSION

So, what about submission then? Is that a word with good associations for you? Or is it a rather unpleasant word? I used to think that submission could best be summed up as: "*Just shut up and do as you're told.*" It is typically seen as an issue of one will over another, or two wills clashing in opposition.

In the system-based thinking of the world, external compliance is the primary thing: "Just do as you're told no matter how you feel about it." Yet the relational perspective of the Kingdom emphasises the heart. Our heart and our actions are supposed to line up. If we obey unwillingly – with our heart out of sync with our actions – then we are, in a sense, a hypocrite and no longer walking in Father-righteousness.

Once again, we find that the key issue is willingness. In the Kingdom of God, submission is more about attitudes than simply going along with what you are told. Let's take a closer look at what the Bible tells us.

The Greek word for submit, *hupotasso*, literally meant to *put/arrange under*, though it could be used in a variety of ways. Thayer's Lexicon explains that it was a Greek military term meaning "to arrange [troop divisions] in a military fashion under the command of a leader". Yet in non-military use, it was "a voluntary attitude of giving in, cooperating, assuming responsibility, and carrying a burden".[69]

Note the distinction here. In a military context, it was about system-based thinking. There, it's important to know your place and follow the system. However, in the broader context of life, *hupotasso* was much more relational; it was about heart attitudes and a willingness to cooperate.

WILLING TO LET GO

The English word, *submit*, comes from the Latin, *submittere*, meaning to 'let go under'. This starts to touch on some of the other elements in *hupotasso* that were not so clear in the literal meaning of 'put under'.

In a courtroom, both the defence and the prosecution are called to *submit* evidence. They come with respect and humility before the judge and 'let go' of the evidence, leaving it for the judge to evaluate. A similar principle applies when *submitting* an application, proposal, tender for a project, or sample for testing. You present your material and let go, respectfully leaving the decision to someone else. The attitudes of *humility* and *respect* are an integral part of having a *submissive* heart.

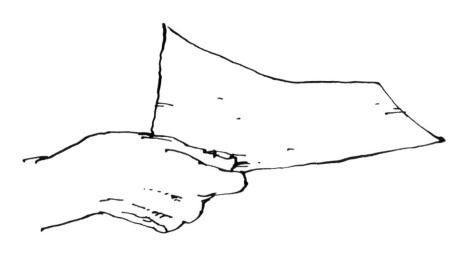

These last examples also illustrate the aspect of *referring* the matter to another for their consideration. This means being *willing* to let them have the last word – or at least to have a say in the matter. This is part of what it means for God to be our 'referee'. This type of submissive heart attitude is relevant for those under authority and those in authority, especially for being a servant-leader like Jesus. Both leaders and followers can learn to refer and let go with humility and respect.

GOD SUBMITS

It is fascinating to see that the Bible has several examples of God himself being submissive. One of the earliest examples is when God plans to destroy Sodom and Gomorrah (Gen 18:16–33). Here, God takes the initiative as he rhetorically asks, "Shall I hide from Abraham what I am about to do?" (v. 17). We then get some insight into God's thoughts and motives: "Abraham will surely become a great and powerful nation, and all nations on earth will be blessed through him" (v. 18).

Why should God *submit* his plans to Abraham? He does not have to, but he *wants* Abraham involved and he desires harmony and unity in the relationship. God is about to do something that should raise questions for Abraham. God has previously told Abraham of his desire to bless all nations, and that Abraham has a role in this (Gen 12:1–3). God seems to anticipate that Abraham will have questions about the impending destruction of a whole people. God is virtually inviting Abraham to question him.

ABRAHAM SUBMITS

What follows is a sort of Middle-Eastern bargaining process, where Abraham questions what God is proposing to do. Yet this is not the arrogant challenge of one who is not willing to submit; Abraham does not question God's authority or ridicule his plans. No, Abraham also exhibits submissiveness as he questions with *humility* and *respect*. This isn't a case of one will struggling against another; this is a case of two wills committed to relationship and the highest good.

Abraham seems to be motivated by a concern for God's reputation among the nations: "Will not the Judge of all the earth do right?" (Gen 18:25). As he proceeds to question God, Abraham is concerned that his questions should not be perceived as a lack of respect. He says things like, "May the Lord not be angry, but let me speak" (v. 30). There is no indication that God resented Abraham's questions either.

Abraham's final expression of submission is his continued willingness to *let go* after asking his final question about ten righteous in the city. As long as Abraham has concerns, he continues to submit his questions to God. But finally, when he is satisfied that God has thought this through, he lets go. He is willing to let God have the last word.

DEEPER UNITY

Even though ten righteous men could not be found, we see that something good has happened in the process: Abraham has started to connect with God's heart for the nations. He has grappled with the apparent tension between God's desire to bless nations and God as judge over the nations. Abraham stepped in as an intercessor for the nations and gained a deeper insight into God's character, seeing that his judgement is not in conflict with his desire to bless.

For God's part, even though Abraham stopped at ten, he goes on to do what he can to rescue the few righteous that are in the cities before bringing judgement. This story is a beautiful example of mutual submission. Two hearts express humility and respect towards each other as they pursue relationship and unity. They gained a deeper unity through the process.

THE TWO BECOME ONE

We could summarise this view of submission in a similar way to our earlier statement about freedom:

> **The biggest key to true submission is a *willing* heart. It all comes down to our willingness to *trust* the Father and give him the last word in all things as we align with his heart.**

When submission and freedom are so closely related, they are almost synonyms. This is part of the radical game change of pursuing Father-life. In the system-thinking of the world, freedom and submission are viewed as opposites. The more you have one, the less you have the other. But that is based on the assumption that the two wills involved are pulling in opposite directions. That is where the tension lies.

> **"** *Our greatest freedom is found in our greatest submission to the Father.*

In the Father-life of the Kingdom, we seek to be aligned with the Father's heart. In so doing, we not only become one with God but we discover that freedom and submission also become one. Our greatest freedom is found in our greatest submission to the Father. As he reveals his true goodness, we learn to faithfully trust him, aligning our hearts with his, as we pursue Father-righteousness.

Isn't this what we see in the life of Jesus? His desire to glorify the Father and do only what he saw the Father doing kept him in full submission to the Father's will. Yet because this was his own desire, he also walked in total freedom.

RELATING TO LAWS

Is this view of submission something that only applies to our relationship with God? Or is this another case where we can't separate 'spiritual' matters from daily life? Let me answer with an example, before looking at some Scriptures.

Some years ago, a law was introduced making it illegal to hold a mobile phone while driving. Before that, I was aware of the possible danger, so I had only occasionally used my phone while driving, and only then with great care. Because I felt I had been exercising enough care, I found it challenging to willingly submit to this new law. I felt wrongly judged by the law. I hadn't been careless, so why should I stop?

Something was stirred deep within me. What was it? It was a deep-rooted conviction that *I alone* am the best judge of what is best for me in any given situation. (Have you ever felt that same conviction?) It produces thoughts like: "Hey, I should be the one to judge whether I am being careful or not. What do those lawmakers know, tucked away in some government office?" Yet that primal urge to decide for myself, which can sound so convincing, goes all the way back to a place called Eden. Listening to it will undermine relationships with those around us, and ultimately, with our heavenly Father.

I struggled for a while to willingly submit to that new law. But one thing that helped was to shift the focus from the law to the relationships. I have no idea who those lawmakers are, but hey, it's a dirty job and someone has to do it. I can imagine I *might* have done things differently if I was in their position. But I'm not in their position, and I haven't had access to the accident statistics and other documentation they have considered. Can I at least respect them for trying to do a good job? I know if ever I was in their position I would want people to respect whatever laws were passed. In any case, I'm glad I live in a country that values order and safety.

All of those considerations helped me to comply, which I thought I had done willingly and not purely out of legal obligation. However, I soon started to notice when friends used their phone while driving. I caught myself thinking, "They shouldn't do that." There is something about system-righteousness that gets offended when someone else gets away with something we refrain from doing. This was a clear warning that my heart still needed some realignment.

RESPECT FOR THOSE BEHIND THE LAWS

Earlier, we looked briefly at King David's view of the Law and the beauty he saw in it (Chapter 13). One of the keys for David was the great respect, admiration, and adoration he had for the One behind the Law. Yet how can we respect the lawgivers in our societies, or the policymakers and rule-makers in our workplaces and schools – especially if they are not godly?

One of the clearest passages in the New Testament about submitting to earthly authority comes from Peter:

> Submit yourselves for the Lord's sake to every human authority: whether to the emperor, as the supreme authority, or to governors … Live as free people, but do not use your freedom as a cover-up for evil; live as God's slaves. Show proper respect to everyone, love the family of believers, fear God, honour the emperor. (1 Pet 2:13–17, see also 18–25)

Notice how he promotes living as free people within a framework of submission. One of the most surprising things about this passage, however, is that Peter is writing to believers suffering under Nero's horrific persecution of Christians. Even so, Peter tells them to submit to, respect, and even honour this same cruel emperor. But Peter gives a context here; we are to honour human authority "for the Lord's sake". If we Christians are known as rebellious law-breakers, that gives God a bad name – just as unruly children can give their parents a bad name. Also, how can we honour God whom we don't see if we can't honour those we can see?

SUBMITTING TO THE FATHER

We can tie this back to righteous living and having God as our reference point (Chapter 14). Part of living in Father-righteousness means honouring the frameworks that are around us. We should not put ourselves *under* them, but we can live freely *within* them when he is our source of identity. Ultimately, our willingness to submit to earthly authority becomes an extension of our willingness to let the Father be the reference point and referee in our lives. We know that humans may fail us, but God can be trusted.

Trusting that he really is God means letting him have the last word in all things. Perhaps you've heard it said: If Jesus is not Lord of all, then he is not Lord at all. Living in submission to our heavenly Father requires obedience. Yet we must not take obedience out of context or let it be our aim. It is simply part of the framework for righteous living and the freedom it leads to.

Our greatest freedom is found in submitting to right relationship with God. The freedom becomes richer as we learn to live in Father-righteousness.

—

KEY POINTS

- The world's idea of absolute freedom is a myth; true freedom is always within some defined boundaries.
- In the Kingdom, freedom and submission both depend on our willingness to trust the Father and let him have the last word in all things.
- There is no tension between submission and freedom when there is a desire for unity and harmony in the relationship.

REFLECTION AND RESPONSE

Who will you allow (or not allow) to set limits on your freedom? Be honest; are there any earthly authorities you resist? What about God himself? (Take a moment with these questions before proceeding.)

Is it possible for any earthly authority to stop you from truly being free when you live in Father-freedom? Take a moment in prayer to express your willingness to trust the Father and give him the last word in all things.

21

LIVING RIGHTEOUSLY BY FAITH

M ost of our theology about righteousness focuses on coming into right relationship with God (justification). Little attention is given to the verses that call us to live in Father-righteousness. To stay rightly aligned with the Father and focused on him, we must learn the art of realigning.

STAYING ON COURSE

Have you ever tried rowing a small boat? It can take a bit of getting used to. You can't see clearly where you are going because you sit facing backwards. Pulling the oars evenly on every stroke is quite impossible, so minor adjustments are continually needed to hold a steady course. You also need to do the occasional check over your shoulder to see if you need to adjust your course. It takes some concentration at first, but the continual adjustments soon become second nature.

Imagine you have just rowed across a small lake to a beach on the other side. How did it go? Are you glad to be at your destination? Did you enjoy the trip? Or do you collapse on the beach feeling like an absolute failure because of all the times you needed to correct your course?

The continual need for small corrections is a normal part of rowing, not a sign of failure. When you are focused on your goal, the number of corrections you need to make is immaterial. Getting to your destination and enjoying the journey is what it is all about.

Life is supposed to be like that, too. Making small corrections should become second nature to us. Even significant course corrections are no reason to feel defeated.

A SENSE OF DEFEAT

Yet why do so many Christians feel a sense of defeat when they need to repent? Why do we dislike being shown areas where we may be out of line? Is it because we are more focused on our performance than what we are aiming at?

I see in my life how system-thinking can lead me to focus on standards and achievement. To recognise a need for realignment then becomes an admission of failure. So, what happens if anyone – including my heavenly Father – tries to correct me or questions my motives? I would either receive that as judgement or reject them with self-justification and resentment. My defensiveness or sense of condemnation would come from thoughts of what's 'OK' or 'not OK'.

A SENSE OF PURPOSE

In contrast, Father-righteousness pursues healthy relationships and good fruit. As we seek to live in tune with God and others, we will value the awareness of any need for realignment. We will naturally *want* to know whether our actions are producing the desired good fruit or damaging a relationship. If we are off target, we will *value* revelation, insight, and corrective feedback.

Receiving help is not something we can take credit for. It doesn't need to be a source of condemnation either, if we truly desire to correct our aim. Even our response in realigning should give no grounds for pride or shame. What credit can we take for simply responding willingly to what we have been shown? What shame is there in choosing what is truly good? What pride is there in simply pursuing what we value and desire?

This lifestyle of realigning with the Father is not about passivity or striving to fix ourselves. Our responsiveness is driven by our faithful trust in the Father as we pursue relationship. Having a revelation of God's goodness – His total acceptance and high ideals – frees us to pursue him even in our imperfection and failings. It also gives us a sense of purpose when we are inspired to be like him.

GETTING BACK ON TRACK

I am a divergent thinker; my thoughts can easily wander off on all sorts of side-tracks. Therefore, you can imagine my sense of defeat as a young Christian trying to maintain the 'normal' Christian disciplines of having regular times of Bible reading and prayer. Sometimes, I would forget to do these even when planned. That certainly made me feel like a failure. Sometimes I would be praying or reading my Bible and suddenly discover that my thoughts were miles away and had been for some time.

If I am aiming at performing well and conforming to the pattern of being a 'good' Christian, then my awareness of being off track is already an admission of poor performance. On the other hand, I could reject the sense of defeat and condemnation and just say, "It's OK. It's no big deal." But then I would not aim to do better. If I am genuinely aiming at my heavenly Father, wanting to be like him and to pursue relationship with him, then the awareness that I am off track is valuable information. It allows me to re-affirm my desire to focus on him as I redirect my thoughts to what I had aimed to do.

Writing this book has been a real challenge as well. Writing isn't my preferred method of communication. Even when I manage to keep my thoughts focused on the task at hand, I often need to re-evaluate and realign. I might start looking into something or following a line of thought, only to discover it was leading me nowhere or needed rewriting. I could be tempted to feel frustrated or think I had just wasted my time. But sometimes, you need to look into something before you decide whether or not it is significant.

Repentance doesn't need to be about turning from sin, as such. The focus is not what we turn *from*, or about feeling sorry. The focus is who we turn *towards*. Repentance is about re-affirming our true values and goals, in response to fresh insight about the direction we are heading. Realigning our hearts and minds should be as natural as breathing – or the subtle corrections while rowing.

BEING PURE WHILE STILL IMPERFECT

A major aspect of the Father-life is keeping the focus on the heart. Then, as his children, we can be rightly aligned with our Father in terms of heart integrity – even while growing more aligned with his values, attitudes, and purposes. As long as we respond wholeheartedly to the revelation we have of the Father, then we are rightly aligned with him, even though we still need to grow. In this sense, we can be fully righteous in God's eyes even though we are not technically perfect.

King David was known for his heart purity. God described him as "a man after his own heart" (1 Sam 13:14, also Acts 13:22). That means David's heart was *like* God's heart.[70] The Hebraic concept of 'heart' was very broad. The word here referred to the whole inner life, including mind, will, and 'heart' as we know it. It is a powerful statement to say David's heart, mind, and will were like God's.

Yet, how can we reconcile that statement with some of David's failings, such as the episode with Bathsheba? (2 Sam 11 & 12) There is one thing David was an expert at: the art of realigning. The moment he realised his heart was out of line, he responded quickly and *wholeheartedly*. David had a teachable heart. In the Father's eyes, David's heart was pure, though imperfect. David maintained a pure heart by responding well to fresh revelation of his imperfections.

THE ART OF REALIGNING

As far as I can see, the art of realigning our hearts isn't a complicated science. It only requires two things: *evidence* and *willingness*. These are the same two

> **❝** *Repentance is not so much about what we turn from, but who we turn towards.*

ingredients we talked about concerning faith (Chapter 11). Therefore, realigning our hearts towards the Father is also an act of faith (and faithfulness), as we continue to respond willingly to the evidence he gives.

Evidence: To realign, we must first have *evidence* or *awareness* of being out of alignment. How can we realign without seeing the need? David was blind about being off course with Bathsheba until confronted by Nathan. Similarly, while I was leading the team in Greece, I was blissfully unaware that I was treating others harshly (Chapter 2). God, in his grace, does not immediately confront us with every issue. Yet now and then, the Spirit of the Father shines his pure light into our lives, giving us evidence that something is out of line in our hearts. Other times, someone else may stir our awareness (though not always with grace).

Willingness: As soon as the evidence is clear, we must be *willing to accept it.* This is where we need the Father's eyes of grace, so we can see our failings as he does – neither being overwhelmed nor brushing them aside. We start by agreeing with his judgement of our situation, accepting it to be just and fair. Then we need the *willingness to realign.* This is where we need to practice the art of letting go. We agree to let God have the last word as we submit to him.

This might sound like a technical analysis, but it is a very relational process. Repentance comes more naturally the more we are willing to trust God (faith) and are committed to pursuing relationship (faithfulness).

AIMING AT CONSISTENCY

Now that we have looked at repentance and how it is connected to faith, we have a foundation for understanding how repentance is essential in *living righteously by faith* – the title of this chapter. So, how does repentance connect with righteous living?

Repentance is about restoring *consistency;* we aim for consistency within ourselves and in our relationships. The biblical view of righteousness has a strong element of *consistency* and *straightness* to it (Chapter 14). This sense of straightness is not about the perfection of achievement, but the consistency of a heart that maintains a pure aim.

Here are some small examples of where the Father has revealed my lack of consistency:

- Pretending to not hear something it was inconvenient to hear
- Appearing to listen in a conversation while my mind is elsewhere
- Treating other's property carelessly
- Not returning borrowed things in reasonable time
- Not following up on things I said I would do

This is not about some new form of puritanism or 'tithing your herbs' (Luke 11:42). This is about our relationships being healthy and alive. Don't focus on the details of what is 'correct'. Focus on your heavenly Father, and desire to be consistent because he is consistent. Just respond well whenever you discover inconsistency.

THE GIFT OF CONSCIENCE

To help highlight inconsistency in our lives, the Father has given us a precious gift: the conscience. It is mentioned 32 times in the New Testament, yet I have rarely heard a sermon about the conscience. It is regularly misunderstood and not valued. I once even heard a preacher say to ignore the conscience because it only brings condemnation.

The Apostle Paul mentions the conscience 23 times,[71] and it is central to some of his teachings (e.g. 1 Corinthians 8 and 10). He also made the claim: "I strive always to keep my conscience clear before God and man" (Acts 24:16).

I used to think of the conscience more as an inbuilt list of *dos and don'ts*. But what if it is more like a simple integrity checker, warning us of inconsistency when things don't line up? The way the conscience works, then, will be dependent on whether we are focused on the 'fence' or the 'well' (Chapter 17). Are we focused on a system of what is 'OK', or on God himself?

Under system-thinking, the conscience warns you when you are not following the system, so the conscious works to keep you in compliance. (That would easily be perceived as condemnation and slavery.) But if we are focused on the Father of Life, then the conscience can be a wonderful servant to help us live in tune with him.

DRIFTING OFF COURSE

Ideally, our conscience will help us to realign. Scripture warns us, however, that our conscience can be either oversensitive (1 Cor 10:27–29) or desensitised (1 Tim 4:2). King David's conscience must have been desensitised, as he failed to realise he had gone way off track with Bathsheba.

I can only imagine how David might have slowly drifted off course. I doubt that it happened suddenly. Perhaps one evening, he catches a passing glimpse of Bathsheba bathing. He just needs to quickly double-check: "Is that what I thought I saw?" A subtle flutter stirs in his conscience, but his attention is elsewhere. Anyway, it's no big deal; isn't he just enjoying the view? Soon, he finds himself drawn to the palace roof at a certain time of evening – perhaps he will 'accidentally' catch another glimpse of her.

Ignoring the subtle stirrings of our conscience can desensitise it. In David's case, once confronted, he was fully aware his conscience needed restoring. We can read part of his sincere response to God in Psalm 51: "Create in me a pure heart, O God and renew a steadfast spirit within me" (v. 10). (The Hebraic concepts of 'heart' and 'spirit' include what we call 'conscience'.[72])

THE HEART IS DECEITFUL

I used to find it hard to relate to David's failure, though I think I better understand him now. I've had to do some realigning myself, even while working on the last chapters of this book.

I'm sure I must have ignored my conscience at some point, but I don't recall doing so. It was probably 'no big deal'. But soon, I had developed an unhealthy habit of being curious about news items that were a bit macabre, or the latest gossip, or something a bit racy. I should have realised something was wrong when I started to hide what I was watching or reading if someone came into the room. I thought I had learnt a lot about maintaining a clear conscience, but I was obviously missing some important signals and not fully conscious of the Father's presence. My conscience was still quite alert in many other ways, yet there were clearly some areas where I had lost sensitivity.

The heart is deceitful! (Jer 17:9) Therefore, we should never be presumptuous about our heart purity. David was so deceived that he didn't even realise he was a murderer until Nathan confronted him.

Finally, one day, I too was jarred awake; I knew I had crossed a line. Although, *crossing the line* was not the issue. My heart was *out of line* and had been for some time. I had been valuing things that were not in line with the Father's values. I had turned from his target and had found my own. To use other biblical imagery, I had turned from the Father's fresh springs of living water to drink from "broken cisterns" I had dug for myself (Jer 2:13).

Once I was aware of it, I thought it would be easy to get back on track. Yet re-sensitising the conscience after months or years of drifting is a process. In that process, the Bible is essential. It is our ultimate reference point for aligning with the character and values of God. While trying to realign, however, any new awareness of drifting can easily stir a sense of weakness or defeat. All we can do is keep responding to the awareness we have – and keep saying *yes* to the Father as we realign with his values.

VALUING GROWTH AND RELATIONSHIP

How could a good Father allow us to drift off course? Well, he isn't as concerned about perfect performance as he is about inner growth and relationship. Allowing us to drift can help us grow. It helps us see what is in our hearts. It helps us to be humble and have grace for others. It also helps us to reaffirm our trust in God and our dependence on him as we realign.

Similarly, earthly parents will sometimes just watch their child struggle to do something, as it is important for children to discover things for themselves or realise they need help.

Even if we have consciously gone out of line – when it is our fault alone and not because God has withheld revelation – the solution is the same: Turn to the Father in trust. Each time we reaffirm our commitment to the relationship it also grows deeper:

> No discipline seems pleasant at the time, but painful. Later on,
> however, it produces *a harvest of righteousness and peace* for those who
> have been trained by it. (Heb 12:11)

I don't know about you, but I want that *harvest of righteousness and peace* in my life, even if it will cost something.

RELATIONAL FAITHFULNESS, NOT WORKS

Our *faithfulness* towards the Father is essential in living righteously and growing in Father-righteousness. This is clearly stated in Habakkuk: "the righteous person will live by his *faithfulness*" (2:4). Some translations say, "by his faith".

As mentioned earlier (Chapter 12), the Hebraic ideas of *faith* and *faithfulness* are inseparably connected. The Hebrew root here is *emunah*, which literally means *firmness* (to be firm). Yet typically, in terms of relationships or character, its figurative meaning is faithfulness, fidelity, stability, or steadiness. This relational firmness – this steadfast trust, this faithfulness – gains expression every time we realign with the Father. Each act of realignment affirms and strengthens the relationship.

In system-thinking, faith and faithfulness seem to be at odds. Then our 'faith' is all about what God does for us and our 'faithfulness' is what we do in response. Faithfulness to a *system* – any *nomos*-system of rules, norms, expectations or ideas of what is 'right' – is all about our own efforts and performance. That is works-faithfulness.

Faithfulness towards the Father, however, is all about looking to him as the source, trusting him, and being *willing* to let go and let him have the last word. It is a natural continuation of our initial willingness to put our trust in him. True relational faithfulness is ongoing faith, just as married life is a continuation of getting married. Inner faith gains expression in living faithfully. This is a key to understanding the Letter of James.[73] In relational-thinking, faith and faithfulness are practically synonyms.

What about the Father's faithfulness towards us, then? Is that also an expression of his faith? Yes, God has *faith* in us! He believes in the potential he sees in us. He knows our 'God-given' potential. He has faith in our ability to respond to him and to grow. Why would he do so much on our behalf, if not for the fact that he believes in our potential to respond to what he does?

LIVING CONSISTENT LIVES

Let's close this chapter by paraphrasing the above verse from Habakkuk, based on the root meanings *straight* and *firm*. It basically says: The one who is *straight* (rightly aligned in God's eyes, in right relationship, *having inner consistency of heart*) will be so because of being *firm* (steadfast, trusting, faithful, *relationally consistent*).

As we aim to be straight/firm/consistent, we aim to be consistent within ourselves (our words, actions, motives, and values), consistent towards others (right attitudes towards them, treat them as we would be treated), and consistent with our Father (in tune with his character and values). The only way that is possible is by *consistently trusting* God, as we allow his Spirit to lead us. Truly, the righteous shall live by faithfulness.

This approach to life is all about God; it is all centred on him. Just like rowing, it is about where you are going and not how many corrections you make on the way. As we continue to realign ourselves with the Father, more and more of his Father-life will flow in us and through us. In time, we should see signs of spiritual growth. We will seek to better understand that process in the next chapter.

—

KEY POINTS

- Realigning our heart with the Father is a natural part of living the Father-life.
- The conscience is a precious gift to help us maintain consistency, in our character and relationships.
- Aiming at consistency and being quick to realign are natural expressions of our desire to faithfully remain in relationship with God.

REFLECTION AND RESPONSE

Are you aware of any areas where you have allowed your conscience to be desensitised? Or perhaps it is oversensitive and focused on the 'correct' behaviour of following a system. Either way, you may find that you value things that are not in line with the Father's values. Consider that briefly and ask for the Father's revelation.

Now, look to God with the expectation that he is always willing to help you grow in whatever area he highlights. First, thank him for his goodness and grace. Then be ready in the coming days and weeks to continue realigning with him, as you say *yes* to him and all that he values.

22

SPIRITUAL GROWTH

We have previously talked about the need for us to 'garden' righteousness. What needs to happen for us to know fruitfulness in our relationship with God and for others to recognise the fruit of the Spirit in us? One key in this process is allowing the Father to teach us the art of making good decisions.

THE MYSTERY OF GROWTH

Have you ever watched a time-lapse video of a flower blossoming or a fern unfolding? There is a fascinating beauty about the way plants grow and develop. Yet, how do plants actually grow?

Most people are aware that plants need light, moisture, air, proper temperature, and nutrients. A skilled gardener can provide the right amounts of each. Yet, do these things cause growth?

All the right conditions are quite useless if the plant is already dead or otherwise unresponsive. The life of a plant does not come from its environment. Such things are simply a 'framework' for growth. The way the plant responds to these things is hidden and mysterious. Deep within, growth comes as DNA replicates and cells divide.

SPIRITUAL GROWTH

How does spiritual growth happen? Is it just a matter of having the right conditions for growth? Do we grow spiritually simply by engaging in the right sort of activities, such as prayer, worship, and Bible reading? Just like with plants, external activities or influences can provide a framework for growth or stimulate growth. Yet the actual growth happens somewhere deep within the core of our being.

In understanding the essence of spirituality, A. W. Tozer suggests considering at least twenty inspiring spiritual figures from the Bible or church history. Whether you think of Moses, Ruth, King David, Mary, Paul, St. Francis, Martin Luther or Corrie Ten Boom, what quickly stands out is how different they all are in personality, giftings, calling, and circumstances. Yet, as Tozer observes, they all have one quality: spiritual receptivity.[74]

Their spirits were alive and responsive to the Spirit of God – they didn't just follow a system of 'spirituality'. They had an awareness of God and a longing for him. More importantly, there was an inner response to God that gained expression in their actions. They were 'spiritual' because of their receptivity and responsiveness to *the Spirit*.

This core dynamic can also be described as our *willingness* towards God, which we identified as a key in many earlier chapters. We also saw that God, in his goodness, helps us to be willing. Interestingly, my wife uses the word 'willing' to describe a plant that adapts easily to a new environment and doesn't need a lot of nurture in order to grow and flourish. Our willingness – our receptivity and responsiveness to God – is essential if our relationship with God is to grow stronger. It is our continual willingness towards God that allows us to remain in him and him in us (John 15:4).

In our oneness with the Father of Life, is there some way that his 'DNA' is replicated in the 'cells' of our spirit? I once heard someone say that the most spiritual thing you are going to do today is make decisions. I agree, because at the core of our being are our attitudes, motives, and desires, and these shape our decisions and actions. When we allow our God-inspired attitudes and values to be expressed in our decisions, then his 'DNA' is woven into in our lives.

MAKING GOOD DECISIONS

Learning the art of making good decisions is key to our spiritual growth and fruitfulness. Yet our understanding of what defines a 'good decision' needs to be shaped by the Father's focus on the heart.

Let me put this another way: Have you ever made a bad decision? Perhaps, no matter how good your intentions may have been, a decision led to an undesirable outcome. A failure to hit the target, however, doesn't necessarily mean that we failed to aim at the target.

What if our assessment of a 'good decision' is limited only to our aiming and the way we make the decision? Good decisions will always involve good motives, attitudes, and objectives – things that carry the Father's DNA as we aim at his 'target'. They will also have a good process, in openness and humility, and with due consideration of others. Loving God and neighbour are essential elements in all good decisions.

Do you see how a 'good decision' is defined differently when looking from the perspective of the Father's focus on the heart? It is not about the result. A good decision is any decision that is shaped by the Father's goodness (which is both firm and warm) and seeks to express his goodness by promoting Father-life. In other words, any truly good decisions will always be made in the context of our trust relationship with our heavenly Father.

THE BEST DECISION

The best decision we can make is to put our trust in God. Yet that is not the type of decision we can simply make at some point then put out of mind. That decision needs to be nurtured and kept alive. Once we have decided to trust the Father of Life, whether it was last year or last week, we need to stand by our decision and maintain the trust relationship. All our later decisions, big and small, can either undermine or affirm our trust in God.

Whether or not I am consciously making decisions, I have found it meaningful to occasionally just say in my spirit, "Yes, Father, I trust you. I am willing to give you the last word in all things." Affirming our willingness regularly can help us stay in the right frame of heart and mind, so that we have the responsivity Tozer spoke of.

BETWEEN THE PAST AND THE FUTURE

Our life unfolds in real time, in an unbroken timeline of small moments moving us forward from our past to our future. Our trust in the Father is what keeps this process on track with his heart and purposes. The enemy of our souls, however, is out to derail our trust. Distorted views of our past or future easily influence our decisions in the present, stunting our growth and leaving us with far less than life in abundance.

Past failings and disappointments can bring guilt, shame, and fear into the daily decisions we make. Similarly, any bitterness or resentment towards others for their past failings clouds our ability to choose what is good. The resulting bad decisions don't carry the DNA or our true Father. They are like cancer cells that spread death rather than life. An example of this is someone with 'a chip on their shoulder' allowing past hurts to shape their identity, words, and actions. This type of cancer, however, isn't always so obvious, and we all have traces of it.

In terms of our future, worldly desires give us false ideas about what is worth aiming for or pursuing. We end up choosing our own targets and pursue approval, popularity, material wealth, or something else. When our values, desires, and goals in life are at odds with the Father's aspirations, we end up pursuing a non-life. The wrong sort of DNA is sown into our lives and the fruit is not good.

Fortunately, we have a loving Father who understands the challenges we face. He is able to sympathise with our weakness and his grace gives us the help we need. Through Jesus, the Father has given us two precious gifts to help us with these issues of past and future.

TWO PRECIOUS GIFTS

Have you ever wondered why we use two elements to celebrate the Lord's Supper? Wouldn't it be enough to just have one symbol to remind us that Jesus died for us? Yet we have the bread and the wine, representing the body and the blood of Jesus.

Significantly, these two elements symbolise the objective and subjective sides of the relationship. One helps us to maintain the framework for the relationship and the other helps us to keep pursuing life in the relationship. Both are important for our covenant relationship with God.

THE BLOOD: This addresses our past. The objective historical facts of things said and done in sin can't be changed. The only thing that can help is for someone to take responsibility for our actions. The objective fact that Jesus' blood was shed as the once-for-all sacrifice is God's gift for dealing with the objective facts of our past. The blood of Jesus is also the eternal evidence that the Father looks to the heart. When God sees a change of heart – when we trust in the blood of Jesus, repent and confess – his view of our past changes. We can then be free from any shame, guilt, fear, or recent bad decision that seek to bind us to our past. It can also free us to forgive and release others from their debts towards us. The blood means that our decisions today don't need to be influenced by past failures, disappointments, and wounds. No matter how many bad decisions we have made lately, the blood can free us to make good decisions now. The blood enables us to repair and maintain the right framework for Father-life.

THE BODY: This has a broader application. Jesus' final surrender at the Cross was only possible because he had given his body to the Father during his whole life. The continual subjective choice of bowing to the Father and valuing him above all else is uniquely significant. Jesus' whole life was a continual 'yes' to the Father. As we remain 'in' the body of Jesus – subjectively dying to self, surrendering to him, taking up our cross to follow him – we learn to reject all worldly visions for our future. The Father's aspirations for us become our target in life and our vision for the future. When our desires are aligned towards the Father, good decisions come naturally and Father-life flows.

The covenant meal is a way for us to celebrate our covenant relationship with God. Through it, we affirm our 'yes' to him. Our commitment is not simply to stay in relationship, but to pursue a healthy relationship. Even when we are not celebrating communion, we can weave these two elements of the blood and the body into the fabric of our lives as we allow them to shape our decisions.

AN ORGANIC PROCESS

This isn't an unrealistic goal. Don't think that you now need to be hyper-aware about every decision you make, constantly checking your motives. This is not about doing everything 'right' and complying with a system. Father-life is more organic and relational – like the father and child in the garden. It is about how we respond and learn from our bad decisions, and how the Father's values become a natural element in the way we live.

Don't try to overanalyse your every decision. Most of our decisions happen subconsciously, so we often only realise later if we have had impure motives. Just keep the focus on your relationship with God and that will help you to respond well when things come to the surface.

However, when you find yourself consciously evaluating a decision – whether important or mundane – try to shift the focus to the heart. We easily focus on external things and we pray for God to show us which is the right option. Instead, let's invite the Spirit to illuminate our heart. What motivations, values or attitudes are influencing our decisions? If you discover anything in your heart that is not in line with the Father's heart, deal with that first.

For example, while considering which car to buy, I realise that I have a selfish motivation influencing my preference. Once I have allowed the Father to help me deal with that impure motive, he may lead me to buy that car anyway. Having good motives for what we do produces good fruit.

Together with Paul, I pray that God "may bring to fruition your every desire for goodness and your every deed prompted by faith" (2 Thes 1:11).

CLEAR OBJECTIVES

Jesus gives an interesting example of a bad decision in the parable of the talents (Matt 25:14–30). The third servant did not trust his master and was afraid of being responsible for so much money.[75] This fear motivated him to play safe and aim to stay out of trouble. In contrast, the other two servants shared their master's values and had his interests at heart. While their objective was growth, the third servant simply aimed at balancing the books.

I used to be troubled by this parable, because the third servant does not seem to have done anything 'wrong' – he took care of the money and gave it all back. Yet Father-righteousness is not about 'balancing the books', it is about releasing life and being fruitful. The third servant broke no laws and did no 'wrong', yet he did nothing 'right' in terms of Father-righteousness. He was neither hot nor cold.

Let Father-life be your goal and you will not be lukewarm. True sons and daughters of God do not simply aim to stay out of trouble. They seek to release Father-life. Having this clear objective as we make decisions helps us see beyond the short-term action we are considering to the long-term fruit it may bring. In contrast, simple yes-or-no decisions – to do or not to do – focus on the immediate action rather than the heart or the fruit.

When facing areas of sin in my life, it didn't help to simply think: "Will I, or won't I?" This just increased my focus on the issue and did not lead to breakthrough. Learning to stop and consider my heart and what I was aiming at was revolutionary. Keeping in mind my deeper desire to live in unity with my Father consistently led to better choices.

Even secular philosophers have concluded that freedom of choice isn't simply about being able to respond to the impulses of our desires. Rather, the greater freedom is when we are free to choose which desire we will respond to.[76] We need to learn to ignore our sinful appetites in favour of our deeper values and long-term desires. The Bible calls this 'dying to self', yet it is also a process of discovering who we really are. Knowing *whose* we are helps us to choose to grow into *who* we are.

Paul calls this "to put off your old self" (a corrupted understanding of who we are, with "deceitful desires"), while we "put on the new self, created to be like God in true righteousness and holiness" (Eph 4:22–24). That is who we really are, sons and daughters of God who bear his image!

SPIRITUAL PRACTICES

Consistently making such good decisions will not be easy, and doing so is only possible by the Spirit within, who helps us to desire and do what is good (Phil 2:13). However, growth in this area can be easier if we have some good frameworks in place to help us. Throughout the ages, Christians have recognised the value of spiritual practices such as prayer, Bible reading, meditation, worship, sharing life with other believers, and engaging in ministry. As mentioned earlier, following patterns of activity cannot impart life, but such things can support life and promote growth. This only happens, however, when done with the right sort of motivation.

If we do something simply because we 'should' or because it is the 'right' thing to do, we often end up doing it half-heartedly, unwillingly, or by sheer willpower alone. That allows bad DNA to be sown into our life. There are a few things we actually 'should' do – like loving God and neighbour – but such things are also *good*. Wholeheartedly desiring to do what is good leads to much better fruit. When we act out of our God-given desires, then his DNA becomes evident in our life.

SPIRITUAL GROWTH IN CONTEXT

Whatever spiritual practices you find fruitful, recognise the value of family. We live in a world that is saturated with ideas of individualistic self-help. In the Father's Kingdom, spiritual growth is not an individual exercise or about self-improvement. Our heavenly Father values family, and he intends for human growth and development to happen in the context of loving relationships. Find others who can encourage, support, and challenge you.

Furthermore, the Father aspires for his sons and daughters to become fathers and mothers. Find mature believers who know what it means to be a spiritual parent and learn from them. In time, you can also look for those you can parent.

The Bible talks a lot about being disciples and making disciples. It is a very similar concept to being *huios* sons and daughters. It isn't simply about following a system. Rather, it is a very relational form of growth driven by aspirations.

Being a disciple means the world is our classroom. We need the boss who is difficult, the colleague who causes problems for us, and the friend who let us down – just as a bodybuilder needs the challenge of weights. In such

> **❝** *Being a disciple means the world is our classroom.*

situations, we learn to desire the Father's ways higher than our ways. We won't always get it right, but that is not the point. We are out in the garden with our Father, and he is teaching us.

When Jesus explains the parable of the weeds, he says, "The one who sowed the good seed is the Son of Man. The field is the world, and the good seed stands for the people of the kingdom" (Matt 13:37–38). A farmer sows in anticipation of growth. God has sown us into his world that we too may mature and be fruitful. And in the real world, storms may come and 'weeds' are present.

SANCTIFICATION

This process of letting the Father's DNA shape our lives is also known as sanctification (growing in holiness). This is a key part of the Father's aspirations for his children. Through being holy, we reflect his character and values – then we are truly '*huios*' sons and daughters. Jesus has gone ahead and paved the way for us by going through sanctification himself: "For them I sanctify myself, that they too may be truly sanctified" (John 17:19).

It is strange to consider Jesus being sanctified. Wasn't he always holy? Certainly! Yet in keeping himself holy, he had to *learn* obedience: "Although he was a son, he learned obedience through what he suffered" (Heb 5:8 ESV).

We also, although we are sons and daughters, need to learn obedience – and it will involve suffering. Living the Father-life means dying to self, as we choose to follow our God-given desires rather than our worldly desires. We will also, at times, be misunderstood or considered politically incorrect – or even be persecuted. Yet we can learn to say, like Paul, "our present sufferings are not worth comparing with the glory that will be revealed in us" (Rom 8:18).

In Romans 6, Paul explains how we can grow in holiness. He starts by talking about dying to sin, that we may live a new resurrection life (v. 1–4). He goes on to talk about the importance of the choices we make. We are to no longer allow sinful desires to direct us, but rather, connect with our deeper motivations and become 'slaves' to obedience (v. 16). As we, like Jesus, learn obedience, this will lead us into righteous living (v. 16). Continuing to offer ourselves as 'slaves' to Father-righteousness leads to holiness (v. 19).

This 'slavery' is *not* an exercise in self-improvement driven by willpower and determination. That would feed the ego and destroy life. Rather, it is a work of the Spirit released through our willingness and driven by our God-given desires. In contrast to checklist-holiness, relational holiness flows from the inside and produces life. Spiritual fruit become evident, such as "love, joy, peace, forbearance, kindness, goodness, faithfulness, gentleness and self-control" (Gal 5:22–23).

Sanctification is a very organic process that happens naturally as we pursue a life in harmony with our heavenly Father. As we keep turning to the body and blood of Jesus – maintaining the framework for life and pursuing life in the framework – the Father's DNA is woven into our lives and we discover a new way of being human.

Father-life is ultimately all about the Father. As we learn to value him and choose his ways above ours, our worship of God grows deeper. Worshipping the Father is our final topic.

—

KEY POINTS
- Spiritual growth happens as we allow the Father to shape our decisions and weave his DNA into our lives.
- The body and blood of Jesus help us to maintain the right frameworks for good relationships with God and others and to pursue life in those relationships.
- Being clear about our deeper God-given desires helps us to choose them as we die to our worldly appetites. This is how we grow in holiness.

REFLECTION AND RESPONSE

Take a moment to reflect on this verse. Consider what it means regarding the decisions you make each day, and then respond in prayer:

Remain in me, as I also remain in you.
No branch can bear fruit by itself;
it must remain in the vine.
neither can you bear fruit
unless you remain in me. (John 15:4)

If appropriate, find a way to celebrate communion, preferably with others. Let this be a part of your ongoing 'yes' to the Father and the family he has given you.

23

WORSHIPPING THE FATHER

To be human as God intends means learning the art of living a God-centred life. Then our whole life becomes an expression of worship. To grasp this, we need a biblical understanding of 'worship'.

WHAT IS WORSHIP?

Many years ago, I read a book about worship. I don't remember much of the content or who wrote it, but I recall one key thought: *The essence of worship is standing in awe of God.* There is something beautiful about the way little children look up to their parents with awe, wonder, and trust. There is something about being in awe – overwhelmed by a sense of wonder and mystery, left speechless – that naturally leads to expressions of worship. The biblical concept of worship is more closely tied to speechlessness than it is to words and music.

In recent years, there has been a growing interest in 'worship', with a worship movement impacting the church globally. But our concept of worship seems to have gradually shifted; it has become increasingly synonymous with music or a particular type of experience. If you are going to a meeting and you hear it will start with a time of worship, you can assume there will be some musicians on a stage leading the congregation in song. You may even anticipate some sort of encounter with God, or that you will be ministered to through the worship. Sometimes, I wonder if we treat worship more like a consumer product for *us* to enjoy, rather than something we give to God.

Whether or not our songs are an expression of 'worship', in the biblical sense, depends on our heart. Songs may help us to worship, but only if our hearts are in awe of God and bowing to him.

BIBLICAL WORSHIP

In the Bible, the Hebrew and Greek words that are usually translated as worship don't carry any meaning of music or words. The core idea is about *bowing*, which has more to do with body language. Throughout the Bible, we see that an inner bowing of the heart will sometimes gain expression in physical bowing, kneeling, or prostrating. At other times, a surrendered heart will be expressed in some form of *sacrifice* or *service*.

When the wise men came to the infant Jesus, "they bowed down and worshipped him" (Matt 2:11). They didn't break out in song; they prostrated themselves. The Greek word here, *proskuneó*, carries the meaning "to fall down/prostrate oneself, to adore on one's knees".[77] When Abraham was willing to sacrifice Isaac (bowing his will to God in obedient sacrifice), he told his servants they were going to "worship" (Gen 22:5). Here again, in the Hebrew language, the word *shachah* builds on the idea of bowing or prostrating.

In the New Testament, we see that some of the themes of bowing, laying down, and sacrifice are reinterpreted with an increased focus on the heart. For example, we are exhorted to be a "living sacrifice" (Rom 12:1). This builds on the inner bowing of our will towards God.

VARIOUS FORMS OF WORSHIP

In Chapter 19, we explored some of the many forms of giving and receiving. Similarly, we could talk about the varied ways of bowing in worship. No, I'm not referring to different body postures, although they can be appropriate expressions. I mean things like putting our trust in God the Father, bowing our will to him, and letting him have the last word.

Our English word *worship* is a contraction of *worth-ship*. Anytime we express his worth to us – looking up to him, embracing his values or letting him be our inspiration – that is a form of bowing in worship.

In many of the topics we have explored, we identified *willingness* as a key in our relationship with the Father. Having a *willing* heart towards God is one of the deepest forms of bowing. Again, that is worship. We can similarly apply this understanding of 'worth-ship' to all of the previous topics:

- When we look to the Father as the *source of life* – not just the origin, but the ongoing source – and as we actively draw on his life, we worship.
- Each time we turn from our own targets and focus on the *Father's target* for our lives, we worship.
- Whenever we open ourselves to the Father's firm and warm *goodness*, allowing him to shape our character, and whenever we choose to meet others with that same goodness, we worship the Father and glorify him.

- Each act of pursuing *relationship* with the Father affirms his value to us; that too, is worship.
- When we *aspire* to be like our heavenly Father, to be with him, doing what he is doing, we worship him.
- Every time we are willing to let the Father *persuade* us of his faithfulness, and every time we are willing to *trust* him and 'get in the wheelbarrow' with him, we worship.
- When we pursue *Father-righteousness*, having the Father as our reference point and referee, we worship.
- Allowing ourselves to become an *extension* of his Father-righteousness is also worship and his glory is revealed.
- Whenever we seek to view others with the Father's *eyes of grace*, meeting them with his *giving-and-receiving* life, we worship and bring glory to his name.
- Each time we are willing to let go, willingly *submitting* our lives to the Father's will and purposes, we bow our lives in worship.
- Every act of *repentance* and realignment towards the Father and his values is worship.

IN SPIRIT AND TRUTH

In the encounter with the Samaritan woman (John 4), we see how she tries to draw Jesus into a discussion about the right *place* for worship. Jesus shifts the focus from the outer expression to inner life, where true worship happens: "the hour is coming, and is now here, when the *true worshipers* will worship the Father in *spirit* and *truth*, for the Father is seeking such people to worship him" (4:23 ESV).

Some translations and commentaries have interpreted the word *spirit* as "the Spirit". Yet many of the more literal translations simply use "spirit", referring to the spirit of the person. Either way, it is clearly about inner life rather than outer expression. I think we sometimes make too much of a distinction between our spirit and the Spirit of God within us. We think that if it is God, then it is not us; if it is us, then it is not God. Ideally, there should be no distinction. Our spirit should be in tune with the Spirit of the Father. Any true worship in our spirit will be energised by the Spirit.

We should also be careful to not read too much into Jesus' choice of the word *spirit*. He is not necessarily highlighting some specific 'spiritual' aspect of our inner life in isolation from others. This is likely a reference to the whole inner life, including mind, will, and heart. Again, the various components of our inner life will ideally be in tune with each other.

Then we have the word *truth*. We must not limit our view of truth to objective statements. Truth is about consistency. In terms of *objective* facts, they are true if they are consistent with reality. People can also be true. You are *true to your word* when you *subjectively* choose to live consistently with what you have said, even if it turns out to be inconvenient. Living consistent lives and being true (faithful) are essential to true worship. It isn't enough to just have some true statements in the songs we sing.

Jesus could have argued that the worship in Jerusalem was *right* or *correct* in terms of the God-prescribed ceremonies. Yet he knew that much of the worship there was not *true* – some people were just out for personal gain (Mk 11:15–17), others were hypocritical or full of pride (Lk 18:9–14). That is not *true* worship; there is a lack of consistency and integrity.

For my part, I have sung songs of commitment, proclaiming, "I surrender all". Then the next day, I have struggled to let God have the last word in a small matter. I have sung of how precious God is, then later in the week, I have been unwilling to value his ways above mine. I have sung of desiring God's presence and wanting intimacy. Yet afterwards, I have ignored his presence in my daily life, and been unwilling to listen to the intimate whispers of his Spirit. These examples all show a lack of consistency. My words may have been sincere, but my life of worship has proven to be less than *true*.

Did I just raise the bar too high? Well, this is not about performance and attaining the ideal. We just need to be clear about what we are aiming for and ready to realign when we become aware of inconsistencies in our life.

THE HEART OF GOD'S GLORY

Another aspect of true worship is that we are truly in awe of God. Are we really in awe of our heavenly Father, or is he just nice to have around? Perhaps a fresh revelation of his glory would help us to be in awe of him.

Imagine being with Moses as he encounters God's glory. Can you picture the burning bush, the staff that became a snake, the parting of the sea, bitter water that became sweet, water from a rock, the victory while Moses' hands were raised, the Mount Sinai encounter (with cloud, thunder, lightning, billows of smoke and trumpet blasts), the tablets of stone, another mountaintop experience for *forty days* in a cloud of glory, the regular encounters at the tent of meeting where God appeared in a cloud and spoke with Moses face to face – and those are just some of the highlights!

Yet, when Moses later asks, "Now show me your glory" (Ex 33:18), God shifts the focus from outer manifestations to who he is. He responds by declaring, "I will cause all my *goodness* to pass in front of you" (v. 19).

Hopefully, we have understood by now that our heavenly Father looks to our heart. Yet we also should *look to his heart*. Any outer manifestations of his glory – goosebumps, glory clouds, or gold dust – are only signs; they are not his actual glory. God's glory – his greatness, the most magnificent thing about him – is his actual *being*. And the core of his being is his *goodness*.

As we 'bow' to his goodness – allowing it to flood our lives, permeating our values, our attitudes, our actions and our relationships – we get to know him in the deepest way possible. More than just *knowledge* about his goodness, or an *experience* of his goodness, we get *inside* his goodness and meet others with his heart. As we experience the Father in this intimate way, Father-life flows and our very lives become a symphony of harmonious worship.

A LIFE OF WORSHIP

It is not merely our songs, but our very lives, that are to be sweet music to God. The more we consistently align with the Father as our 'conductor', the more our hearts and lives will be in harmony and producing sweet music. Such music will reach not just the Father's ears, but also the ears of those around us.

I find it significant that when Paul tells the Ephesian believers to "Sing and make music from your heart to the Lord" (5:19), he does so in the context of instructions about how to live well with others (Eph 4–6). Our musical harmony has greater meaning when our lives are filled with relational harmony.

The deeper we go in living the Father-life, the more we discover that some words, which at first appear to be in tension, are actually closely related:

> **"** *This is to my Father's glory,*
> *that you bear much fruit.*

holiness and love; justice and mercy; steadfastness and grace; freedom and submission. These all become synonyms in the Father. They still have their distinct meanings, yet they are all tied together. The connection isn't technical or semantic; the strong connection is the One who gives each of these words its richest meaning. In light of who the Father is, *all* of these words come together in unity.

The Father is glorified when we live life with the harmony he intended. As we allow these various elements of Father-life to be established in our lives, we become more whole, more in tune, and more alive.

Take a moment to imagine the multiplied impact, as whole groups of Christians start to live in harmony with God and each other in this deep way. Soon, whole societies would be impacted. Imagine being a part of a growing movement of Father-life!

FLOURISHING LIFE

All that is truly alive has some form of growth and reproduction. This life dynamic is just as true of Father-life. Father-life seeks to flood our lives with his goodness. Yet it is not content to just fill *us*; it presses outward; it seeks to overflow. Father-life looks for ways of pressing through our sometimes thick exterior, like dandelions pushing through asphalt.

Allow Father-life to explode through your life – be fruitful! Fruitfulness was one of the first commands in the Bible (Gen 1:22). Fruitfulness is also worship: "This is to my Father's glory, that you bear much fruit" (John 15:8a). Father-life can't be kept in a jar – it has to grow, or it dies.

St. Irenaeus is quoted as saying: *The glory of God is man fully alive.*[78] We are fully alive when Father-life flows through us and bears fruit. Such fruit will hopefully be evident as the fruit of the Spirit (love, joy, peace, etc.) and in the fruitfulness of discipling others to trust the Father. The more that happens, the more the Father is glorified.

FULLNESS OF LIFE

This book has only briefly addressed a variety of topics. Much more could be said on each of these topics and many others, such as prayer, the Holy Spirit, parenting, acts of justice and mercy, etc. Your task, as you continue to grow, is to keep everything rightly connected with the Father, and with the other aspects of life. Father-life does not recognise our usual sacred/secular divide. All of life is potentially spiritual as we bring Father-life into it. Aim for wholeness and fullness in life.

Your life is one of the Father's precious gifts to the world. As you allow him to release his life through you, grace and blessing will flow. Then your life, your family, your church, and the world are all enriched. Be fruitful and help others to be fruitful, that the Father may be glorified!

As mentioned in Chapter 15, if all you manage to do in life is pay your debts and 'balance the books', then the sum total of your life is zero. Don't let that happen; release the Father's gift in you. Let your life be all that God intended, in a generous overflow of Father-life.

May Father-life fruitfulness grow in you and in your relationships – in your family, your church, your workplace and your free-time activities. May you impact and disciple many in knowing and loving the Father. Embrace the adventure of relationship with the Father of Life, as he develops and grows his family on Earth. Don't hold back. Let the Father's eternal, resurrection-life flow freely. Eternal life has already started.

—

KEY POINTS

- The biblical view of worship builds on the concept of bowing. We can bow our hearts to the Father by trusting him, letting him be our reference point and by aspiring to be like him.
- Perhaps the most glorious thing about God is his holy, loving *goodness*; this is the essence of his being.
- Worshipping the Father in spirit and truth leads us into greater wholeness, a deeper relationship with him and a more fruitful life.

REFLECTION AND RESPONSE

Has your view of worship been expanded or redefined? In what areas would you like to grow in your worship of the Father? Invite his Spirit to increase your awareness of these things in the coming weeks and months.

FURTHER REFLECTION AND APPLICATION

Now that you have finished the book, it might prove valuable to do a quick review. This can help you to apply the things you have learnt. You can quickly browse through each chapter, or read through the Key Points at the end of each chapter. How is the Father speaking to you in all of this? Take some time to process, journal, pray, or respond in any other way that seems meaningful. Pray also about how you might share some new insights with others, that Father-life may flow through you.

—

CONTACT THE AUTHOR

Please give your feedback about this book through the author's website. You can also order further copies of *Father-Life*, obtain electronic versions, explore other material or resources, and contact the author.

www.fathersimage.eu

SUGGESTIONS FOR STUDY

My hope is that you will really get a hold of the message of this book. More than that, I pray that the message will also get a hold of you and influence the way you live. Reading is one thing, yet reflecting and processing can lead to greater fruit and lasting growth. When you put in the effort of reading this book, it does not take much extra effort to get more out of it through study.

You will be able to proceed at your own pace through personal study. If you are able to do a group study with others, you will have the added benefit of synergy and fellowship. Either way, here are some suggestions to help you engage with the material.

Please note, however, that these are just *suggestions*. Part of the message of this book is that life does not come through simply following a system. Feel free to adapt these suggestions and go with whatever proves most fruitful.

PERSONAL STUDY

As you start

- **Read** – Read the Author's Note and the start of Part One.
- **Reflect** – What are your desires, hopes or expectations? Is there anything in particular you hope to get out of this book or would like to see God do in your life?
- **Pray** – Ask your heavenly Father to give you what you need.

For each chapter

- **Intro** – After reading the chapter title and opening paragraph, pause to reflect and pray.
- **Read** – As you read, make notes and/or underline sections that are key for you.
- **Endnotes** – Take a moment to look up some of the endnotes.
- **Breaks** – Be sensitive to the leading of the Spirit to put the book aside for a moment as you respond in prayer or process in some other way.
- **Review** – As you read the Key Points at the end of each chapter, consider if you would like to add some points that were key for you. Do you have any issues with the chapter or questions that have come up? Who might help you to pursue those questions?
- **Application** – Take some time for the suggested reflection/application activity. Consider keeping a journal of what you are learning and how you hope to apply it.

Bible study

As an additional activity, consider doing some Bible study for each chapter of the book, or at least some of the chapters.

- **Review** – Quickly review the chapter, identifying any Scripture passages or key verses.
- **Select** – Choose at least one verse or passage that stood out to you and take some time to look at it more closely.
- **Context** – Make sure to understand the context of the passage. Check your own Bible and see what else is being said in that

section. Even just looking at a few verses before and after a passage will often bring greater understanding.

- **Message** – What does this passage tell you about God? What can we learn about ourselves/others and how we should live?
- **Foundation** – Do you agree with how the verse/passage was presented in the book? Was it faithful to the Scriptures? Do you have a firm basis for your views, or would it be good to dig some more?

At the end of the book

- **Conclusions** – Spend some time with the closing reflection and application at the end of the last chapter. Seriously consider the challenge to share some of what you have learnt with others.

GROUP STUDY

Group study can be combined with personal reading or may include group reading. Reading aloud seems to be a dying art, yet it is an active way of engaging with a text and can bring an extra dynamic into a group.

For group reading, have one person read at a time. You can use the subheadings in the text to mark the switch to the next reader. Allow for any brief questions or clarifications, but save discussion questions for after the reading.

The format is flexible. If there is enough time, the group could read through and respond to one or two chapters in each gathering. If group time is limited, participants could read a chapter or two at home then gather to share, reflect, and pray for one another. Alternatively, it may work well to have a combination of home reading and group reading. (For example, read a chapter at home, meet to share about it, and then read the next chapter in the group.) The group gatherings could be in person or using an online video platform.

Having a group leader can help the group to operate well within their given timeframe, stay on topic, and stir the participants' interest for the coming chapter. Ideally, the leader will help the group to honour their given framework, while being sensitive to the Spirit and seeking to bring life into the format.

The process for group study can be based on the **outline above** for personal study, though some adaptation will be necessary. Here are a few **additional suggestions** for groups:

Group gatherings

- **Group reading** – Take turns at reading a section at a time. (Be sensitive to those who struggle to read aloud.) Save discussion questions for after the reading.
- **Endnotes** – The group leader could prepare by going through the chapter and looking for any interesting information in the endnotes to bring to the group's attention.

Final session

- **Review** – In the closing session, take time to quickly review the whole book. Look at the Key Points after each chapter, and allow participants to share any personal highlights.
- **Conclusions** – Allow time for participants to reflect on what God has been doing in their life through this process. Are further changes necessary? Share with and pray for each other.
- **Share the blessings** – In closing, each participant can consider what insights from this book they can share with others. Ask God to show you at least one or two specific individuals you can share with and how you can initiate contact.
- **Commissioning** – Pray together for God's blessing over your desire to live in and spread Father-life. Pray that your life in him would bear much fruit!
- **Continue** – Consider continuing to gather as a group or find some other way you can continue to encourage and support one another.

My prayer for you is "that our God
may make you worthy of his calling, and
that by his power he may bring to fruition
your every desire for goodness and your
every deed prompted by faith"

2 Thes 1:11

ENDNOTES

— 1 —

1   For other examples of verses which call us to believe in the One who raised Jesus, see 1 Peter 1:21 and Romans 10:9.

2   For example, Dr. Walter Martin has identified the Resurrection as "the central truth of the early apostles' preaching" and "the energizing force which spread the gospel across the face of the earth". [Walter R. Martin, *Essential Christianity*, Baker, 1980, p. 63.]
Similarly, Clifford and Johnson have observed that the Resurrection is "the central theme of the speeches and sermons in the book of Acts". [Ross Clifford, Philip Johnson, *The Cross Is Not Enough: Living as Witnesses to the Resurrection*, Baker, 2012, p. 27.]
N. T. Wright has observed, "Resurrection is not a fancy way of saying 'going to heaven when you die'. ... none of the resurrection stories in the gospels or Acts speaks of the event proving that some kind of afterlife exists. ... when Jesus rose again God's whole new creation emerged from the tomb, introducing a world full of new potential and possibility." [Tom Wright (Nicholas Thomas Wright), *Simply Christian: Why Christianity Makes Sense*, Society for Promoting Christian Knowledge, 2006.]

— 2 —

3   Some examples: Deut 32:6; 32:18–19; Is 63:16; Is 64:8; Mal 2:10.

4   Marianne Meye Thompson, *The Promise of the Father: Jesus and God in the New Testament*, Westminster John Knox Press, 2000, p. 39.

— 3 —

5   "A complete transformation takes place when the New Testament uses hamartia to denote the determination of human nature in hostility to God." [Gerhard Kittel (ed.), *Theological Dictionary of the New Testament, 10 volume set (TDNT)*, 1964, William B. Eerdmans Publishing Company, vol. 1, p. 295.] See pages 293–295 for other source material.

— 4 —

6   Liberalism refers to any view that emphasises or absolutises individual liberty. In this context, and in the rest of this book, it is used in contrast to legalism. Usage here isn't connected with liberalism in politics or economics, nor is it directly related to *liberal theology*.

7　Oswald Chambers, *Christian Disciplines (Abridged and updated language edition)*, 2013, Discovery House.

— 7 —

8　Susan Pinker, *The secret to living longer may be your social life*, TED Talks, 2017. https://www.ted.com/talks/susan_pinker_the_secret_to_living_longer_may_be_your_social_life (accessed 13 May 2019).

9　*Epigenetics and Child Development: How Children's Experiences Affect Their Genes*, Center on the Developing Child, Havard University, https://developingchild.harvard.edu/resources/what-is-epigenetics-and-how-does-it-relate-to-child-development/ (accessed 9 August 2021).
Epigenetics: Your DNA is not your destiny, BBC Reel, https://www.youtube.com/watch?v=Hrl9_GwNLGI (accessed 9 August 2021).

— 8 —

10　Brother Lawrence (Nicholas Herman), Joseph de Beaufort (ed.), *The Practice of the Presence of God: The Best Rule of Holy Life*, public domain.

11　ibid, https://www.ccel.org/ccel/lawrence/practice (accessed 2 July 2018).

12　The fact that Paul is referring to the present dynamics of the relationship isn't immediately obvious in all translation of Romans 5:10–11. For example: "how much more, having been reconciled, shall we be saved through his life!" (v. 10b, NIV). The Greek verb for 'shall be saved' is in the future tense, yet the context suggests that Paul is giving assurance of God's ongoing work in the *immediate* future, as needs arise in our day to day lives. The *Amplified Bible, Classic Edition* (AMPCE) spells this out: "it is much more [certain], now that we are reconciled, that we shall be saved (daily delivered from sin's dominion) through His [resurrection] life." Here, we see that Paul's mention of "having been reconciled" (NIV) can be seen as a reference to the current state of being reconciled – having an active relationship. This comes out even more clearly in verse 11 of the *Amplified Bible* (AMP): "we have now received and enjoy [our] reconciliation."

13　According to the Jewish Encyclopedia: "The oldest known interpretation of the Song is allegorical: the Midrash and the Targum represent it as depicting the relations between God and Israel." [The Jewish Encyclopedia, Funk & Wagnalls, 1906, Vol. 11, p. 466.] Throughout Church history there have been many leading figures, from at least as early as Origen (3rd Century) and Augustine, who have viewed the Song of Songs as allegory also at the individual level. In such cases, it is important to understand the limitations of the parallels.

— 9 —

14　Various Bible translations and commentaries have divided views on this verse, many preferring the interpretation, "in my Father's house". The word "house" is not in the Greek text, though it was assumed in an early Syriac translation. Even if the text is read as "house", we see that the young Jesus was not content to just be *in* the temple gazing at its grandeur; he was *engaged in* his Father's affairs.

15 A similar grief is expressed in Jesus' lament over Jerusalem in Matthew 23:37. God desired to gather his people as a hen gathers her chicks, yet they were unresponsive and unwilling.

16 A similar grief is expressed in Luke 19:41–44 as Jesus wept over Jerusalem. The people of Jerusalem were known for their religious piety, yet they barely knew God and "did not recognise the time of God's coming" (v. 44).

— 10 —

17 The pronunciation of *huios* is something like *hwee-oss*.

18 Gerhard **Kittel** (ed.), *Theological Dictionary of the New Testament, Abridged in One Volume (**TDNTa**)*, 1985, William B. Eerdmans Publishing Company, p. 1209.

19 Scripture has many examples of *huios* being used metaphorically. For example: sons of the kingdom (Matt 8:12), of light (Luke 16:8), of the wicked one (Matt 13:38), of the devil (Acts 13:10), of the Pharisees (Matt 12:27, Acts 23:6), of thunder (Mark 3:17), Mark as "son" of Paul (1 Pet 5:13).

20 The word *huios* is gender specific, referring literally to a 'son'. Of course, it is very much tied in to the cultural and historical context at the time of Jesus, where sons typically became heirs. Yet it is also clear from its figurative use in the Bible that both sons and daughters of God are called to be 'sons'. It is a metaphor. So the women will just have to get used to the idea of being a 'son' of God, while we men try to see ourselves as part of the 'bride' of Christ.

21 Many Bible translations often use "child" also for *huios*, probably in an attempt to be gender neutral.

22 Jewish coming of age ceremony for boys, typically when they are 13 years old. In Bible times, the son became legally responsible for his own actions and could now formally represent his father in business matters.

23 Several sources, including: James C. Walters, *Paul, Adoption, and Inheritance*, in J. Paul Sampley (ed.), *Paul in the Greco-Roman World: A Handbook* (A&C Black, 2003), pp. 42–76.

24 Interestingly, a similar form of adoption (of adult male heirs) is practised in Japanese culture, even in our day. [John W. Traphagan (ed.) and John Knight (ed.), *Demographic Change and the Family in Japan's Aging Society*, State University of New York Press, 2003, p. 9.]

25 Lewis (Lew) Wallace, *Ben-Hur: A Tale of the Christ*, Harper & Brothers, 1880. Considered one of the most influential Christian books of the nineteenth century. Various film versions of the story have adapted some details of the adoption.

26 James C. Walters, *Paul, Adoption, and Inheritance*, in J. Paul Sampley (ed.), *Paul in the Greco-Roman World: A Handbook*, A&C Black, 2003, p. 56–57.

— 11 —

27 Many interpret this from Ephesians 2:8, though others understand the "gift of God" as referring to salvation.

28 This seems to be part of the message of Romans 12:3, though not all translations express it this way.

29 While this story has been adapted to serve as an illustration, some of the facts behind the story are just as amazing. Charles Blondin was the first person to cross Niagara Falls by tightrope on 30th June 1859. He later crossed 16 more times and performed various feats, such as pushing a wheelbarrow. On one occasion he carried his manager, Harry Colcord, on his back. At the Crystal Palace in England, he crossed a tightrope 50 meters above the ground while pushing his five-year-old daughter, Adele, in a wheelbarrow. She sat there confidently trusting her father while scattering rose petals on the large crowd below. The British Home Secretary promptly banned repetitions of the feat. Blondin complied, yet I doubt that he felt he had put his daughter's life at risk. The drawing in this book is based on an actual photo of Blondin in action at Niagara Falls, with a wheelbarrow strapped to his waist.

— 12 —

30 Bruce Olson, *Bruchko*, Charisma House, 2006, p. 127. (Originally published 1973.)

— 13 —

31 Timothy Keller, *King's Cross: The Story of the World in the Life of Jesus*, Hodder & Stoughton, 2011. (Also published as *Jesus the King: Understanding the Life and Death of the Son of God*, Penguin, 2013.) See Chapter Seven, *The Stain*.

32 The Greek text uses the word meaning 'righteousness', therefore many of the more literal translations, such as the ESV, say: "practice righteousness". Many other translations, such as the NIV, say: "do what is right".

33 See Acts 23:6 and Philippians 3:5.

34 For example: Romans 1:17; 4:3; Galatians 3:6; 3:11.

35 See Psalm 119 verses 7, 62, 75, 106, 138, 144, 160, 164 and 172.

36 Similar views are expressed by Professor Elizabeth Achtemeier. See: Elizabeth R Achtemeier, *Righteousness in the Old Testament*, in George Arthur Buttrick, *The Interpreter's Dictionary of the Bible*, Abingdon Press, 1962, 4:80.

37 Some examples: Psalm 7:8 (integrity); Psalm 33:1 (uprightness); Psalm 36:6 (justice); Psalm 7:11 (wrath).

38 Not all translations express this as "practice righteousness", yet that is the direct meaning in the Greek text. (See also Endnote 32.)

— 14 —

39 Kittel also identifies inner consistency and relational faithfulness as key elements of God's righteousness. The righteousness of God means, "he is consistent in himself and unswervingly faithful to his covenant promise. He does not merely dispense justice as the righteous God; he also grants salvation." (This was said in relation to use of the Greek word *dikaios* in the Septuagint.) [Gerhard Kittel (ed.), *Theological Dictionary of the New Testament, Abridged in One Volume (TNDTa)*, 1985, William B. Eerdmans Publishing Company, p. 169.]

40 From Old English, *wise* can carry the meaning 'way of proceeding', 'manner' or 'direction', and this meaning is still evident in words such as likewise, otherwise, clockwise and lengthwise.

41 R. B. Girdlestone, *Synonyms of the Old Testament*, Hendrickson Publishers, 2000, p. 118.

42 One of the clearest links between righteousness and straightness in the New Testament is when Paul called a magician an "enemy of all righteousness" as he was "making crooked the straight paths of the Lord" (Acts 13:10).

43 For example, in Chapter 10, we mentioned Paul's use of the word 'adoption'. Old Testament Hebrew does not have a word for adoption, as legal adoption was not practiced in Hebraic culture. Adoption was informal; orphans were taken in and fostered by others but maintained their original family identity. Meanwhile, 'adoption' in the Greco-Roman world carried a strong sense of a change of status and allegiance, a meaning which Paul clearly draws upon.

44 About 300 years before the New Testament was written, the Septuagint (a translation of the Old Testament into Greek) had firmly established the practice of expressing Hebraic thought with Greek words. For example, the Greek word for sin, *hamartia*, which we looked at in Chapter 3. In Greek thought *hamartia* could refer to any form of human failing. The writers of the Septuagint and the New Testament, however, used *hamartia* to convey the Hebraic concept of rebellion against God. Christians do something similar when we use the word 'God' while talking with non-Christians. Society at large has distorted stereotype concepts of 'God', and the word has non-Christian origins, yet we use the same word to convey fresh concepts.

45 Kittel, *TDNTa*, pp. 169, 646.

46 Kittel, *TDNTa*, p. 173.

— 15 —

47 The word 'become' in this verse implies *a process of growth*. It is translated from the Greek word *'ginomai'*, a verb which essentially means 'to become' or 'to come into being'. The English words 'gene' and 'genetics' are based on the same Greek root. According to M Vincent, *"ginomai means to come into being/ manifestation* implying *motion, movement, or growth"*. Similarly, Peter uses this word when he says that through God's promises we "may become partakers of the divine nature" (ESV). Peter goes on to call us to "make every effort" to grow in a number of areas, including goodness (moral excellence), insight, kindness and love (see 2 Pet 1:3–8).

48 Fred **Skolnik** (ed.), **Encyclopedia Judaica**, *Second Edition*, Thomson Gale, 2007, vol. 17, p. 308.
With this understanding in mind, Paul's message in Romans 3:23 is probably not only referring to the afterlife, as often assumed.

49 Skolnik, *Encyclopedia Judaica*, p. 307

50 "The man who is righteous tries to preserve the peace and prosperity of the community by fulfilling the commands of God in regard to others." This includes helping those in need and addressing issues of injustice. [Harold Stigers, *sedeq – justice, rightness*, in R. Laird Harris (ed.), *Theological Wordbook of the Old Testament (TWOT)*, Moody Press, 1980, vol. 2, p. 753.]
    "Righteous action results in social stability and ultimately in peace: And the work of righteousness shall be peace (Isa. 32:17; cf. Hos. 10:12; Avot 2:7)." [Skolnik, *Encyclopedia Judaica*, p. 307.]

51 For many other great insights about being salt and light in the world, see materials by Ken Chua, entitled *Empowered to Influence*, available through Simply Mobilizing. Find out more: https://simplymobilizing.com/courses/empowered-to-influence/

— 16 —

52 Also known as *cognitive fluency* or *processing fluency*. These terms appear in areas such as sociology, psychology, cognitive neuroscience, and marketing.

53 There are many examples of Aramaic words and phrases in the New Testament, and they are typically followed by a translation (e.g. Mark 3:17; 5:41; 7:34; John 20:16; Matt 27:46). The translation given for *Abba* is simply *Father*.
    One of the strongest supporters of the 'Daddy' view was the esteemed German scholar, Joachim Jeremias. He promoted the idea of "babbling" baby talk widely in several publications during the 1960s. Yet his view has since been thoroughly challenged by many leading scholars. Jeremias himself later tried to correct his earlier assertion. He described it as "a piece of inadmissible naivety", adding the explanation, "even grown-up sons addressed their father as *abba*". [Joachim Jeremias, *The Prayers of Jesus*, trans. Bowden and Burchard, SCM Press, 1967, p. 63.]
    One of the more thorough assessments of this topic is found in: James Barr, *Abba Isn't Daddy*, The Journal of Theological Studies, Vol. 39, No. 1 (April 1988), pp. 28–47.

54 Sir William Robertson Nicoll (ed.), *Expositor's Greek Testament*, Hodder and Stoughton, 1897, p. 835. Comments with reference to John 16:8.

55 Paul uses *nomos* over 120 times in the New Testament, including over 30 times in Galatians.

56 Kittel, *TDNTa*, p. 646. Secondarily, *nomos* could also refer to a basic principle (like the *law* of gravity), defining how things seem to work.

57 Sociologist Peter Berger uses the term *nomos* to refer to the norms of behaviour within any society. Berger notes that once a pattern of behaviour becomes so normal that it is assumed, then it takes on the nature of an absolute. [Peter Berger, *The Sacred Canopy: Elements of a Sociological Theory of Religion*, Open Road Media, 2011.]

58 Timothy Ashworth observes that Paul's use of *nomos* "carries meaning in a subtle and flexible way". This means, "there are always several meanings operating even though one of the meanings can be very much to the fore in a particular context". [Timothy Ashworth, *Paul's Necessary Sin: the Experience of Liberation*, Ashgate, 2006, pp. 67–68.]

59 The context suggests Paul is speaking generally, not just of the Jews, when he says "we" (Gal 3:23). He has just spoken of what was promised as being "given to those who believe" (3:22) which applies to all believers. Verse 23 builds on this by referring back to "this faith" (of any believer).

60 Based on Young's Literal Translation and the Greek text. There are no clear indications in the Greek text that Paul is referring exclusively to *the Nomos* (Torah).

61 See, for example, Matthew 7:24.

— 17 —

62 The terms 'bounded sets' and 'centred sets', originally from mathematics, are also used by sociologists to describe contrasting ways of thinking and relating in groups. These terms were later applied to missiology by Paul Hiebert as early as 1978 and can be found in his book *Anthropological Reflections on Missiological Issues*. The terms are now widely used in teaching about church planting and discipleship.

63 For part of his story, see https://www.ted.com/talks/daryl_davis_why_i_as_a_black_man_attend_kkk_rallies (accessed 27 July 2021)

64 See, for example, Matthew 18:15–17.

— 18 —

65 Where *impute* has been used in this passage, it too has typically been viewed by theologians only in an objective way, as an accounting term. Yet *impute* can also be understood in a subjective way. When Juliet says to Romeo, "therefore pardon me, and not *impute* this yielding to light love," she is addressing his view of her and how he is to consider her, despite her apparent failings. [William Shakespeare, *Romeo and Juliet*, Act 2 Scene 2]

66 Romans 8:18 – "I *consider* [*logizomai*] that our present sufferings are not worth comparing with the glory that will be revealed in us." In Paul's subjective view, the future glory is more significant than the present trials.

67 "It is clear that in Rom 4:6, 11, 'righteousness reckoned' must be understood in the light of the context, 'faith reckoned for righteousness,' vv. 3, 5, 9, 22. 'For' in these places is *eis*, which does not mean 'instead of,' but 'with a view to.'" [*Righteousness* in William Edwy Vine, *An Expository Dictionary of New Testament Words*, F. H. Revell, 1940.]

68 For more details on *charis* in the New Testament, see Jim B. McClure, *Grace Revisited*, Trailblazer Bookshop, 2010, p. 11.

69   Joseph Henry Thayer (ed.), *Thayer's Greek-English Lexicon of the New Testament*, Baker Book House, 1977.

21

70   The Hebrew text has a single word with the meaning "as heart of him" – David's heart was *as/like* the heart of God. In saying "a heart *after* God's heart", *after* is used in the same sense as when God made man "in our image, *after* our likeness" (Gen 1:26 KJV). It is not about being *after* God in the sense of desiring or pursuing God. Although these things were evident in David's life, they are clearly not the meaning of this phrase.

71   In addition to 21 references in his letters, Paul refers to conscience twice in the record of Acts.

72   The Hebrew text of the Old Testament does not have a specific word for conscience but refers to it in various indirect ways, such as *integrity of heart* (clear conscience), *heart-stricken* (conscience-stricken), etc.

73   In particular, see James 2:14–26.

22

74   A. W. Tozer, *The Pursuit of God*, Authentic Media, 2012, p. 43–44.

75   A talent was a lot of money. Think of the annual wage of a labourer, then multiply that by twenty.

76   Harry G. Frankfurt uses the term 'first order desires' to describe our normal appetites to act in certain ways. In contrast, 'second order desires' are when we recognise that we have conflicting desires and we have a preference about which desire should be acted upon. Freedom to act on a first-order desire is merely freedom of action. A person has free will only when they are able to prefer one desire over another, thereby not doing something they might otherwise have done. (Author's paraphrase of the concepts.)

23

77   Colin Brown (ed.), *The New International Dictionary of New Testament Theology*, Zondervan, 1986.

78   The original Latin, *Gloria Dei est vivens homo*, can also be translated as: *The glory of God is living man.*